Rust Atomics and Locks
Low-Level Concurrency in Practice

Mara Bos

Beijing · Boston · Farnham · Sebastopol · Tokyo

Rust Atomics and Locks

by Mara Bos

Copyright © 2023 Mara Bos. All rights reserved.

Published by O'Reilly Media, Inc., 1005 Gravenstein Highway North, Sebastopol, CA 95472.

O'Reilly books may be purchased for educational, business, or sales promotional use. Online editions are also available for most titles (*https://oreilly.com*). For more information, contact our corporate/institutional sales department: 800-998-9938 or *corporate@oreilly.com*.

Acquisitions Editor: Suzanne McQuade	**Indexer:** Ellen Troutman-Zaig
Development Editor: Shira Evans	**Interior Designer:** David Futato
Production Editor: Elizabeth Faerm	**Cover Designer:** Karen Montgomery
Copyeditor: Liz Wheeler	**Illustrator:** Kate Dullea
Proofreader: Penelope Perkins	

December 2022:   First Edition

Revision History for the First Edition

2022-12-14:   First Release
2023-01-27:   Second Release

See *https://oreilly.com/catalog/errata.csp?isbn=9781098119447* for release details.

978-1-098-11944-7

[LSI]

To all the Rust contributors who were waiting for me to review their code while I was busy writing this book.

And to my loved ones, too, of course. ♥

In loving memory of
Amélia Ada Louise, 1994–2021

Table of Contents

Foreword

This book provides an excellent overview of low-level concurrency in the Rust language, including threads, locks, reference counts, atomics, mailboxes/channels, and much else besides. It digs into issues with CPUs and operating systems, the latter summarizing challenges inherent in making concurrent code work correctly on Linux, macOS, and Windows. I was particularly happy to see that Mara illustrates these topics with working Rust code. It wraps up by discussing semaphores, lock-free linked lists, queued locks, sequence locks, and even RCU.

So what does this book offer someone like myself, who has been slinging C code for almost 40 years, most recently in the nether depths of the Linux kernel?

I first learned of Rust from any number of enthusiasts and Linux-related conferences. Nevertheless, I was happily minding my own business until I was called out by name in a Rust-related LWN article, "Using Rust for Kernel Development" (*https://oreil.ly/OnlX8*). Thus prodded, I wrote a blog series entitled "So You Want to Rust the Linux Kernel?" (*https://oreil.ly/eiedc*). This blog series sparked a number of spirited discussions, a few of which are visible in the series' comments.

In one such discussion, a long-time Linux-kernel developer who has also written a lot of Rust code told me that when writing concurrent code in Rust, you should write it the way Rust wants you to. I have since learned that although this is great advice, it leaves open the question of exactly what Rust wants. This book gives excellent answers to this question, and is thus valuable both to Rust developers wishing to learn concurrency and to developers of concurrent code in other languages who would like to learn how best to do so in Rust.

I of course fall into this latter category. However, I must confess that many of the spirited discussions about Rust concurrency remind me of my parents' and grandparents' long-ago complaints about the inconvenient safety features that were being added to power tools such as saws and drills. Some of those safety features are now ubiquitous, but hammers, chisels, and chainsaws have not changed all that much. It was not at all easy to work out which mechanical safety features would stand the test of time, so I recommend approaching software safety features with an attitude of profound humility. And please understand that I am addressing the proponents of such features as well as their detractors.

Which brings us to another group of potential readers, the Rust skeptics. While I do believe that most Rust skeptics are doing the community a valuable service by pointing out opportunities for improvement, all but the most Rust-savvy of skeptics would benefit from reading this book. If nothing else, doing so would enable them to provide sharper and better-targeted criticisms.

Then there are those dyed-in-the-wool non-Rust developers who would prefer to implement Rust's concurrency-related safety mechanisms in their own favorite language. This book will give them a deeper understanding of the Rust mechanisms that they would like to replicate, or, better yet, improve upon.

Finally, any number of Linux-kernel developers are noting the progress that Rust is making toward being included in the Linux kernel; for example, see Jonathan Corbet's article, "Next Steps for Rust in the Kernel" (*https://oreil.ly/MLrT5*). As of October 2022, this is still an experiment, but one that is being taken increasingly seriously. In fact, seriously enough that Linus Torvalds has accepted the first bits of Rust-language support into version 6.1 of the Linux kernel.

Whether you are reading this book to expand your Rust repertoire to include concurrency, to expand your concurrency repertoire to include Rust, to improve your existing non-Rust environment, or just to look at concurrency from a different viewpoint, I wish you the very best on your journey!

— Paul E. McKenney
Meta Platforms Kernel Team
Meta
October 2022

Preface

Rust has played, and keeps playing, a significant role in making systems programming more accessible. However, low-level concurrency topics such as atomics and memory ordering are still often thought of as somewhat mystical subjects that are best left to a very small group of experts.

While working on Rust-based real-time control systems and the Rust standard library over the past few years, I found that many of the available resources on atomics and related topics only cover a small part of the information I was looking for. Many resources focus entirely on C and C++, which can make it hard to form the connection with Rust's concept of (memory and thread) safety and type system. The resources that cover the details of the abstract theory, like C++'s memory model, often only vaguely explain how it relates to actual hardware, if at all. There are many resources that cover every detail of the actual hardware, such as processor instructions and cache coherency, but forming a holistic understanding often requires collecting bits and pieces of information from many different places.

This book is an attempt to put relevant information in one place, connecting it all together, providing everything you need to build your own correct, safe, and ergonomic concurrency primitives, while understanding enough about the underlying hardware and the role of the operating system to be able to make design decisions and basic optimization trade-offs.

Who This Book Is For

The primary audience for this book is Rust developers who want to learn more about low-level concurrency. Additionally, this book can also be suitable for those who are not very familiar with Rust yet, but would like to know what low-level concurrency looks like from a Rust perspective.

It is assumed you know the basics of Rust, have a recent Rust compiler installed, and know how to compile and run Rust code using `cargo`. Rust concepts that are important for concurrency are briefly explained when relevant, so no prior knowledge about Rust concurrency is necessary.

Overview of the Chapters

This book consists of ten chapters. Here's what to expect from each chapter, and what to look forward to:

Chapter 1 — Basics of Rust Concurrency
> This chapter introduces all the tools and concepts we need for basic concurrency in Rust, such as threads, mutexes, thread safety, shared and exclusive references, interior mutability, and so on, which are foundational to the rest of the book.
>
> For experienced Rust programmers who are familiar with these concepts, this chapter can serve as a quick refresher. For those who know these concepts from other languages but aren't very familiar with Rust yet, this chapter will quickly fill you in on any Rust-specific knowledge you might need for the rest of the book.

Chapter 2 — Atomics
> In the second chapter we'll learn about Rust's atomic types and all their operations. We start with simple load and store operations, and build our way up to more advanced *compare-and-exchange loops*, exploring each new concept with several real-world use cases as usable examples.
>
> While *memory ordering* is relevant for every atomic operation, that topic is left for the next chapter. This chapter only covers situations where *relaxed* memory ordering suffices, which is the case more often than one might expect.

Chapter 3 — Memory Ordering
> After learning about the various atomic operations and how to use them, the third chapter introduces the most complicated topic of the book: memory ordering.
>
> We'll explore how the memory model works, what *happens-before relationships* are and how to create them, what all the different memory orderings mean, and why *sequentially consistent ordering* might not be the answer to everything.

Chapter 4 — Building Our Own Spin Lock
> After learning the theory, we put it to practice in the next three chapters by building our own versions of several common concurrency primitives. The first of these chapters is a short one, in which we implement a *spin lock*.
>
> We'll start with a very minimal version to put *release and acquire memory ordering* to practice, and then we'll explore Rust's concept of *safety* to turn it into an ergonomic and hard-to-misuse Rust data type.

Chapter 5 — Building Our Own Channels
> In Chapter 5, we'll implement from scratch a handful of variations of a *one-shot channel*, a primitive that can be used to send data from one thread to another.

Starting with a very minimal but entirely unsafe version, we'll work our way through several ways to design a safe interface, while considering design decisions and their consequences.

Chapter 6 — Building Our Own "Arc"

For the sixth chapter, we'll take on a more challenging memory ordering puzzle. We're going to implement our own version of atomic reference counting from scratch.

After adding support for *weak pointers* and optimizing it for performance, our final version will be practically identical to Rust's standard std::sync::Arc type.

Chapter 7 — Understanding the Processor

The seventh chapter is a deep dive into all the low-level details. We'll explore what happens at the processor level, what the *assembly instructions* behind the atomic operations look like on the two most popular processor architectures, what caching is and how it affects the performance of our code, and we'll find out what remains of the memory model at the hardware level.

Chapter 8 — Operating System Primitives

In Chapter 8 we acknowledge that there are things we can't do without the help of the operating system's *kernel* and learn what functionality is available on Linux, macOS, and Windows.

We'll discuss the concurrency primitives that are available through *pthreads* on POSIX systems, find out what we can do with the Windows API, and learn what the Linux *futex syscall* does.

Chapter 9 — Building Our Own Locks

Using what we've learned in the previous chapters, in Chapter 9 we're going to build several implementations of a *mutex, condition variable,* and *reader-writer lock* from scratch.

For each of these, we'll start with a minimal but complete version, which we'll then attempt to optimize in various ways. Using some simple benchmark tests, we'll find out that our attempts at optimization don't always increase performance, while we discuss various design trade-offs.

Chapter 10 — Ideas and Inspiration

The final chapter makes sure you don't fall into a void after finishing the book, but are instead left with ideas and inspiration for things to build and explore with your new knowledge and skills, perhaps kicking off an exciting journey further into the depths of low-level concurrency.

Code Examples

All code in this book is written for and tested using Rust 1.66.0, which was released on December 15, 2022. Earlier versions do not include all features used in this book. Later versions, however, should work just fine.

For brevity, the code examples do not include use statements, except for the first time a new item from the standard library is introduced. As a convenience, the following prelude can be used to import everything necessary to compile any of the code examples in this book:

```
#[allow(unused)]
use std::{
    cell::{Cell, RefCell, UnsafeCell},
    collections::VecDeque,
    marker::PhantomData,
    mem::{ManuallyDrop, MaybeUninit},
    ops::{Deref, DerefMut},
    ptr::NonNull,
    rc::Rc,
    sync::{*, atomic::{*, Ordering::*}},
    thread::{self, Thread},
};
```

Supplemental material, including complete versions of all code examples, is available at *https://marabos.nl/atomics/*.

You may use all example code offered with this book for any purpose.

Attribution is appreciated, but not required. An attribution usually includes the title, author, publisher, and ISBN. For example: "*Rust Atomics and Locks* by Mara Bos (O'Reilly). Copyright 2023 Mara Bos, 978-1-098-11944-7."

Conventions Used in This Book

The following typographical conventions are used in this book:

Italic
Used for new terms, URLs, and emphasis.

`Constant width`
Used for program listings, as well as within paragraphs to refer to program elements such as variable or function names, data types, statements, and keywords.

This element signifies a tip or suggestion.

 This element signifies a general note.

 This element indicates a warning or caution.

Contact Information

O'Reilly has a web page for this book, where errata, examples, and any additional information are listed. It is available at *https://oreil.ly/rust-atomics-and-locks*.

Email *bookquestions@oreilly.com* to comment or ask technical questions about this book. If you wish to reuse content from this book, and you feel your reuse falls outside fair use or the permission given in this Preface, feel free to contact O'Reilly at *permissions@oreilly.com*.

For news and information about O'Reilly, visit *https://oreilly.com*.

Follow O'Reilly on Twitter: *https://twitter.com/oreillymedia*.

Follow the author on Twitter: *https://twitter.com/m_ou_se*.

Acknowledgments

I'd like to thank everyone who had a part in the creation this book. Many people provided support and useful input, which has been incredibly helpful. In particular, I'd like to thank Amanieu d'Antras, Aria Beingessner, Paul McKenney, Carol Nichols, and Miguel Raz Guzmán Macedo for their invaluable and thoughtful feedback on the early drafts. I'd also like to thank everyone at O'Reilly, and in particular my editors, Shira Evans and Zan McQuade, for their inexhaustible enthusiasm and support.

CHAPTER 1

Basics of Rust Concurrency

Long before multi-core processors were commonplace, operating systems allowed for a single computer to run many programs concurrently. This is achieved by rapidly switching between processes, allowing each to repeatedly make a little bit of progress, one by one. Nowadays, virtually all our computers and even our phones and watches have processors with multiple cores, which can truly execute multiple processes in parallel.

Operating systems isolate processes from each other as much as possible, allowing a program to do its thing while completely unaware of what any other processes are doing. For example, a process cannot normally access the memory of another process, or communicate with it in any way, without asking the operating system's kernel first.

However, a program can spawn extra *threads of execution*, as part of the same *process*. Threads within the same process are not isolated from each other. Threads share memory and can interact with each other through that memory.

This chapter will explain how threads are spawned in Rust, and all the basic concepts around them, such as how to safely share data between multiple threads. The concepts explained in this chapter are foundational to the rest of the book.

 If you're already familiar with these parts of Rust, feel free to skip ahead. However, before you continue to the next chapters, make sure you have a good understanding of threads, interior mutability, Send and Sync, and know what a mutex, a condition variable, and thread parking are.

Threads in Rust

Every program starts with exactly one thread: the main thread. This thread will execute your main function and can be used to spawn more threads if necessary.

In Rust, new threads are spawned using the std::thread::spawn function from the standard library. It takes a single argument: the function the new thread will execute. The thread stops once this function returns.

Let's take a look at an example:

```
use std::thread;

fn main() {
    thread::spawn(f);
    thread::spawn(f);

    println!("Hello from the main thread.");
}

fn f() {
    println!("Hello from another thread!");

    let id = thread::current().id();
    println!("This is my thread id: {id:?}");
}
```

We spawn two threads that will both execute f as their main function. Both of these threads will print a message and show their *thread id*, while the main thread will also print its own message.

Thread ID

The Rust standard library assigns every thread a unique identifier. This identifier is accessible through Thread::id() and is of the type ThreadId. There's not much you can do with a ThreadId other than copying it around and checking for equality. There is no guarantee that these IDs will be assigned consecutively, only that they will be different for each thread.

If you run our example program above several times, you might notice the output varies between runs. This is the output I got on my machine during one particular run:

```
Hello from the main thread.
Hello from another thread!
This is my thread id:
```

Surprisingly, part of the output seems to be missing.

What happened here is that the main thread finished executing the main function before the newly spawned threads finished executing their functions.

Returning from main will exit the entire program, even if other threads are still running.

In this particular example, one of the newly spawned threads had just enough time to get to halfway through the second message, before the program was shut down by the main thread.

If we want to make sure the threads are finished before we return from main, we can wait for them by *joining* them. To do so, we have to use the JoinHandle returned by the spawn function:

```
fn main() {
    let t1 = thread::spawn(f);
    let t2 = thread::spawn(f);

    println!("Hello from the main thread.");

    t1.join().unwrap();
    t2.join().unwrap();
}
```

The .join() method waits until the thread has finished executing and returns a std::thread::Result. If the thread did not successfully finish its function because it panicked, this will contain the panic message. We could attempt to handle that situation, or just call .unwrap() to panic when joining a panicked thread.

Running this version of our program will no longer result in truncated output:

```
Hello from the main thread.
Hello from another thread!
This is my thread id: ThreadId(3)
Hello from another thread!
This is my thread id: ThreadId(2)
```

The only thing that still changes between runs is the order in which the messages are printed:

```
Hello from the main thread.
Hello from another thread!
Hello from another thread!
This is my thread id: ThreadId(2)
This is my thread id: ThreadId(3)
```

Rather than passing the name of a function to `std::thread::spawn`, as in our example above, it's far more common to pass it a *closure*. This allows us to capture values to move into the new thread:

```
let numbers = vec![1, 2, 3];

thread::spawn(move || {
    for n in &numbers {
        println!("{n}");
    }
}).join().unwrap();
```

Here, ownership of `numbers` is transferred to the newly spawned thread, since we used a `move` closure. If we had not used the `move` keyword, the closure would have captured `numbers` by reference. This would have resulted in a compiler error, since the new thread might outlive that variable.

Since a thread might run until the very end of the program's execution, the `spawn` function has a `'static` lifetime bound on its argument type. In other words, it only accepts functions that may be kept around forever. A closure capturing a local variable by reference may not be kept around forever, since that reference would become invalid the moment the local variable ceases to exist.

Getting a value back out of the thread is done by returning it from the closure. This return value can be obtained from the `Result` returned by the `join` method:

```
let numbers = Vec::from_iter(0..=1000);

let t = thread::spawn(move || {
    let len = numbers.len();
    let sum = numbers.iter().sum::<usize>();
    sum / len  ❶
});

let average = t.join().unwrap();  ❷
```

```
    println!("average: {average}");
```

Here, the value returned by the thread's closure (❶) is sent back to the main thread through the join method (❷).

If numbers had been empty, the thread would've panicked while trying to divide by zero (❶), and join would've returned that panic message instead, causing the main thread to panic too because of unwrap (❷).

Thread Builder

The std::thread::spawn function is actually just a convenient shorthand for std::thread::Builder::new().spawn().unwrap().

A std::thread::Builder allows you to set some settings for the new thread before spawning it. You can use it to configure the stack size for the new thread and to give the new thread a name. The name of a thread is available through std::thread::cur rent().name(), will be used in panic messages, and will be visible in monitoring and debugging tools on most platforms.

Additionally, Builder's spawn function returns an std::io::Result, allowing you to handle situations where spawning a new thread fails. This might happen if the operating system runs out of memory, or if resource limits have been applied to your program. The std::thread::spawn function simply panics if it is unable to spawn a new thread.

Scoped Threads

If we know for sure that a spawned thread will definitely not outlive a certain scope, that thread could safely borrow things that do not live forever, such as local variables, as long as they outlive that scope.

The Rust standard library provides the std::thread::scope function to spawn such *scoped threads*. It allows us to spawn threads that cannot outlive the scope of the closure we pass to that function, making it possible to safely borrow local variables.

How it works is best shown with an example:

```
let numbers = vec![1, 2, 3];

thread::scope(|s| {        ❶
    s.spawn(|| {           ❷
        println!("length: {}", numbers.len());
    });
    s.spawn(|| {           ❷
        for n in &numbers {
```

```
            println!("{n}");
        }
    });
}); ❸
```

❶ We call the `std::thread::scope` function with a closure. Our closure is directly
    executed and gets an argument, s, representing the scope.

❷ We use s to spawn threads. The closures can borrow local variables like numbers.

❸ When the scope ends, all threads that haven't been joined yet are automatically
    joined.

This pattern guarantees that none of the threads spawned in the scope can outlive the
scope. Because of that, this scoped `spawn` method does not have a `'static` bound on
its argument type, allowing us to reference anything as long as it outlives the scope,
such as numbers.

In the example above, both of the new threads are concurrently accessing numbers.
This is fine, because neither of them (nor the main thread) modifies it. If we were
to change the first thread to modify numbers, as shown below, the compiler wouldn't
allow us to spawn another thread that also uses numbers:

```
let mut numbers = vec![1, 2, 3];

thread::scope(|s| {
    s.spawn(|| {
        numbers.push(1);
    });
    s.spawn(|| {
        numbers.push(2); // Error!
    });
});
```

The exact error message depends on the version of the Rust compiler, since it's often
improved to produce better diagnostics, but attempting to compile the code above
will result in something like this:

```
error[E0499]: cannot borrow `numbers` as mutable more than once at a time
  --> example.rs:7:13
   |
4  |         s.spawn(|| {
   |                 -- first mutable borrow occurs here
5  |             numbers.push(1);
   |             ------- first borrow occurs due to use of `numbers` in closure
   |
7  |         s.spawn(|| {
   |                 ^^ second mutable borrow occurs here
8  |             numbers.push(2);
   |             ------- second borrow occurs due to use of `numbers` in closure
```

The Leakpocalypse

Before Rust 1.0, the standard library had a function named `std::thread::scoped` that would directly spawn a thread, just like `std::thread::spawn`. It allowed non-`'static` captures, because instead of a `JoinHandle`, it returned a `JoinGuard` which joined the thread when dropped. Any borrowed data only needed to outlive this `JoinGuard`. This seemed safe, as long as the `JoinGuard` got dropped at some point.

Just before the release of Rust 1.0, it slowly became clear that it's not possible to guarantee that something will be dropped. There are many ways, such as creating a cycle of reference-counted nodes, that make it possible to forget about something, or *leak* it, without dropping it.

Eventually, in what some people refer to as "The Leakpocalypse," the conclusion was made that the design of a (safe) interface cannot rely on the assumption that objects will always be dropped at the end of their lifetime. Leaking an object might reasonably result in leaking more objects (e.g., leaking a `Vec` will also leak its elements), but it may not result in undefined behavior. Because of this conclusion, `std::thread::scoped` was no longer deemed safe and was removed from the standard library. Additionally, `std::mem::forget` was upgraded from an `unsafe` function to a *safe* function, to emphasize that forgetting (or leaking) is always a possibility.

Only much later, in Rust 1.63, a new `std::thread::scope` function was added with a new design that does not rely on `Drop` for correctness.

Shared Ownership and Reference Counting

So far we've looked at transferring ownership of a value to a thread using a move closure ("Threads in Rust" on page 2) and borrowing data from longer-living parent threads ("Scoped Threads" on page 5). When sharing data between two threads where neither thread is guaranteed to outlive the other, neither of them can be the owner of that data. Any data shared between them will need to live as long as the longest living thread.

Statics

There are several ways to create something that's not owned by a single thread. The simplest one is a `static` value, which is "owned" by the entire program, instead of an individual thread. In the following example, both threads can access X, but neither of them owns it:

```
static X: [i32; 3] = [1, 2, 3];
```

```
thread::spawn(|| dbg!(&X));
thread::spawn(|| dbg!(&X));
```

A static item has a constant initializer, is never dropped, and already exists before the main function of the program even starts. Every thread can borrow it, since it's guaranteed to always exist.

Leaking

Another way to share ownership is by *leaking* an allocation. Using `Box::leak`, one can release ownership of a `Box`, promising to never drop it. From that point on, the `Box` will live forever, without an owner, allowing it to be borrowed by any thread for as long as the program runs.

```
let x: &'static [i32; 3] = Box::leak(Box::new([1, 2, 3]));

thread::spawn(move || dbg!(x));
thread::spawn(move || dbg!(x));
```

The `move` closure might make it look like we're moving ownership into the threads, but a closer look at the type of x reveals that we're only giving the threads a *reference* to the data.

 References are Copy, meaning that when you "move" them, the original still exists, just like with an integer or boolean.

Note how the `'static` lifetime doesn't mean that the value lived since the start of the program, but only that it lives to the end of the program. The past is simply not relevant.

The downside of leaking a `Box` is that we're *leaking memory*. We allocate something, but never drop and deallocate it. This can be fine if it happens only a limited number of times. But if we keep doing this, the program will slowly run out of memory.

Reference Counting

To make sure that shared data gets dropped and deallocated, we can't completely give up its ownership. Instead, we can *share ownership*. By keeping track of the number of owners, we can make sure the value is dropped only when there are no owners left.

The Rust standard library provides this functionality through the `std::rc::Rc` type, short for "reference counted." It is very similar to a `Box`, except cloning it will not allocate anything new, but instead increment a counter stored next to the contained value. Both the original and cloned Rc will refer to the same allocation; they *share ownership*.

```
use std::rc::Rc;

let a = Rc::new([1, 2, 3]);
let b = a.clone();

assert_eq!(a.as_ptr(), b.as_ptr()); // Same allocation!
```

Dropping an Rc will decrement the counter. Only the last Rc, which will see the counter drop to zero, will be the one dropping and deallocating the contained data.

If we were to try to send an Rc to another thread, however, we would run into the following compiler error:

```
error[E0277]: `Rc` cannot be sent between threads safely
    |
8   |       thread::spawn(move || dbg!(b));
    |                     ^^^^^^^^^^^^^^^^
```

As it turns out, Rc is not *thread safe* (more on that in "Thread Safety: Send and Sync" on page 16). If multiple threads had an Rc to the same allocation, they might try to modify the reference counter at the same time, which can give unpredictable results.

Instead, we can use std::sync::Arc, which stands for "atomically reference counted." It's identical to Rc, except it guarantees that modifications to the reference counter are indivisible *atomic* operations, making it safe to use it with multiple threads. (More on that in Chapter 2.)

```
use std::sync::Arc;

let a = Arc::new([1, 2, 3]); ❶
let b = a.clone(); ❷

thread::spawn(move || dbg!(a)); ❸
thread::spawn(move || dbg!(b)); ❸
```

❶ We put an array in a new allocation together with a reference counter, which starts at one.

❷ Cloning the Arc increments the reference count to two and provides us with a second Arc to the same allocation.

❸ Both threads get their own Arc through which they can access the shared array. Both decrement the reference counter when they drop their Arc. The last thread to drop its Arc will see the counter drop to zero and will be the one to drop and deallocate the array.

Naming Clones

Having to give every clone of an Arc a different name can quickly make the code quite cluttered and hard to follow. While every clone of an Arc is a separate object, each clone represents the same shared value, which is not well reflected by naming each one differently.

Rust allows (and encourages) you to *shadow* variables by defining a new variable with the same name. If you do that in the same scope, the original variable cannot be named anymore. But by opening a new scope, a statement like let a = a.clone(); can be used to reuse the same name within that scope, while leaving the original variable available outside the scope.

By wrapping a closure in a new scope (with {}), we can clone variables before moving them into the closure, without having to rename them.

```
let a = Arc::new([1, 2, 3]);

let b = a.clone();

thread::spawn(move || {
    dbg!(b);
});

dbg!(a);
```

```
let a = Arc::new([1, 2, 3]);

thread::spawn({
    let a = a.clone();
    move || {
        dbg!(a);
    }
});

dbg!(a);
```

The clone of the Arc lives in the same scope. Each thread gets its own clone with a different name.

The clone of the Arc lives in a different scope. We can use the same name in each thread.

Because ownership is shared, reference counting pointers (Rc<T> and Arc<T>) have the same restrictions as shared references (&T). They do not give you mutable access to their contained value, since the value might be borrowed by other code at the same time.

For example, if we were to try to sort the slice of integers in an Arc<[i32]>, the compiler would stop us from doing so, telling us that we're not allowed to mutate the data:

```
error[E0596]: cannot borrow data in an `Arc` as mutable
   |
 6 |     a.sort();
   |     ^^^^^^^^
```

Borrowing and Data Races

In Rust, values can be borrowed in two ways:

Immutable borrowing

Borrowing something with & gives an *immutable reference*. Such a reference can be copied. Access to the data it references is shared between all copies of such a reference. As the name implies, the compiler doesn't normally allow you to *mutate* something through such a reference, since that might affect other code that's currently borrowing the same data.

Mutable borrowing

Borrowing something with &mut gives a *mutable reference*. A mutable borrow guarantees it's the only active borrow of that data. This ensures that mutating the data will not change anything that other code is currently looking at.

These two concepts together fully prevent *data races*: situations where one thread is mutating data while another is concurrently accessing it. Data races are generally *undefined behavior*, which means the compiler does not need to take these situations into account. It will simply assume they do not happen.

To clarify what that means, let's take a look at an example where the compiler can make a useful assumption using the borrowing rules:

```
fn f(a: &i32, b: &mut i32) {
    let before = *a;
    *b += 1;
    let after = *a;
    if before != after {
        x(); // never happens
    }
}
```

Here, we get an immutable reference to an integer, and store the value of the integer both before and after incrementing the integer that b refers to. The compiler is free to assume that the fundamental rules about borrowing and data races are upheld, which means that b can't possibly refer to the same integer as a does. In fact, nothing in the entire program can mutably borrow the integer that a refers to as long as a is borrowing it. Therefore, the compiler can easily conclude that *a will not change and the condition of the if statement will never be true, and can completely remove the call to x from the program as an optimization.

It's impossible to write a Rust program that breaks the compiler's assumptions, other than by using an unsafe block to disable some of the compiler's safety checks.

Undefined Behavior

Languages like C, C++, and Rust have a set of rules that need to be followed to avoid something called *undefined behavior*. For example, one of Rust's rules is that there may never be more than one mutable reference to any object.

In Rust, it's only possible to break any of these rules when using unsafe code. "Unsafe" doesn't mean that the code is incorrect or never safe to use, but rather that the compiler is not validating for you that the code is safe. If the code does violate these rules, it is called *unsound*.

The compiler is allowed to assume, without checking, that these rules are never broken. When broken, this results in something called *undefined behavior*, which we need to avoid at all costs. If we allow the compiler to make an assumption that is not actually true, it can easily result in more wrong conclusions about different parts of your code, affecting your whole program.

As a concrete example, let's take a look at a small snippet that uses the get_unchecked method on a slice:

```
let a = [123, 456, 789];
let b = unsafe { a.get_unchecked(index) };
```

The get_unchecked method gives us an element of the slice given its index, just like a[index], but allows the compiler to assume the index is always within bounds, without any checks.

This means that in this code snippet, because a is of length 3, the compiler may assume that index is less than three. It's up to us to make sure its assumption holds.

If we break this assumption, for example if we run this with index equal to 3, anything might happen. It might result in reading from memory whatever was stored in the bytes right after a. It might cause the program to crash. It might end up executing some entirely unrelated part of the program. It can cause all kinds of havoc.

Perhaps surprisingly, undefined behavior can even "travel back in time," causing problems in code that precedes it. To understand how that can happen, imagine we had a match statement before our previous snippet, as follows:

```
match index {
    0 => x(),
    1 => y(),
    _ => z(index),
}

let a = [123, 456, 789];
let b = unsafe { a.get_unchecked(index) };
```

Because of the unsafe code, the compiler is allowed to assume index is only ever 0, 1, or 2. It may logically conclude that the last arm of our match statement will only ever match a 2, and thus that z is only ever called as z(2). That conclusion might be used not only to optimize the match, but also to optimize z itself. This can include throwing out unused parts of the code.

If we execute this with an index of 3, our program might attempt to execute parts that have been optimized away, resulting in completely unpredictable behavior, long before we get to the unsafe block on the last line. Just like that, undefined behavior can propagate through a whole program, both backwards and forwards, in often very unexpected ways.

When calling any unsafe function, read its documentation carefully and make sure you fully understand its *safety requirements*: the assumptions you need to uphold, as the caller, to avoid undefined behavior.

Interior Mutability

The borrowing rules as introduced in the previous section are simple, but can be quite limiting—especially when multiple threads are involved. Following these rules makes communication between threads extremely limited and almost impossible, since no data that's accessible by multiple threads can be mutated.

Luckily, there is an escape hatch: *interior mutability*. A data type with interior mutability slightly bends the borrowing rules. Under certain conditions, those types can allow mutation through an "immutable" reference.

In "Reference Counting" on page 8, we've already seen one subtle example involving interior mutability. Both Rc and Arc mutate a reference counter, even though there might be multiple clones all using the same reference counter.

As soon as interior mutable types are involved, calling a reference "immutable" or "mutable" becomes confusing and inaccurate, since some things can be mutated through both. The more accurate terms are "shared" and "exclusive": a *shared reference* (&T) can be copied and shared with others, while an *exclusive reference* (&mut T) guarantees it's the only *exclusive borrowing* of that T. For most types, shared references do not allow mutation, but there are exceptions. Since in this book we will mostly be working with these exceptions, we'll use the more accurate terms in the rest of this book.

Keep in mind that interior mutability only bends the rules of shared borrowing to allow mutation when shared. It does not change anything about exclusive borrowing. Exclusive borrowing still guarantees that there are no other active borrows. Unsafe code that results in more than one active exclusive reference to something always invokes undefined behavior, regardless of interior mutability.

Let's take a look at a few types with interior mutability and how they can allow mutation through shared references without causing undefined behavior.

Cell

A `std::cell::Cell<T>` simply wraps a `T`, but allows mutations through a shared reference. To avoid undefined behavior, it only allows you to copy the value out (if `T` is `Copy`), or replace it with another value as a whole. In addition, it can only be used within a single thread.

Let's take a look at an example similar to the one in the previous section, but this time using `Cell<i32>` instead of `i32`:

```
use std::cell::Cell;

fn f(a: &Cell<i32>, b: &Cell<i32>) {
    let before = a.get();
    b.set(b.get() + 1);
    let after = a.get();
    if before != after {
        x(); // might happen
    }
}
```

Unlike last time, it is now possible for the `if` condition to be true. Because a `Cell<i32>` has interior mutability, the compiler can no longer assume its value won't change as long as we have a shared reference to it. Both `a` and `b` might refer to the same value, such that mutating through `b` might affect `a` as well. It may still assume, however, that no other threads are accessing the cells concurrently.

The restrictions on a `Cell` are not always easy to work with. Since it can't directly let us borrow the value it holds, we need to move a value out (leaving something in its place), modify it, then put it back, to mutate its contents:

```
fn f(v: &Cell<Vec<i32>>) {
    let mut v2 = v.take(); // Replaces the contents of the Cell with an empty Vec
    v2.push(1);
    v.set(v2); // Put the modified Vec back
}
```

RefCell

Unlike a regular `Cell`, a `std::cell::RefCell` does allow you to borrow its contents, at a small runtime cost. A `RefCell<T>` does not only hold a `T`, but also holds a counter that keeps track of any outstanding borrows. If you try to borrow it while it is already mutably borrowed (or vice-versa), it will panic, which avoids undefined behavior. Just like a `Cell`, a `RefCell` can only be used within a single thread.

Borrowing the contents of RefCell is done by calling borrow or borrow_mut:

```
use std::cell::RefCell;

fn f(v: &RefCell<Vec<i32>>) {
    v.borrow_mut().push(1); // We can modify the `Vec` directly.
}
```

While Cell and RefCell can be very useful, they become rather useless when we need to do something with multiple threads. So let's move on to the types that are relevant for concurrency.

Mutex and RwLock

An RwLock or *reader-writer lock* is the concurrent version of a RefCell. An RwLock<T> holds a T and tracks any outstanding borrows. However, unlike a RefCell, it does not panic on conflicting borrows. Instead, it blocks the current thread—putting it to sleep—while waiting for conflicting borrows to disappear. We'll just have to patiently wait for our turn with the data, after the other threads are done with it.

Borrowing the contents of an RwLock is called *locking*. By *locking* it we temporarily block concurrent conflicting borrows, allowing us to borrow it without causing data races.

A Mutex is very similar, but conceptually slightly simpler. Instead of keeping track of the number of shared and exclusive borrows like an RwLock, it only allows exclusive borrows.

We'll go more into detail on these types in "Locking: Mutexes and RwLocks" on page 18.

Atomics

The atomic types represent the concurrent version of a Cell, and are the main topic of Chapters 2 and 3. Like a Cell, they avoid undefined behavior by making us copy values in and out as a whole, without letting us borrow the contents directly.

Unlike a Cell, though, they cannot be of arbitrary size. Because of this, there is no generic Atomic<T> type for any T, but there are only specific atomic types such as AtomicU32 and AtomicPtr<T>. Which ones are available depends on the platform, since they require support from the processor to avoid data races. (We'll dive into that in Chapter 7.)

Since they are so limited in size, atomics often don't directly contain the information that needs to be shared between threads. Instead, they are often used as a tool to make it possible to share other—often bigger—things between threads. When atomics are used to say something about other data, things can get surprisingly complicated.

UnsafeCell

An UnsafeCell is the primitive building block for interior mutability.

An UnsafeCell<T> wraps a T, but does not come with any conditions or restrictions to avoid undefined behavior. Instead, its get() method just gives a raw pointer to the value it wraps, which can only be meaningfully used in unsafe blocks. It leaves it up to the user to use it in a way that does not cause any undefined behavior.

Most commonly, an UnsafeCell is not used directly, but wrapped in another type that provides safety through a limited interface, such as Cell or Mutex. All types with interior mutability—including all types discussed above—are built on top of UnsafeCell.

Thread Safety: Send and Sync

In this chapter, we've seen several types that are not *thread safe*, types that can only be used on a single thread, such as Rc, Cell, and others. Since that restriction is needed to avoid undefined behavior, it's something the compiler needs to understand and check for you, so you can use these types without having to use unsafe blocks.

The language uses two special traits to keep track of which types can be safely used across threads:

Send
    A type is Send if it can be sent to another thread. In other words, if ownership of a value of that type can be transferred to another thread. For example, Arc<i32> is Send, but Rc<i32> is not.

Sync
    A type is Sync if it can be shared with another thread. In other words, a type T is Sync if and only if a shared reference to that type, &T, is Send. For example, an i32 is Sync, but a Cell<i32> is not. (A Cell<i32> is Send, however.)

All primitive types such as i32, bool, and str are both Send and Sync.

Both of these traits are *auto traits*, which means that they are automatically implemented for your types based on their fields. A struct with fields that are all Send and Sync, is itself also Send and Sync.

The way to opt out of either of these is to add a field to your type that does not implement the trait. For that purpose, the special std::marker::PhantomData<T>

---

type often comes in handy. That type is treated by the compiler as a T, except it doesn't actually exist at runtime. It's a zero-sized type, taking no space.

Let's take a look at the following struct:

```
use std::marker::PhantomData;

struct X {
    handle: i32,
    _not_sync: PhantomData<Cell<()>>,
}
```

In this example, X would be both Send and Sync if handle was its only field. However, we added a zero-sized PhantomData<Cell<()>> field, which is treated as if it were a Cell<()>. Since a Cell<()> is not Sync, neither is X. It is still Send, however, since all its fields implement Send.

Raw pointers (*const T and *mut T) are neither Send nor Sync, since the compiler doesn't know much about what they represent.

The way to opt in to either of the traits is the same as with any other trait; use an impl block to implement the trait for your type:

```
struct X {
    p: *mut i32,
}

unsafe impl Send for X {}
unsafe impl Sync for X {}
```

Note how implementing these traits requires the unsafe keyword, since the compiler cannot check for you if it's correct. It's a promise you make to the compiler, which it will just have to trust.

If you try to move something into another thread which is not Send, the compiler will politely stop you from doing that. Here is a small example to demonstrate that:

```
fn main() {
    let a = Rc::new(123);
    thread::spawn(move || { // Error!
        dbg!(a);
    });
}
```

Here, we try to send an Rc<i32> to a new thread, but Rc<i32>, unlike Arc<i32>, does not implement Send.

If we try to compile the example above, we're faced with an error that looks something like this:

```
error[E0277]: `Rc<i32>` cannot be sent between threads safely
  --> src/main.rs:3:5
   |
3  |       thread::spawn(move || {
   |       ^^^^^^^^^^^^^ `Rc<i32>` cannot be sent between threads safely
   |
   = help: within `[closure]`, the trait `Send` is not implemented for `Rc<i32>`
note: required because it's used within this closure
  --> src/main.rs:3:19
   |
3  |       thread::spawn(move || {
   |                     ^^^^^^^
note: required by a bound in `spawn`
```

The thread::spawn function requires its argument to be Send, and a closure is only Send if all of its captures are. If we try to capture something that's not Send, our mistake is caught, protecting us from undefined behavior.

Locking: Mutexes and RwLocks

The most commonly used tool for sharing (mutable) data between threads is a *mutex*, which is short for "mutual exclusion." The job of a mutex is to ensure threads have exclusive access to some data by temporarily blocking other threads that try to access it at the same time.

Conceptually, a mutex has only two states: locked and unlocked. When a thread locks an unlocked mutex, the mutex is marked as locked and the thread can immediately continue. When a thread then attempts to lock an already locked mutex, that operation will *block*. The thread is put to sleep while it waits for the mutex to be unlocked. Unlocking is only possible on a locked mutex, and should be done by the same thread that locked it. If other threads are waiting to lock the mutex, unlocking will cause one of those threads to be woken up, so it can try to lock the mutex again and continue its course.

Protecting data with a mutex is simply the agreement between all threads that they will only access the data when they have the mutex locked. That way, no two threads can ever access that data concurrently and cause a data race.

Rust's Mutex

The Rust standard library provides this functionality through std::sync::Mutex<T>. It is generic over a type T, which is the type of the data the mutex is protecting. By making this T part of the mutex, the data can only be accessed through the mutex, allowing for a safe interface that can guarantee all threads will uphold the agreement.

To ensure a locked mutex can only be unlocked by the thread that locked it, it does not have an unlock() method. Instead, its lock() method returns a special type called a MutexGuard. This guard represents the guarantee that we have locked the mutex. It behaves like an exclusive reference through the DerefMut trait, giving us exclusive access to the data the mutex protects. Unlocking the mutex is done by dropping the guard. When we drop the guard, we give up our ability to access the data, and the Drop implementation of the guard will unlock the mutex.

Let's take a look at an example to see a mutex in practice:

```rust
use std::sync::Mutex;

fn main() {
    let n = Mutex::new(0);
    thread::scope(|s| {
        for _ in 0..10 {
            s.spawn(|| {
                let mut guard = n.lock().unwrap();
                for _ in 0..100 {
                    *guard += 1;
                }
            });
        }
    });
    assert_eq!(n.into_inner().unwrap(), 1000);
}
```

Here, we have a Mutex<i32>, a mutex protecting an integer, and we spawn ten threads to each increment the integer one hundred times. Each thread will first lock the mutex to obtain a MutexGuard, and then use that guard to access the integer and modify it. The guard is implicitly dropped right after, when that variable goes out of scope.

After the threads are done, we can safely remove the protection from the integer through into_inner(). The into_inner method takes ownership of the mutex, which guarantees that nothing else can have a reference to the mutex anymore, making locking unnecessary.

Even though the increments happen in steps of one, a thread observing the integer would only ever see multiples of 100, since it can only look at the integer when the mutex is unlocked. Effectively, thanks to the mutex, the one hundred increments together are now a single indivisible—atomic—operation.

To clearly see the effect of the mutex, we can make each thread wait a second before unlocking the mutex:

```rust
use std::time::Duration;

fn main() {
    let n = Mutex::new(0);
    thread::scope(|s| {
        for _ in 0..10 {
            s.spawn(|| {
                let mut guard = n.lock().unwrap();
                for _ in 0..100 {
                    *guard += 1;
                }
                thread::sleep(Duration::from_secs(1)); // New!
            });
        }
    });
    assert_eq!(n.into_inner().unwrap(), 1000);
}
```

When you run the program now, you will see that it takes about 10 seconds to complete. Each thread only waits for one second, but the mutex ensures that only one thread at a time can do so.

If we drop the guard—and therefore unlock the mutex—before sleeping one second, we will see it happen in parallel instead:

```rust
fn main() {
    let n = Mutex::new(0);
    thread::scope(|s| {
        for _ in 0..10 {
            s.spawn(|| {
                let mut guard = n.lock().unwrap();
                for _ in 0..100 {
                    *guard += 1;
                }
                drop(guard); // New: drop the guard before sleeping!
                thread::sleep(Duration::from_secs(1));
            });
        }
    });
    assert_eq!(n.into_inner().unwrap(), 1000);
}
```

With this change, this program takes only about one second, since now the 10 threads can execute their one-second sleep at the same time. This shows the importance of keeping the amount of time a mutex is locked as short as possible. Keeping a mutex locked longer than necessary can completely nullify any benefits of parallelism, effectively forcing everything to happen serially instead.

Lock Poisoning

The unwrap() calls in the examples above relate to *lock poisoning*.

A Mutex in Rust gets marked as *poisoned* when a thread panics while holding the lock. When that happens, the Mutex will no longer be locked, but calling its lock method will result in an Err to indicate it has been poisoned.

This is a mechanism to protect against leaving the data that's protected by a mutex in an inconsistent state. In our example above, if a thread would panic after incrementing the integer fewer than 100 times, the mutex would unlock and the integer would be left in an unexpected state where it is no longer a multiple of 100, possibly breaking assumptions made by other threads. Automatically marking the mutex as poisoned in that case forces the user to handle this possibility.

Calling lock() on a poisoned mutex still locks the mutex. The Err returned by lock() contains the MutexGuard, allowing us to correct an inconsistent state if necessary.

While lock poisoning might seem like a powerful mechanism, recovering from a potentially inconsistent state is not often done in practice. Most code either disregards poison or uses unwrap() to panic if the lock was poisoned, effectively propagating panics to all users of the mutex.

Lifetime of the MutexGuard

While it's convenient that implicitly dropping a guard unlocks the mutex, it can sometimes lead to subtle surprises. If we assign the guard a name with a let statement (as in our examples above), it's relatively straightforward to see when it will be dropped, since local variables are dropped at the end of the scope they are defined in. Still, not explicitly dropping a guard might lead to keeping the mutex locked for longer than necessary, as demonstrated in the examples above.

Using a guard *without* assigning it a name is also possible, and can be very convenient at times. Since a MutexGuard behaves like an exclusive reference to the protected data, we can directly use it without assigning a name to the guard first. For example, if you have a Mutex<Vec<i32>>, you can lock the mutex, push an item into the Vec, and unlock the mutex again, in a single statement:

```
list.lock().unwrap().push(1);
```

Any temporaries produced within a larger expression, such as the guard returned by lock(), will be dropped at the end of the statement. While this might seem obvious and reasonable, it leads to a common pitfall that usually involves a match, if let, or while let statement. Here is an example that runs into this pitfall:

```
if let Some(item) = list.lock().unwrap().pop() {
    process_item(item);
}
```

If our intention was to lock the list, pop an item, unlock the list, and *then* process the item after the list is unlocked, we made a subtle but important mistake here. The temporary guard is not dropped until the end of the entire if let statement, meaning we needlessly hold on to the lock while processing the item.

Perhaps surprisingly, this does not happen for a similar if statement, such as in this example:

```
if list.lock().unwrap().pop() == Some(1) {
    do_something();
}
```

Here, the temporary guard does get dropped before the body of the if statement is executed. The reason is that the condition of a regular if statement is always a plain boolean, which cannot borrow anything. There is no reason to extend the lifetime of temporaries from the condition to the end of the statement. For an if let statement, however, that might not be the case. If we had used front() rather than pop(), for example, item would be borrowing from the list, making it necessary to keep the guard around. Since the borrow checker is only really a check and does *not* influence when or in what order things are dropped, the same happens when we use pop(), even though that wouldn't have been necessary.

We can avoid this by moving the pop operation to a separate let statement. Then the guard is dropped at the end of that statement, before the if let:

```
let item = list.lock().unwrap().pop();
if let Some(item) = item {
    process_item(item);
}
```

Reader-Writer Lock

A mutex is only concerned with exclusive access. The MutexGuard will provide us an exclusive reference (&mut T) to the protected data, even if we only wanted to look at the data and a shared reference (&T) would have sufficed.

A reader-writer lock is a slightly more complicated version of a mutex that understands the difference between exclusive and shared access, and can provide either. It has three states: unlocked, locked by a single *writer* (for exclusive access), and locked by any number of *readers* (for shared access). It is commonly used for data that is often read by multiple threads, but only updated once in a while.

The Rust standard library provides this lock through the std::sync::RwLock<T> type. It works similarly to the standard Mutex, except its interface is mostly split in two parts. Instead of a single lock() method, it has a read() and write() method for locking as either a reader or a writer. It comes with two guard types, one for readers and one for writers: RwLockReadGuard and RwLockWriteGuard. The former only implements Deref to behave like a shared reference to the protected data, while the latter also implements DerefMut to behave like an exclusive reference.

It is effectively the multi-threaded version of RefCell, dynamically tracking the number of references to ensure the borrow rules are upheld.

Both Mutex<T> and RwLock<T> require T to be Send, because they can be used to send a T to another thread. An RwLock<T> additionally requires T to also implement Sync, because it allows multiple threads to hold a shared reference (&T) to the protected data. (Strictly speaking, you can create a lock for a T that doesn't fulfill these requirements, but you wouldn't be able to share it between threads as the lock itself won't implement Sync.)

The Rust standard library provides only one general purpose RwLock type, but its implementation depends on the operating system. There are many subtle variations between reader-writer lock implementations. Most implementations will block new readers when there is a writer waiting, even when the lock is already read-locked. This is done to prevent *writer starvation*, a situation where many readers collectively keep the lock from ever unlocking, never allowing any writer to update the data.

Mutexes in Other Languages

Rust's standard Mutex and RwLock types look a bit different than those you find in other languages like C or C++.

The biggest difference is that Rust's Mutex<T> *contains* the data it is protecting. In C++, for example, std::mutex does not contain the data it protects, nor does it even know what it is protecting. This means that it is the responsibility of the user to remember which data is protected and by which mutex, and ensure the right mutex is locked every time "protected" data is accessed. This is useful to keep in mind when reading code involving mutexes in other languages, or when communicating with programmers who are not familiar with Rust. A Rust programmer might talk about "the data inside the mutex," or say things like "wrap it in a mutex," which can be confusing to those only familiar with mutexes in other languages.

If you really need a stand-alone mutex that doesn't contain anything, for example to protect some external hardware, you can use Mutex<()>. But even in a case like that, you are probably better off defining a (possibly zero-sized) type to interface with that hardware and wrapping that in a Mutex instead. That way, you are still forced to lock the mutex before you can interact with the hardware.

Waiting: Parking and Condition Variables

When data is mutated by multiple threads, there are many situations where they would need to wait for some event, for some condition about the data to become true. For example, if we have a mutex protecting a Vec, we might want to wait until it contains anything.

While a mutex does allow threads to wait until it becomes unlocked, it does not provide functionality for waiting for any other conditions. If a mutex was all we had, we'd have to keep locking the mutex to repeatedly check if there's anything in the Vec yet.

Thread Parking

One way to wait for a notification from another thread is called *thread parking*. A thread can *park* itself, which puts it to sleep, stopping it from consuming any CPU cycles. Another thread can then *unpark* the parked thread, waking it up from its nap.

Thread parking is available through the std::thread::park() function. For unparking, you call the unpark() method on a Thread object representing the thread that you want to unpark. Such an object can be obtained from the join handle returned by spawn, or by the thread itself through std::thread::current().

Let's dive into an example that uses a mutex to share a queue between two threads. In the following example, a newly spawned thread will consume items from the queue, while the main thread will insert a new item into the queue every second. Thread parking is used to make the consuming thread wait when the queue is empty.

```rust
use std::collections::VecDeque;

fn main() {
    let queue = Mutex::new(VecDeque::new());

    thread::scope(|s| {
        // Consuming thread
        let t = s.spawn(|| loop {
            let item = queue.lock().unwrap().pop_front();
            if let Some(item) = item {
                dbg!(item);
            } else {
                thread::park();
            }
        });

        // Producing thread
        for i in 0.. {
            queue.lock().unwrap().push_back(i);
            t.thread().unpark();
            thread::sleep(Duration::from_secs(1));
```

```
        }
    });
}
```

The consuming thread runs an infinite loop in which it pops items out of the queue to display them using the dbg macro. When the queue is empty, it stops and goes to sleep using the park() function. If it gets unparked, the park() call returns, and the loop continues, popping items from the queue again until it is empty. And so on.

The producing thread produces a new number every second by pushing it into the queue. Every time it adds an item, it uses the unpark() method on the Thread object that refers to the consuming thread to unpark it. That way, the consuming thread gets woken up to process the new element.

An important observation to make here is that this program would still be theoretically correct, although inefficient, if we remove parking. This is important, because park() does not guarantee that it will only return because of a matching unpark(). While somewhat rare, it might have *spurious wake-ups*. Our example deals with that just fine, because the consuming thread will lock the queue, see that it is empty, and directly unlock it and park itself again.

An important property of thread parking is that a call to unpark() *before* the thread parks itself does not get lost. The request to unpark is still recorded, and the next time the thread tries to park itself, it clears that request and directly continues without actually going to sleep. To see why that is critical for correct operation, let's go through a possible ordering of the steps executed by both threads:

1. The consuming thread—let's call it C—locks the queue.

2. C tries to pop an item from the queue, but it is empty, resulting in None.

3. C unlocks the queue.

4. The producing thread, which we'll call P, locks the queue.

5. P pushes a new item onto the queue.

6. P unlocks the queue again.

7. P calls unpark() to notify C that there are new items.

8. C calls park() to go to sleep, to wait for more items.

While there is most likely only a very brief moment between releasing the queue in step 3 and parking in step 8, steps 4 through 7 could potentially happen in that moment before the thread parks itself. If unpark() would do nothing if the thread wasn't parked, the notification would be lost. The consuming thread would still be waiting, even if there were an item in the queue. Thanks to unpark requests getting saved for a future call to park(), we don't have to worry about this.

However, unpark requests don't stack up. Calling `unpark()` two times and then calling `park()` two times afterwards still results in the thread going to sleep. The first `park()` clears the request and returns directly, but the second one goes to sleep as usual.

This means that in our example above it's important that we only park the thread if we've seen the queue is empty, rather than park it after every processed item. While it's extremely unlikely to happen in this example because of the huge (one second) sleep, it's possible for multiple `unpark()` calls to wake up only a single `park()` call.

Unfortunately, this does mean that if `unpark()` is called right after `park()` returns, but before the queue gets locked and emptied out, the `unpark()` call was unnecessary but still causes the next `park()` call to instantly return. This results in the (empty) queue getting locked and unlocked an extra time. While this doesn't affect the correctness of the program, it does affect its efficiency and performance.

This mechanism works well for simple situations like in our example, but quickly breaks down when things get more complicated. For example, if we had multiple consumer threads taking items from the same queue, the producer thread would have no way of knowing which of the consumers is actually waiting and should be woken up. The producer will have to know exactly when a consumer is waiting, and what condition it is waiting for.

Condition Variables

Condition variables are a more commonly used option for waiting for something to happen to data protected by a mutex. They have two basic operations: *wait* and *notify*. Threads can wait on a condition variable, after which they can be woken up when another thread notifies that same condition variable. Multiple threads can wait on the same condition variable, and notifications can either be sent to one waiting thread, or to all of them.

This means that we can create a condition variable for specific events or conditions we're interested in, such as the queue being non-empty, and wait on that condition. Any thread that causes that event or condition to happen then notifies the condition variable, without having to know which or how many threads are interested in that notification.

To avoid the issue of missing notifications in the brief moment between unlocking a mutex and waiting for a condition variable, condition variables provide a way to *atomically* unlock the mutex and start waiting. This means there is simply no possible moment for notifications to get lost.

The Rust standard library provides a condition variable as `std::sync::Condvar`. Its `wait` method takes a `MutexGuard` that proves we've locked the mutex. It first unlocks the mutex and goes to sleep. Later, when woken up, it relocks the mutex and returns a new `MutexGuard` (which proves that the mutex is locked again).

It has two notify functions: `notify_one` to wake up just one waiting thread (if any), and `notify_all` to wake them all up.

Let's modify the example we used for thread parking to use `Condvar` instead:

```
use std::sync::Condvar;

let queue = Mutex::new(VecDeque::new());
let not_empty = Condvar::new();

thread::scope(|s| {
    s.spawn(|| {
        loop {
            let mut q = queue.lock().unwrap();
            let item = loop {
                if let Some(item) = q.pop_front() {
                    break item;
                } else {
                    q = not_empty.wait(q).unwrap();
                }
            };
            drop(q);
            dbg!(item);
        }
    });

    for i in 0.. {
        queue.lock().unwrap().push_back(i);
        not_empty.notify_one();
        thread::sleep(Duration::from_secs(1));
    }
});
```

We had to change a few things:

- We now not only have a `Mutex` containing the queue, but also a `Condvar` to communicate the "not empty" condition.

- We no longer need to know which thread to wake up, so we don't store the return value from `spawn` anymore. Instead, we notify the consumer through the condition variable with the `notify_one` method.

- Unlocking, waiting, and relocking is all done by the `wait` method. We had to restructure the control flow a bit to be able to pass the guard to the `wait` method, while still dropping it before processing an item.

Now we can spawn as many consuming threads as we like, and even spawn more later, without having to change anything. The condition variable takes care of delivering the notifications to whichever thread is interested.

If we had a more complicated system with threads that are interested in different conditions, we could define a Condvar for each condition. For example, we could define one to indicate the queue is non-empty and another one to indicate it is empty. Then each thread would wait for whichever condition is relevant to what they are doing.

Normally, a Condvar is only ever used together with a single Mutex. If two threads try to concurrently wait on a condition variable using two different mutexes, it might cause a panic.

A downside of a Condvar is that it only works when used together with a Mutex, but for most use cases that is perfectly fine, as that's exactly what's already used to protect the data anyway.

Both thread::park() and Condvar::wait() also have a variant with a time limit: thread::park_timeout() and Condvar::wait_timeout(). These take a Duration as an extra argument, which is the time after which it should give up waiting for a notification and unconditionally wake up.

Summary

- Multiple threads can run concurrently within the same program and can be spawned at any time.

- When the main thread ends, the entire program ends.

- Data races are undefined behavior, which is fully prevented (in safe code) by Rust's type system.

- Data that is Send can be sent to other threads, and data that is Sync can be shared between threads.

- Regular threads might run as long as the program does, and thus can only borrow 'static data such as statics and leaked allocations.

- Reference counting (Arc) can be used to share ownership to make sure data lives as long as at least one thread is using it.

- Scoped threads are useful to limit the lifetime of a thread to alllow it to borrow non-'static data, such as local variables.

- &T is a *shared* reference. &mut T is an *exclusive* reference. Regular types do not allow mutation through a shared reference.

- Some types have interior mutability, thanks to UnsafeCell, which allows for mutation through shared references.

- Cell and RefCell are the standard types for single-threaded interior mutability. Atomics, Mutex, and RwLock are their multi-threaded equivalents.

- Cell and atomics only allow replacing the value as a whole, while RefCell, Mutex, and RwLock allow you to mutate the value directly by dynamically enforcing access rules.

- Thread parking can be a convenient way to wait for some condition.

- When a condition is about data protected by a Mutex, using a Condvar is more convenient, and can be more efficient, than thread parking.

CHAPTER 2

Atomics

The word *atomic* comes from the Greek word ἄτομος, meaning *indivisible*, something that cannot be cut into smaller pieces. In computer science, it is used to describe an operation that is indivisible: it is either fully completed, or it didn't happen yet.

As mentioned in "Borrowing and Data Races" on page 11, multiple threads concurrently reading and modifying the same variable normally results in undefined behavior. However, atomic operations do allow for different threads to safely read and modify the same variable. Since such an operation is indivisible, it either happens completely before or completely after another operation, avoiding undefined behavior. Later, in Chapter 7, we'll see how this works at the hardware level.

Atomic operations are the main building block for anything involving multiple threads. All the other concurrency primitives, such as mutexes and condition variables, are implemented using atomic operations.

In Rust, atomic operations are available as methods on the standard atomic types that live in `std::sync::atomic`. They all have names starting with `Atomic`, such as `AtomicI32` or `AtomicUsize`. Which ones are available depends on the hardware architecture and sometimes operating system, but almost all platforms provide at least all atomic types up to the size of a pointer.

Unlike most types, they allow modification through a shared reference (e.g., `&AtomicU8`). This is possible thanks to interior mutability, as discussed in "Interior Mutability" on page 13.

Each of the available atomic types has the same interface with methods for storing and loading, methods for atomic "fetch-and-modify" operations, and some more advanced "compare-and-exchange" methods. We'll discuss them in detail in the rest of this chapter.

But, before we can dive into the different atomic operations, we briefly need to touch upon a concept called *memory ordering*:

Every atomic operation takes an argument of type `std::sync::atomic::Ordering`, which determines what guarantees we get about the relative ordering of operations. The simplest variant with the fewest guarantees is `Relaxed`. `Relaxed` still guarantees consistency on a single atomic variable, but does not promise anything about the relative order of operations between different variables.

What this means is that two threads might see operations on different variables happen in a different order. For example, if one thread writes to one variable first and then to a second variable very quickly afterwards, another thread might see that happen in the opposite order.

In this chapter we'll only look at use cases where this is not a problem and simply use `Relaxed` everywhere without going more into detail. We'll discuss all the details of memory ordering and the other available memory orderings in Chapter 3.

Atomic Load and Store Operations

The first two atomic operations we'll look at are the most basic ones: `load` and `store`. Their function signatures are as follows, using `AtomicI32` as an example:

```
impl AtomicI32 {
    pub fn load(&self, ordering: Ordering) -> i32;
    pub fn store(&self, value: i32, ordering: Ordering);
}
```

The `load` method atomically loads the value stored in the atomic variable, and the `store` method atomically stores a new value in it. Note how the `store` method takes a shared reference (&T) rather than an exclusive reference (&mut T), even though it modifies the value.

Let's take a look at some realistic use cases for these two methods.

Example: Stop Flag

The first example uses an `AtomicBool` for a *stop flag*. Such a flag is used to inform other threads to stop running.

```
use std::sync::atomic::AtomicBool;
use std::sync::atomic::Ordering::Relaxed;

fn main() {
    static STOP: AtomicBool = AtomicBool::new(false);

    // Spawn a thread to do the work.
    let background_thread = thread::spawn(|| {
```

```
        while !STOP.load(Relaxed) {
            some_work();
        }
    });

    // Use the main thread to listen for user input.
    for line in std::io::stdin().lines() {
        match line.unwrap().as_str() {
            "help" => println!("commands: help, stop"),
            "stop" => break,
            cmd => println!("unknown command: {cmd:?}"),
        }
    }

    // Inform the background thread it needs to stop.
    STOP.store(true, Relaxed);

    // Wait until the background thread finishes.
    background_thread.join().unwrap();
}
```

In this example, the background thread is repeatedly running some_work(), while the main thread allows the user to enter some commands to interact with the program. In this simple example, the only useful command is stop to make the program stop.

To make the background thread stop, the atomic STOP boolean is used to communicate this condition to the background thread. When the foreground thread reads the stop command, it sets the flag to true, which is checked by the background thread before each new iteration. The main thread waits until the background thread is finished with its current iteration using the join method.

This simple solution works great as long as the flag is regularly checked by the background thread. If it gets stuck in some_work() for a long time, that can result in an unacceptable delay between the stop command and the program quitting.

Example: Progress Reporting

In our next example, we process 100 items one by one on a background thread, while the main thread gives the user regular updates on the progress:

```
use std::sync::atomic::AtomicUsize;

fn main() {
    let num_done = AtomicUsize::new(0);

    thread::scope(|s| {
        // A background thread to process all 100 items.
        s.spawn(|| {
            for i in 0..100 {
                process_item(i); // Assuming this takes some time.
```

```
            num_done.store(i + 1, Relaxed);
        }
    });

    // The main thread shows status updates, every second.
    loop {
        let n = num_done.load(Relaxed);
        if n == 100 { break; }
        println!("Working.. {n}/100 done");
        thread::sleep(Duration::from_secs(1));
    }
});

    println!("Done!");
}
```

This time, we use a scoped thread ("Scoped Threads" on page 5), which will automatically handle the joining of the thread for us, and also allow us to borrow local variables.

Every time the background thread finishes processing an item, it stores the number of processed items in an `AtomicUsize`. Meanwhile, the main thread shows that number to the user to inform them of the progress, about once per second. Once the main thread sees that all 100 items have been processed, it exits the scope, which implicitly joins the background thread, and informs the user that everything is done.

Synchronization

Once the last item is processed, it might take up to one whole second for the main thread to know, introducing an unnecessary delay at the end. To solve this, we can use thread parking ("Thread Parking" on page 24) to wake the main thread from its sleep whenever there is new information it might be interested in.

Here's the same example, but now using `thread::park_timeout` rather than `thread::sleep`:

```
fn main() {
    let num_done = AtomicUsize::new(0);

    let main_thread = thread::current();

    thread::scope(|s| {
        // A background thread to process all 100 items.
        s.spawn(|| {
            for i in 0..100 {
                process_item(i); // Assuming this takes some time.
                num_done.store(i + 1, Relaxed);
                main_thread.unpark(); // Wake up the main thread.
            }
        });
```

```
        // The main thread shows status updates.
        loop {
            let n = num_done.load(Relaxed);
            if n == 100 { break; }
            println!("Working.. {n}/100 done");
            thread::park_timeout(Duration::from_secs(1));
        }
    });

    println!("Done!");
}
```

Not much has changed. We've obtained a handle to the main thread through `thread::current()`, which is now used by the background thread to unpark the main thread after every status update. The main thread now uses `park_timeout` rather than `sleep`, such that it can be interrupted.

Now, any status updates are immediately reported to the user, while still repeating the last update every second to show that the program is still running.

Example: Lazy Initialization

The last example before we move on to more advanced atomic operations is about *lazy initialization*.

Imagine there is a value x, which we are reading from a file, obtaining from the operating system, or calculating in some other way, that we expect to be constant during a run of the program. Maybe x is the version of the operating system, or the total amount of memory, or the 400th digit of tau. It doesn't really matter for this example.

Since we don't expect it to change, we can request or calculate it only the first time we need it, and remember the result. The first thread that needs it will have to calculate the value, but it can store it in an atomic `static` to make it available for all threads, including itself if it needs it again later.

Let's take a look at an example of this. To keep things simple, we'll assume x is never zero, so that we can use zero as a placeholder before it has been calculated.

```
use std::sync::atomic::AtomicU64;

fn get_x() -> u64 {
    static X: AtomicU64 = AtomicU64::new(0);
    let mut x = X.load(Relaxed);
    if x == 0 {
        x = calculate_x();
        X.store(x, Relaxed);
    }
    x
}
```

The first thread to call get_x() will check the static X and see it is still zero, calculate its value, and store the result back in the static to make it available for future use. Later, any call to get_x() will see that the value in the static is nonzero, and return it immediately without calculating it again.

However, if a second thread calls get_x() while the first one is still calculating x, the second thread will also see a zero and also calculate x in parallel. One of the threads will end up overwriting the result of the other, depending on which one finishes first. This is called a *race*. Not a *data race*, which is undefined behavior and impossible in Rust without using unsafe, but still a race with an unpredictable winner.

Since we expect x to be constant, it doesn't matter who wins the race, as the result will be the same regardless. Depending on how much time we expect calculate_x() to take, this might be a very good or very bad strategy.

If calculate_x() is expected to take a long time, it's better if threads wait while the first thread is still initializing X, to avoid unnecessarily wasting processor time. You could implement this using a condition variable or thread parking ("Waiting: Parking and Condition Variables" on page 24), but that quickly gets too complicated for a small example. The Rust standard library provides exactly this functionality through std::sync::Once and std::sync::OnceLock, so there's usually no need to implement these yourself.

Fetch-and-Modify Operations

Now that we've seen a few use cases for the basic load and store operations, let's move on to more interesting operations: the *fetch-and-modify* operations. These operations modify the atomic variable, but also load (fetch) the original value, as a single atomic operation.

The most commonly used ones are fetch_add and fetch_sub, which perform addition and subtraction, respectively. Some of the other available operations are fetch_or and fetch_and for bitwise operations, and fetch_max and fetch_min which can be used to keep a running maximum or minimum.

Their function signatures are as follows, using `AtomicI32` as an example:

```
impl AtomicI32 {
    pub fn fetch_add(&self, v: i32, ordering: Ordering) -> i32;
    pub fn fetch_sub(&self, v: i32, ordering: Ordering) -> i32;
    pub fn fetch_or(&self, v: i32, ordering: Ordering) -> i32;
    pub fn fetch_and(&self, v: i32, ordering: Ordering) -> i32;
    pub fn fetch_nand(&self, v: i32, ordering: Ordering) -> i32;
    pub fn fetch_xor(&self, v: i32, ordering: Ordering) -> i32;
    pub fn fetch_max(&self, v: i32, ordering: Ordering) -> i32;
    pub fn fetch_min(&self, v: i32, ordering: Ordering) -> i32;
    pub fn swap(&self, v: i32, ordering: Ordering) -> i32; // "fetch_store"
}
```

The one outlier is the operation that simply stores a new value, regardless of the old value. Instead of `fetch_store`, it has been called `swap`.

Here's a quick demonstration showing how `fetch_add` returns the value before the operation:

```
use std::sync::atomic::AtomicI32;

let a = AtomicI32::new(100);
let b = a.fetch_add(23, Relaxed);
let c = a.load(Relaxed);

assert_eq!(b, 100);
assert_eq!(c, 123);
```

The `fetch_add` operation incremented a from 100 to 123, but returned to us the old value of 100. Any next operation will see the value of 123.

The return value from these operations is not always relevant. If you only need the operation to be applied to the atomic value, but are not interested in the value itself, it's perfectly fine to simply ignore the return value.

An important thing to keep in mind is that `fetch_add` and `fetch_sub` implement *wrapping* behavior for overflows. Incrementing a value past the maximum representable value will wrap around and result in the minimum representable value. This is different than the behavior of the plus and minus operators on regular integers, which will panic in debug mode on overflow.

In "Compare-and-Exchange Operations" on page 42, we'll see how to do atomic addition with overflow checking.

But first, let's see some real-world use cases of these methods.

Example: Progress Reporting from Multiple Threads

In "Example: Progress Reporting" on page 33, we used an AtomicUsize to report the progress of a background thread. If we had split the work over, for example, four threads with each processing 25 items, we'd need to know the progress from all four threads.

We could use a separate AtomicUsize for each thread and load them all in the main thread and sum them up, but an easier solution is to use a single AtomicUsize to track the total number of processed items over all threads.

To make that work, we can no longer use the store method, as that would overwrite the progress from other threads. Instead, we can use an atomic add operation to increment the counter after every processed item.

Let's update the example from "Example: Progress Reporting" on page 33 to split the work over four threads:

```
fn main() {
    let num_done = &AtomicUsize::new(0);

    thread::scope(|s| {
        // Four background threads to process all 100 items, 25 each.
        for t in 0..4 {
            s.spawn(move || {
                for i in 0..25 {
                    process_item(t * 25 + i); // Assuming this takes some time.
                    num_done.fetch_add(1, Relaxed);
                }
            });
        }

        // The main thread shows status updates, every second.
        loop {
            let n = num_done.load(Relaxed);
            if n == 100 { break; }
            println!("Working.. {n}/100 done");
            thread::sleep(Duration::from_secs(1));
        }
    });

    println!("Done!");
}
```

A few things have changed. Most importantly, we now spawn four background threads rather than one, and use fetch_add instead of store to modify the num_done atomic variable.

More subtly, we now use a move closure for the background threads, and num_done is now a reference. This is not related to our use of fetch_add, but rather to how we spawn four threads in a loop. This closure captures t to know which of the four threads it is, and thus whether to start at item 0, 25, 50, or 75. Without the move keyword, the closure would try to capture t by reference. That isn't allowed, as it only exists briefly during the loop.

As a move closure, it moves (or copies) its captures rather than borrowing them, giving it a copy of t. Because it also captures num_done, we've changed that variable to be a reference, since we still want to borrow that same AtomicUsize. Note that the atomic types do not implement the Copy trait, so we'd have gotten an error if we had tried to move one into more than one thread.

Closure capture subtleties aside, the change to use fetch_add here is very simple. We don't know in which order the threads will increment num_done, but as the addition is atomic, we don't have to worry about anything and can be sure it will be exactly 100 when all threads are done.

Example: Statistics

Continuing with this concept of reporting what other threads are doing through atomics, let's extend our example to also collect and report some statistics on the time it takes to process an item.

Next to num_done, we're adding two atomic variables, total_time and max_time, to keep track of the amount of time spent processing items. We'll use these to report the average and peak processing times.

```
fn main() {
    let num_done = &AtomicUsize::new(0);
    let total_time = &AtomicU64::new(0);
    let max_time = &AtomicU64::new(0);

    thread::scope(|s| {
        // Four background threads to process all 100 items, 25 each.
        for t in 0..4 {
            s.spawn(move || {
                for i in 0..25 {
                    let start = Instant::now();
                    process_item(t * 25 + i); // Assuming this takes some time.
                    let time_taken = start.elapsed().as_micros() as u64;
                    num_done.fetch_add(1, Relaxed);
                    total_time.fetch_add(time_taken, Relaxed);
                    max_time.fetch_max(time_taken, Relaxed);
                }
            });
        }

        // The main thread shows status updates, every second.
        loop {
            let total_time = Duration::from_micros(total_time.load(Relaxed));
```

```
        let max_time = Duration::from_micros(max_time.load(Relaxed));
        let n = num_done.load(Relaxed);
        if n == 100 { break; }
        if n == 0 {
            println!("Working.. nothing done yet.");
        } else {
            println!(
                "Working.. {n}/100 done, {:?} average, {:?} peak",
                total_time / n as u32,
                max_time,
            );
        }
        thread::sleep(Duration::from_secs(1));
    }
});

println!("Done!");
}
```

The background threads now use `Instant::now()` and `Instant::elapsed()` to measure the time they spend in `process_item()`. An atomic add operation is used to add the number of microseconds to `total_time`, and an atomic max operation is used to keep track of the highest measurement in `max_time`.

The main thread divides the total time by the number of processed items to obtain the average processing time, which it then reports together with the peak time from `max_time`.

Since the three atomic variables are updated separately, it is possible for the main thread to load the values after a thread has incremented `num_done`, but before it has updated `total_time`, resulting in an underestimate of the average. More subtly, because the `Relaxed` memory ordering gives no guarantees about the relative order of operations as seen from another thread, it might even briefly see a new updated value of `total_time`, while still seeing an old value of `num_done`, resulting in an overestimate of the average.

Neither of this is a big issue in our example. The worst that can happen is that an inaccurate average is briefly reported to the user.

If we want to avoid this, we can put the three statistics inside a `Mutex`. Then we'd briefly lock the mutex while updating the three numbers, which no longer have to be atomic by themselves. This effectively turns the three updates into a single atomic operation, at the cost of locking and unlocking a mutex, and potentially temporarily blocking threads.

Example: ID Allocation

Let's move on to a use case where we actually need the return value from `fetch_add`.

Suppose we need some function, `allocate_new_id()`, that gives a new unique number every time it is called. We might use these numbers to identify tasks or other things in our program; things that need to be uniquely identified by something small that can be easily stored and passed around between threads, such as an integer.

Implementing this function turns out to be trivial using `fetch_add`:

```
use std::sync::atomic::AtomicU32;

fn allocate_new_id() -> u32 {
    static NEXT_ID: AtomicU32 = AtomicU32::new(0);
    NEXT_ID.fetch_add(1, Relaxed)
}
```

We simply keep track of the *next* number to give out, and increment it every time we load it. The first caller will get a 0, the second a 1, and so on.

The only problem here is the wrapping behavior on overflow. The 4,294,967,296th call will overflow the 32-bit integer, such that the next call will return 0 again.

Whether this is a problem depends on the use case: how likely is it to be called this often, and what's the worst that can happen if the numbers are not unique? While this might seeem like a huge number, modern computers can easily execute our function that many times within seconds. If memory safety is dependent on these numbers being unique, our implementation above is not acceptable.

To solve this, we can attempt to make the function panic if it is called too many times, like this:

```
// This version is problematic.
fn allocate_new_id() -> u32 {
    static NEXT_ID: AtomicU32 = AtomicU32::new(0);
    let id = NEXT_ID.fetch_add(1, Relaxed);
    assert!(id < 1000, "too many IDs!");
    id
}
```

Now, the `assert` statement will panic after a thousand calls. However, this happens *after* the atomic add operation already happened, meaning that NEXT_ID has already been incremented to 1001 when we panic. If another thread then calls the function, it'll increment it to 1002 before panicking, and so on. Although it might take significantly longer, we'll run into the same problem after 4,294,966,296 panics when NEXT_ID will overflow to zero again.

There are three common solutions to this problem. The first one is to not panic but instead completely abort the process on overflow. The `std::process::abort` function will abort the entire process, ruling out the possibility of anything continuing to call our function. While aborting the process might take a brief moment in which the function can still be called by other threads, the chance of that happening billions of times before the program is truly aborted is negligible.

This is, in fact, how the overflow check in `Arc::clone()` in the standard library is implemented, in case you somehow manage to clone it `isize::MAX` times. That'd take hundreds of years on a 64-bit computer, but is achieveable in seconds if `isize` is only 32 bits.

A second way to deal with the overflow is to use `fetch_sub` to decrement the counter again before panicking, like this:

```
fn allocate_new_id() -> u32 {
    static NEXT_ID: AtomicU32 = AtomicU32::new(0);
    let id = NEXT_ID.fetch_add(1, Relaxed);
    if id >= 1000 {
        NEXT_ID.fetch_sub(1, Relaxed);
        panic!("too many IDs!");
    }
    id
}
```

It's still possible for the counter to very briefly be incremented beyond 1000 when multiple threads execute this function at the same time, but it is limited by the number of active threads. It's reasonable to assume there will never be billions of active threads at once, especially not all simultaneously executing the same function in the brief moment between `fetch_add` and `fetch_sub`.

This is how overflows are handled for the number of running threads in the standard library's `thread::scope` implementation.

The third way of handling overflows is arguably the only truly correct one, as it prevents the addition from happening at all if it would overflow. However, we cannot implement that with the atomic operations we've seen so far. For this, we'll need compare-and-exchange operations, which we'll explore next.

Compare-and-Exchange Operations

The most advanced and flexible atomic operation is the *compare-and-exchange* operation. This operation checks if the atomic value is equal to a given value, and only if that is the case does it replace it with a new value, all atomically as a single operation. It will return the previous value and tell us whether it replaced it or not.

Its signature is a bit more complicated than the ones we've seen so far. Using Atom icI32 as an example, it looks like this:

```
impl AtomicI32 {
    pub fn compare_exchange(
        &self,
        expected: i32,
        new: i32,
        success_order: Ordering,
        failure_order: Ordering
    ) -> Result<i32, i32>;
}
```

Ignoring memory ordering for a moment, it is basically identical to the following implementation, except it all happens as a single, indivisible atomic operation:

```
impl AtomicI32 {
    pub fn compare_exchange(&self, expected: i32, new: i32) -> Result<i32, i32> {
        // In reality, the load, comparison and store,
        // all happen as a single atomic operation.
        let v = self.load();
        if v == expected {
            // Value is as expected.
            // Replace it and report success.
            self.store(new);
            Ok(v)
        } else {
            // The value was not as expected.
            // Leave it untouched and report failure.
            Err(v)
        }
    }
}
```

Using this, we can load a value from an atomic variable, perform any calculation we like, and then only store the newly calculated value if the atomic variable didn't change in the meantime. If we put this in a loop to retry if it did change, we could use this to implement all the other atomic operations, making this the most general one.

To demonstrate, let's increment an AtomicU32 by one without using fetch_add, just to see how compare_exchange is used in practice:

```
fn increment(a: &AtomicU32) {
    let mut current = a.load(Relaxed); ❶
    loop {
        let new = current + 1; ❷
        match a.compare_exchange(current, new, Relaxed, Relaxed) { ❸
            Ok(_) => return, ❹
            Err(v) => current = v, ❺
        }
    }
}
```

❶ First, we load the current value of a.

❷ We calculate the new value we want to store in a, not taking into account potential concurrent modifications of a by other threads.

❸ We use compare_exchange to update the value of a, but *only* if its value is still the same value we loaded before.

❹ If a was indeed still the same as before, it is now replaced by our new value and we are done.

❺ If a was not the same as before, another thread must've changed it in the brief moment since we loaded it. The compare_exchange operation gives us the changed value that a had, and we'll try again using that value instead. The brief moment between loading and updating is so short that it's unlikely for this to loop more than a few iterations.

 If the atomic variable changes from some value A to B and then back to A after the load operation, but before the compare_exchange operation, it would still succeed, even though the atomic variable was changed (and changed back) in the meantime. In many cases, as with our increment example, this is not a problem. However, there are certain algorithms, often involving atomic pointers, for which this can be a problem. This is known as the *ABA problem*.

Next to compare_exchange, there is a similar method named compare_exchange_weak. The difference is that the weak version may still sometimes leave the value untouched and return an Err, even though the atomic value matched the expected value. On some platforms, this method can be implemented more efficiently and should be preferred in cases where the consequence of a spurious compare-and-exchange failure are insignificant, such as in our increment function above. In Chapter 7, we'll dive into the low-level details to find out why the weak version can be more efficient.

Example: ID Allocation Without Overflow

Now, back to our overflow problem in allocate_new_id() from "Example: ID Allocation" on page 41.

To stop incrementing NEXT_ID beyond a certain limit to prevent overflows, we can use compare_exchange to implement atomic addition with an upper bound. Using that idea, let's make a version of `allocate_new_id` that always handles overflow correctly, even in practically impossible situations:

```
fn allocate_new_id() -> u32 {
    static NEXT_ID: AtomicU32 = AtomicU32::new(0);
    let mut id = NEXT_ID.load(Relaxed);
    loop {
        assert!(id < 1000, "too many IDs!");
        match NEXT_ID.compare_exchange_weak(id, id + 1, Relaxed, Relaxed) {
            Ok(_) => return id,
            Err(v) => id = v,
        }
    }
}
```

Now we check and panic *before* modifying NEXT_ID, guaranteeing it will never be incremented beyond 1000, making overflow impossible. We can now raise the upper limit from 1000 to u32::MAX if we want, without having to worry about edge cases in which it might get incremented beyond the limit.

Fetch-Update

The atomic types have a convenience method called `fetch_update` for the compare-and-exchange loop pattern. It's equivalent to a `load` operation followed by a loop that repeats a calculation and `compare_exchange_weak`, just like what we did above.

Using it, we could implement our `allocate_new_id` function with a one-liner:

```
NEXT_ID.fetch_update(Relaxed, Relaxed,
    |n| n.checked_add(1)).expect("too many IDs!")
```

Check out the method's documentation for details.

We'll not use the `fetch_update` method in this book, so we can focus on the individual atomic operations.

Example: Lazy One-Time Initialization

In "Example: Lazy Initialization" on page 35, we looked at an example of lazy initialization of a constant value. We made a function that lazily initializes a value on the first call, but reuses it on later calls. When multiple threads run the function concurrently during the first call, more than one thread might execute the initialization, and they will overwrite each others' result in an unpredictable order.

This is fine for values that we expect to be constant, or when we don't care about changing values. However, there are also use cases where such a value gets initialized to a different value each time, even though we need every invocation of the function within a single run of the program to return the same value.

For example, imagine a function `get_key()` that returns a randomly generated key that's only generated once per run of the program. It might be an encryption key used for communication with the program, which needs to be unique every time the program is run, but stays constant within a process.

This means we cannot simply use a `store` operation after generating a key, since that might overwrite a key generated by another thread just moments ago, resulting in two threads using different keys. Instead, we can use `compare_exchange` to make sure we only store the key if no other thread has already done so, and otherwise throw our key away and use the stored key instead.

Here's an implementation of this idea:

```
fn get_key() -> u64 {
    static KEY: AtomicU64 = AtomicU64::new(0);
    let key = KEY.load(Relaxed);
    if key == 0 {
        let new_key = generate_random_key();  ❶
        match KEY.compare_exchange(0, new_key, Relaxed, Relaxed) {  ❷
            Ok(_) => new_key,  ❸
            Err(k) => k,  ❹
        }
    } else {
        key
    }
}
```

❶ We only generate a new key if KEY was not yet initialized.

❷ We replace KEY with our newly generated key, but only if it is *still* zero.

❸ If we swapped the zero for our new key, we return our newly generated key. New invocations of `get_key()` will return the same new key that's now stored in KEY.

❹ If we lost the race to another thread that initialized KEY before we could, we forget our newly generated key and use the key from KEY instead.

This is a good example of a situation where `compare_exchange` is more appropriate than its weak variant. We don't run our compare-and-exchange operation in a loop, and we don't want to return zero if the operation spuriously fails.

As mentioned in "Example: Lazy Initialization" on page 35, if `generate_ran dom_key()` takes a lot of time, it might make more sense to block threads during initialization, to avoid potentially spending time generating keys that will not be used. The Rust standard library provides such functionality through `std::sync::Once` and `std::sync::OnceLock`.

Summary

- Atomic operations are indivisible; they have either fully completed, or they haven't happened yet.

- Atomic operations in Rust are done through the atomic types in `std::sync::atomic`, such as `AtomicI32`.

- Not all atomic types are available on all platforms.

- The relative ordering of atomic operations is tricky when multiple variables are involved. More in Chapter 3.

- Simple loads and stores are nice for very basic inter-thread communication, like stop flags and status reporting.

- Lazy initialization can be done as a *race*, without causing a *data race*.

- Fetch-and-modify operations allow for a small set of basic atomic modifications that are especially useful when multiple threads are modifying the same atomic variable.

- Atomic addition and subtraction silently wrap around on overflow.

- Compare-and-exchange operations are the most flexible and general, and a building block for making any other atomic operation.

- A *weak* compare-and-exchange operation can be slightly more efficient.

CHAPTER 3

Memory Ordering

In Chapter 2, we briefly touched upon the concept of *memory ordering*. In this chapter, we'll dive into this topic and explore all the available memory ordering options, and, most importantly, when to use which one.

Reordering and Optimizations

Processors and compilers perform all sorts of tricks to make your programs run as fast as possible. A processor might determine that two particular consecutive instructions in your program will not affect each other, and execute them *out of order*, if that is faster, for example. While one instruction is briefly blocked on fetching some data from main memory, several of the following instructions might be executed and finished before the first instruction finishes, as long as that wouldn't change the behavior of your program. Similarly, a compiler might decide to reorder or rewrite parts of your program if it has reason to believe it might result in faster execution. But, again, only if that wouldn't change the behavior of your program.

Let's take a look at the following function as an example:

```
fn f(a: &mut i32, b: &mut i32) {
    *a += 1;
    *b += 1;
    *a += 1;
}
```

Here, the compiler will most certainly understand that the order of these operations does not matter, since nothing happens between these three addition operations that depends on the value of *a or *b. (Assuming overflow checking is disabled.) Because of that, it might reorder the second and third operations, and then merge the first two into a single addition:

```
fn f(a: &mut i32, b: &mut i32) {
    *a += 2;
    *b += 1;
}
```

Later, while executing this function of the optimized compiled program, a processor might for a variety of reasons end up executing the second addition before the first addition, possibly because *b was available in a cache, while *a had to be fetched from the main memory.

Regardless of these optimizations, the result stays the same: *a is incremented by two and *b is incremented by one. The order in which they were incremented is entirely invisible to the rest of your program.

The logic for verifying that a specific reordering or other optimization won't affect the behavior of your program does not take other threads into account. In our example above, that's perfectly fine, as the unique references (&mut i32) guarantee that nothing else can possibly access the values, making other threads irrelevant. The only situation where this is a problem is when mutating data that's shared between threads. Or, in other words, when working with atomics. This is why we have to explicitly tell the compiler and processor what they can and can't do with our atomic operations, since their usual logic ignores interactions between threads and might allow for optimizations that do change the result of your program.

The interesting question is *how* we tell them. If we wanted to precisely spell out exactly what is and isn't acceptable, concurrent programming might become exceedingly verbose and error prone, and maybe even architecture-specific:

```
let x = a.fetch_add(1,
    Dear compiler and processor,
    Feel free to reorder this with operations on b,
    but if there's another thread concurrently executing f,
    please don't reorder this with operations on c!
    Also, processor, don't forget to flush your store buffer!
    If b is zero, though, it doesn't matter.
    In that case, feel free to do whatever is fastest.
    Thanks~ <3
);
```

Instead, we can only pick from a small set of options, represented by the std::sync::atomic::Ordering enum, which every atomic operation takes as an argument. The set of available options is very limited, but has been carefully picked to fit most use cases well. The orderings are very abstract and do not directly reflect the actual compiler and processor mechanisms involved, such as instruction reordering. This makes it possible for your concurrent code to be architecture-independent and future-proof. It allows for verification without knowing the details of every single current and future processor and compiler version.

The available orderings in Rust are:

- Relaxed ordering: `Ordering::Relaxed`
- Release and acquire ordering: `Ordering::{Release, Acquire, AcqRel}`
- Sequentially consistent ordering: `Ordering::SeqCst`

In C++, there is also something called *consume ordering*, which has been purposely omitted from Rust, but is nonetheless interesting to discuss as well.

The Memory Model

The different memory ordering options have a strict formal definition to make sure we know exactly what we're allowed to assume, and for compiler writers to know exactly what guarantees they need to provide to us. To decouple this from the details of specific processor architectures, memory ordering is defined in terms of an abstract *memory model*.

Rust's memory model, which is mostly copied from C++, doesn't match any existing processor architecture, but instead is an abstract model with a strict set of rules that attempt to represent the greatest common denominator of all current and future architectures, while also giving the compiler enough freedom to make useful assumptions while analyzing and optimizing programs.

We've already seen a part of the memory model in action in "Borrowing and Data Races" on page 11, where we talked about how data races result in undefined behavior. Rust's memory model allows for concurrent atomic stores, but considers concurrent non-atomic stores to the same variable to be a data race, resulting in undefined behavior.

On most processor architectures, however, there is actually no difference between an atomic store and a regular non-atomic store, as we'll see in Chapter 7. One could argue that the memory model is more restrictive than necessary, but these strict rules make it easier to reason about a program, both for the compiler and the programmer, and they leave space for future developments.

Happens-Before Relationship

The memory model defines the order in which operations happen in terms of *happens-before relationships*. This means that as an abstract model, it doesn't talk about machine instructions, caches, buffers, timing, instruction reordering, compiler optimizations, and so on, but instead only defines situations where one thing is guaranteed to happen before another thing, and leaves the order of everything else undefined.

The basic happens-before rule is that everything that happens within the same thread happens in order. If a thread is executing f(); g();, then f() *happens-before* g().

Between threads, however, happens-before relationships only occur in a few specific cases, such as when spawning and joining a thread, unlocking and locking a mutex, and through atomic operations that use non-relaxed memory ordering. Relaxed memory ordering is the most basic (and most performant) memory ordering that, by itself, never results in any cross-thread happens-before relationships.

To explore what that means, let's take a look at the following example where we assume a and b are concurrently executed by different threads:

```
static X: AtomicI32 = AtomicI32::new(0);
static Y: AtomicI32 = AtomicI32::new(0);

fn a() {
    X.store(10, Relaxed); ❶
    Y.store(20, Relaxed); ❷
}

fn b() {
    let y = Y.load(Relaxed); ❸
    let x = X.load(Relaxed); ❹
    println!("{x} {y}");
}
```

As mentioned above, the basic happens-before rule is that everything that happens within the same thread happens in order. In this case: ❶ happens-before ❷, and ❸ happens-before ❹, as shown in Figure 3-1. Since we use relaxed memory ordering, there are no other happens-before relationships in our example.

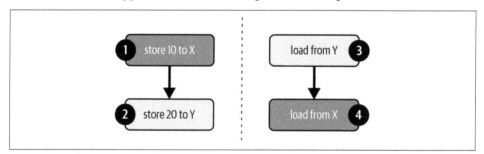

Figure 3-1. The happens-before relationships between atomic operations in the example code

If either of a or b completes before the other starts, the output will be 0 0 or 10 20. If a and b run concurrently, it's easy to see how the output can be 10 0. One way this can happen is if the operations run in this order: ❸❶❷❹.

More interestingly, the output can also be 0 20, even though there is no possible globally consistent order of the four operations that would result in this outcome. When ❸ is executed, there is no happens-before relationship with ❷, which means it could load either 0 or 20. When ❹ is executed, there is no happens-before relationship with ❶, which means it could load either 0 or 10. Given this, the output 0 20 is a valid outcome.

The important and counter-intuitive thing to understand is that operation ❸ loading the value 20 does *not* result in a happens-before relationship with ❷, even though that value is the one stored by ❷. Our intuitive understanding of the concept of "before" breaks down when things don't necessarily happen in a globally consistent order, such as when instruction reordering is involved.

A more practical and intuitive, but less formal, understanding is that from the perspective of the thread executing b, operations ❶ and ❷ might appear to happen in the opposite order.

Spawning and Joining

Spawning a thread creates a happens-before relationship between what happened before the spawn() call, and the new thread. Similarly, joining a thread creates a happens-before relationship between the joined thread and what happens after the join() call.

To demonstrate, the assertion in the following example cannot fail:

```
static X: AtomicI32 = AtomicI32::new(0);

fn main() {
    X.store(1, Relaxed);
    let t = thread::spawn(f);
    X.store(2, Relaxed);
    t.join().unwrap();
    X.store(3, Relaxed);
}

fn f() {
    let x = X.load(Relaxed);
    assert!(x == 1 || x == 2);
}
```

Because of the happens-before relationships formed by the join and spawn operations, we know for sure that the load from X happens after the first store, but before the last store, as visualized in Figure 3-2. However, whether it observes the value before or after the second store is unpredictable. In other words, it could load either 1 or 2, but not 0 or 3.

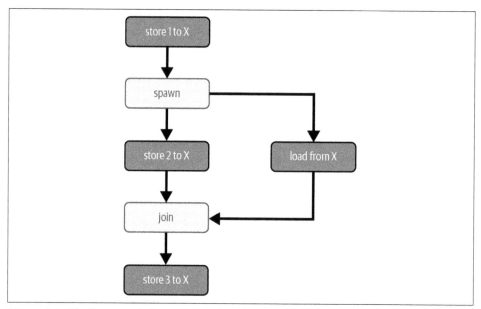

Figure 3-2. The happens-before relationships between the spawn, join, store, and load operations in the example code

Relaxed Ordering

While atomic operations using relaxed memory ordering do not provide any happens-before relationship, they do guarantee a *total modification order* of each individual atomic variable. This means that all modifications *of the same atomic variable* happen in an order that is the same from the perspective of every single thread.

To demonstrate what that means, consider the following example where we assume a and b are concurrently executed by different threads:

```
static X: AtomicI32 = AtomicI32::new(0);

fn a() {
    X.fetch_add(5, Relaxed);
    X.fetch_add(10, Relaxed);
}

fn b() {
    let a = X.load(Relaxed);
    let b = X.load(Relaxed);
    let c = X.load(Relaxed);
    let d = X.load(Relaxed);
    println!("{a} {b} {c} {d}");
}
```

In this example, only one thread modifies X, which makes it easy to see that there's only one possible order of modification of X: 0→5→15. It starts at zero, then becomes five, and is finally changed to fifteen. Threads cannot observe any values from X that are inconsistent with this total modification order. This means that "0 0 0 0", "0 0 5 15", and "0 15 15 15" are some of the possible results from the print statement in the other thread, while an output of "0 5 0 15" or "0 0 10 15" is impossible.

Even if there's more than one possible order of modification for an atomic variable, all threads will agree on a single order.

Let's replace a by two separate functions, a1 and a2, which we assume are each executed by a separate thread:

```
fn a1() {
    X.fetch_add(5, Relaxed);
}

fn a2() {
    X.fetch_add(10, Relaxed);
}
```

Assuming these are the only threads modifying X, there are now two possible modification orders: either 0→5→15, or 0→10→15, depending on which fetch_add operation executes first. Whichever happens, all threads observe the same order. So, even if we have hundreds of additional threads all running our b() function, we know that if one of them prints a 10, the order must be 0→10→15 and none of them can possibly print a 5. And vice versa.

In Chapter 2, we saw several examples of use cases where this total modification order guarantee for individual variables is enough, making relaxed memory ordering sufficient. However, if we try anything more advanced beyond those examples, we'll quickly see we need something stronger than relaxed memory ordering.

Out-of-Thin-Air Values

The lack of ordering guarantees around relaxed memory ordering can lead to some theoretical complications when operations depend on each other in a cyclic way.

To demonstrate, here's a contrived example where two threads load a value from one atomic and store it in the other:

```
static X: AtomicI32 = AtomicI32::new(0);
static Y: AtomicI32 = AtomicI32::new(0);

fn main() {
    let a = thread::spawn(|| {
        let x = X.load(Relaxed);
        Y.store(x, Relaxed);
    });
    let b = thread::spawn(|| {
        let y = Y.load(Relaxed);
        X.store(y, Relaxed);
    });
    a.join().unwrap();
    b.join().unwrap();
    assert_eq!(X.load(Relaxed), 0); // Might fail?
    assert_eq!(Y.load(Relaxed), 0); // Might fail?
}
```

It seems easy to conclude that the values of X and Y will never be anything other than zero, since the store operations only store values that were loaded from these same atomics, which are only ever zero.

If we strictly follow the theoretical memory model, however, we have to come to terms with our cyclic reasoning, and come to the scary conclusion that we might be wrong. In fact, the memory model technically allows for an outcome where both X and Y are 37 in the end, or any other value, making the assertions fail.

Due to the lack of ordering guarantees, the load operations of these two threads might *both* see the result of the store operation of the other thread, allowing for a cycle in the order of operations: we store 37 in Y because we loaded 37 from X, which was stored to X because we loaded 37 from Y, which is the value we stored in Y.

Fortunately, the possibility of such *out-of-thin-air* values is universally considered to be a bug in the theoretical model, and not something you need to take into account in practice. The theoretical problem of how to formalize relaxed memory ordering without the model allowing for such anomalies is an unsolved one. While this is an eyesore for formal verification that keeps many theoreticians up at night, the rest of us can relax in blissful ignorance knowing that this does not happen in practice.

Release and Acquire Ordering

Release and *acquire* memory ordering are used in a pair to form a happens-before relationship between threads. `Release` memory ordering applies to store operations, while `Acquire` memory ordering applies to load operations.

A happens-before relationship is formed when an acquire-load operation observes the result of a release-store operation. In this case, the store and everything before it, happened before the load and everything after it.

When using `Acquire` for a fetch-and-modify or compare-and-exchange operation, it applies only to the part of the operation that loads the value. Similarly, `Release` applies only to the store part of an operation. `AcqRel` is used to represent the combination of `Acquire` and `Release`, which causes both the load to use acquire ordering, and the store to use release ordering.

Let's go over an example to see how that's used in practice. In the following example, we send a 64-bit integer from a spawned thread to the main thread. We use an extra atomic boolean to indicate to the main thread that the integer has been stored and is ready to be read.

```
use std::sync::atomic::Ordering::{Acquire, Release};

static DATA: AtomicU64 = AtomicU64::new(0);
static READY: AtomicBool = AtomicBool::new(false);

fn main() {
    thread::spawn(|| {
        DATA.store(123, Relaxed);
        READY.store(true, Release); // Everything from before this store ..
    });
    while !READY.load(Acquire) { // .. is visible after this loads `true`.
        thread::sleep(Duration::from_millis(100));
        println!("waiting...");
    }
    println!("{}", DATA.load(Relaxed));
}
```

When the spawned thread is done storing the data, it uses a release-store to set the `READY` flag to `true`. When the main thread observes this through its acquire-load operation, a happens-before relationship is established between those two operations, as shown in Figure 3-3. At that point, we know for sure that everything that happened before the release-store to `READY` is visible to everything that happens after the acquire-load. Specifically, when the main thread loads from `DATA`, we know for sure it will load the value stored by the background thread. There's only one possible outcome this program can print on its last line: 123.

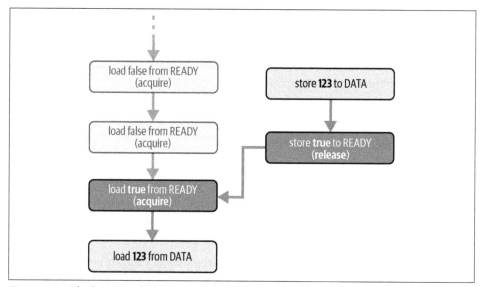

Figure 3-3. The happens-before relationships between atomic operations in the example code, showing the cross-thread relationship formed by the acquire and release operations

If we had used relaxed memory ordering for all operations in this example, the main thread could have seen READY flip to true, while still loading a zero from DATA afterwards.

The names "release" and "acquire" are based on their most basic use case: one thread *releases* data by atomically storing some value to an atomic variable, and another thread *acquires* it by atomically loading that value. This is exactly what happens when we unlock (release) a mutex and subsequently lock (acquire) it on another thread.

In our example, the happens-before relationship from the READY flag guarantees that the store and load operations of DATA cannot happen concurrently. This means that we don't actually need those operations to be atomic.

However, if we simply try to use a regular non-atomic type for our data variable, the compiler will refuse our program, since Rust's type system doesn't allow us to mutate those from one thread when another thread is also borrowing them. The type system does not magically understand the happens-before relationship we've created here. Some unsafe code is necessary to promise to the compiler that we've thought about this carefully and we're sure we're not breaking any rules, as follows:

```
static mut DATA: u64 = 0;
static READY: AtomicBool = AtomicBool::new(false);

fn main() {
    thread::spawn(|| {
        // Safety: Nothing else is accessing DATA,
        // because we haven't set the READY flag yet.
        unsafe { DATA = 123 };
        READY.store(true, Release); // Everything from before this store ..
    });
    while !READY.load(Acquire) { // .. is visible after this loads `true`.
        thread::sleep(Duration::from_millis(100));
        println!("waiting...");
    }
    // Safety: Nothing is mutating DATA, because READY is set.
    println!("{}", unsafe { DATA });
}
```

More Formally

A happens-before relationship is formed when an acquire-load operation observes the result of a release-store operation. But what does that mean?

Imagine that two threads both release-store a seven into the same atomic variable, and a third thread loads a seven from that variable. Does the third thread now have a happens-before relationship with the first thread or the second one? That depends on "which seven" it loaded: the one from thread one or the one from thread two. (Or perhaps an unrelated seven.) This leads us to the conclusion that even though seven equals seven, there is something different about the two sevens from the two threads.

The way to think about this is in terms of the *total modification order* that we talked about in "Relaxed Ordering" on page 54: the ordered list of all modifications that happen to an atomic variable. Even if the same value is written to the same variable more than once, each of these operations represents a separate event in the total modification order of that variable. When we load a value, the value loaded matches a specific point on this per-variable "timeline," which tells us which operation we might be synchronizing with.

For example, if the total modification order of the atomic is

1. Initialized at 0
2. **Release**-store 7 (from thread two)
3. Relaxed-store 6
4. **Release**-store 7 (from thread one)

then acquire-loading a 7 would synchronize with either the release-store from the second event, or the release-store from the last event. However, if we have previously (in terms of happens-before relationships) seen a 6, we know we're seeing the last 7, not the first one, meaning we now have a happens-before relationship with thread one, and not with thread two.

There is one extra detail, which is that a release-stored value may be modified by any number of fetch-and-modify and compare-and-exchange operations, while still resulting in a happens-before relationship with an acquire-load that reads the final result.

For example, imagine an atomic variable with the following total modification order:

1. Initialized at 0
2. **Release**-store 7
3. Relaxed-fetch-and-add 1, changing 7 to 8
4. **Release**-fetch-and-add 1, changing 8 to 9
5. **Release**-store 7
6. Relaxed-swap 10, changing 7 to 10

Now, if we acquire-load a 9 from this variable, we not only establish a happens-before relationship with the fourth operation (that stored this value), but also with the second operation (which stored a 7), even though the third operation used relaxed memory ordering.

Similarly, if we acquire-load a 10 from this variable, which was written by a relaxed operation, we still establish a happens-before relationship with the fifth operation (which stored a 7). Because that was just a regular store operation (not a fetch-and-modify or compare-and-exchange operation), it breaks the chain: we don't establish a happens-before relationship with any of the other operations.

Example: Locking

Mutexes are the most common use case for release and acquire ordering (see "Locking: Mutexes and RwLocks" on page 18). When locking, they use an atomic operation to check if it was unlocked, using acquire ordering, while also (atomically) changing the state to "locked." When unlocking, they set the state back to "unlocked" using release ordering. This means that there will be a happens-before relationship between unlocking a mutex and subsequently locking it.

Here's a demonstration of this pattern:

```
static mut DATA: String = String::new();
static LOCKED: AtomicBool = AtomicBool::new(false);

fn f() {
    if LOCKED.compare_exchange(false, true, Acquire, Relaxed).is_ok() {
        // Safety: We hold the exclusive lock, so nothing else is accessing DATA.
        unsafe { DATA.push('!') };
        LOCKED.store(false, Release);
    }
}

fn main() {
    thread::scope(|s| {
        for _ in 0..100 {
            s.spawn(f);
        }
    });
}
```

As we've briefly seen in "Compare-and-Exchange Operations" on page 42, compare-and-exchange operations take two memory ordering arguments: one for the case where the comparison succeeded and the store happened, and one for the case where the comparison failed and the store did not happen. In f, we attempt to change LOCKED from false to true, and only access DATA if that succeeds. So, we only care about the success memory ordering. If the compare_exchange operation fails, that must be because LOCKED was already set to true, in which case f doesn't do anything. This matches the try_lock operation on a regular mutex.

 An observant reader might have already noticed that the compare-and-exchange operation could also have been a swap operation, since swapping true for true when already locked doesn't change the correctness of the code:

```
// This also works.
if LOCKED.swap(true, Acquire) == false {
    …
}
```

Thanks to the acquire and release memory ordering, we know for sure that no two threads can concurrently access DATA. As visualized in Figure 3-4, any previous access to DATA happened-before the subsequent release-store of false to LOCKED, which in turn happened-before the next acquire-compare-and-exchange (or acquire-swap) operation that changed that false to true, which happened-before the next access to DATA.

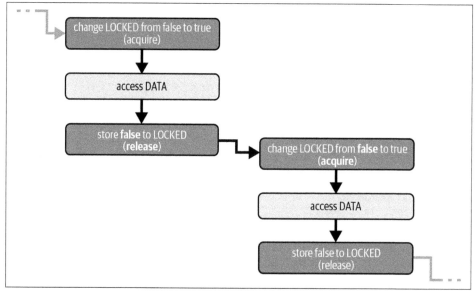

Figure 3-4. The happens-before relationships between atomic operations in the locking example, showing two threads locking and unlocking in sequence

In Chapter 4 we'll turn this concept into a reusable type: a spin lock.

Example: Lazy Initialization with Indirection

In "Example: Lazy One-Time Initialization" on page 45, we implemented lazy initialization of a global variable, using a compare-and-exchange operation to handle situations where multiple threads race to initialize the value concurrently. Because the value was a nonzero 64-bit integer, we were able to use an AtomicU64 to store it, using zero as the placeholder before initializing it.

To do the same for a much larger data type that does not fit in a single atomic variable, we need to look for an alternative.

For this example, let's say we want to maintain the non-blocking behavior, so that threads never wait for another thread, but instead race and take the value from the first thread to complete initialization. This means we still need to be able to go from "uninitalized" to "fully initialized" in a single atomic operation.

As the fundamental theorem of software engineering tells us, every problem in computer science can be solved by adding another layer of indirection, and this problem is no different. Since we can't fit the data into a single atomic variable, we can instead use an atomic variable to store *a pointer* to the data.

An `AtomicPtr<T>` is the atomic version of a `*mut T`: a pointer to T. We can use a null pointer as the placeholder for the initial state, and use a compare-and-exchange operation to atomically replace it with a pointer to a newly allocated, fully initialized T, which can then be read by the other threads.

Since we're not only sharing the atomic variable containing the pointer, but also the data it points to, we can no longer use relaxed memory ordering like in Chapter 2. We need to make sure that allocating and initializing the data does not race with reading it. In other words, we need to use release and acquire ordering on the store and load operations, to make sure the compiler and processor won't break our code by—for example—reordering the store of the pointer and the initialization of the data itself.

This leads us to the following implementation, for some arbitrary data type called Data:

```
use std::sync::atomic::AtomicPtr;

fn get_data() -> &'static Data {
    static PTR: AtomicPtr<Data> = AtomicPtr::new(std::ptr::null_mut());

    let mut p = PTR.load(Acquire);

    if p.is_null() {
        p = Box::into_raw(Box::new(generate_data()));
        if let Err(e) = PTR.compare_exchange(
            std::ptr::null_mut(), p, Release, Acquire
        ) {
            // Safety: p comes from Box::into_raw right above,
            // and wasn't shared with any other thread.
            drop(unsafe { Box::from_raw(p) });
            p = e;
        }
    }

    // Safety: p is not null and points to a properly initialized value.
    unsafe { &*p }
}
```

If the pointer we acquire-load from PTR is non-null, we assume it points to the already initialized data, and construct a reference to that data.

If it's still null, however, we generate new data and store it in a new allocation using Box::new. We then turn this Box into a raw pointer using Box::into_raw, so we can attempt to store it into PTR using a compare-and-exchange operation. If another thread wins the initialization race, compare_exchange fails as PTR is no longer null. If that happens, we turn our raw pointer back into a Box to deallocate it using drop, avoiding a memory leak, and continue with the pointer that the other thread stored in PTR.

The safety comment on the final unsafe block states our assumption that the data it points to has already been initialized. Note how this includes an assumption about the order in which things happened. To make sure our assumption holds, we use release and acquire memory ordering to make sure initializing the data has actually *happened-before* creating a reference to it.

We load a potentially non-null (i.e., initialized) pointer in two places: through the load operation and through the compare_exchange operation when it fails. So, as explained above, we need to use Acquire for both the load memory ordering and the compare_exchange failure memory ordering, to be able to synchronize with the operation that stores the pointer. This store happens when the compare_exchange operation succeeds, so we must use Release as its success ordering.

Figure 3-5 shows a visualization of the operations and happens-before relationships for a situation in which three threads call get_data(). In this situation, thread A and B both observe a null pointer and both attempt to initialize the atomic pointer. Thread A wins that race, causing thread B's compare_exchange operation to fail. Thread C only observes the atomic pointer after it has been initialized by thread A. The end result is that all three threads end up using the box that was allocated by thread A.

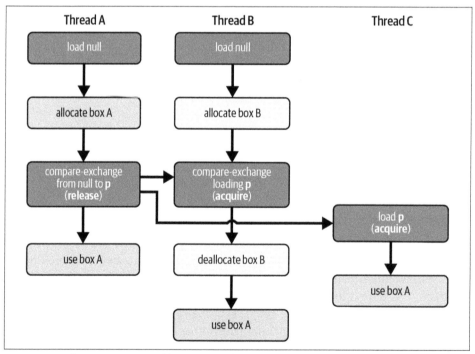

Figure 3-5. The operations and happens-before relationships among three threads calling get_data()

Consume Ordering

Let's take a closer look at the memory ordering in our last example. If we leave the strict memory model aside and think of it in more practical terms, we could say that the release ordering prevents the initialization of the data from being reordered with the store operation that shares the pointer with the other threads. This is important, since otherwise other threads might be able to see the data before it's fully initialized.

Similarly, we could explain the acquire ordering as preventing reordering that would cause the data to be accessed before the pointer is loaded. One might reasonably wonder, however, if that makes any sense in practice. How could the data be accessed before its address is known? We might conclude that something weaker than acquire ordering might suffice. And we would be right: this weaker ordering is called *consume ordering*.

Consume ordering is basically a lightweight—more efficient—variant of acquire ordering, whose synchronizing effects are limited to things that *depend on* the loaded value.

What that means is that if you consume-load a release-stored value x from an atomic variable, then, basically, that store happened before the evaluation of *dependent* expressions like `*x`, `array[x]` or `table.lookup(x + 1)`, but *not* necessarily before independent operations, like reading another variable that we don't need the value of x for.

Now there's good news and bad news.

The good news is that—on all modern processor architectures—consume ordering is achieved with the exact same instructions as relaxed ordering. In other words, consume ordering can be "free," which—at least on some platforms—is not the case for acquire ordering.

The bad news is that no compiler actually implements consume ordering.

As it turns out, not only is this concept of a "dependent" evaluation hard to define, it's even harder to keep such dependencies intact while transforming and optimizing a program. For example, a compiler might be able to optimize x + 2 - x to just 2, effectively dropping the dependency on x. More subtle variations of this issue can happen with more realistic expressions like `array[x]`, if the compiler is able to make any logical deductions about the possible values of x or the array's elements. The issue gets even more complicated when taking control flow into account, like `if` statements or function calls.

Because of this, compilers upgrade consume ordering to acquire ordering, just to be safe. The C++20 standard even explicitly discourages the use of consume ordering, noting that an implementation other than just acquire ordering turned out to be infeasible.

It's possible that a workable definition and implementation of consume ordering might be found in the future. Until that time arrives, however, Rust does not expose Ordering::Consume.

Sequentially Consistent Ordering

The strongest memory ordering is *sequentially consistent* ordering: Ordering::SeqCst. It includes all the guarantees of acquire ordering (for loads) and release ordering (for stores), and *also* guarantees a globally consistent order of operations.

This means that every single operation using SeqCst ordering within a program is part of a single total order that all threads agree on. This total order is consistent with the total modification order of each individual variable.

Since it is strictly stronger than acquire and release memory ordering, a sequentially consistent load or store can take the place of an acquire-load or release-store in a release-acquire pair to form a happens-before relationship. In other words, an acquire-load can not only form a happens-before relationship with a release-store, but also with a sequentially consistent store, and similarly the other way around.

Only when both sides of a happens-before relationship use SeqCst ordering is it guaranteed to be consistent with the single total order of SeqCst operations.

While it might seem like the easiest memory ordering to reason about, SeqCst ordering is almost never necessary in practice. In nearly all cases, regular acquire and release ordering suffice.

Here's an example that depends on sequentially consistent ordered operations:

```
use std::sync::atomic::Ordering::SeqCst;

static A: AtomicBool = AtomicBool::new(false);
static B: AtomicBool = AtomicBool::new(false);

static mut S: String = String::new();

fn main() {
    let a = thread::spawn(|| {
        A.store(true, SeqCst);
        if !B.load(SeqCst) {
            unsafe { S.push('!') };
        }
```

```
    });

    let b = thread::spawn(|| {
        B.store(true, SeqCst);
        if !A.load(SeqCst) {
            unsafe { S.push('!') };
        }
    });

    a.join().unwrap();
    b.join().unwrap();
}
```

Both threads first set their own atomic boolean to `true` to warn the other thread that they are about to access S, and then check the other's atomic boolean to see if they can safely access S without causing a data race.

If both store operations happen before either of the load operations, it's possible that neither thread ends up accessing S. However, it's impossible for *both* threads to access S and cause undefined behavior, since the sequentially consistent ordering guarantees only one of them can win the race. In every possible single total order, the first operation will be a store operation, which prevents the other thread from accessing S.

Virtually all real-world uses of `SeqCst` involve a similar pattern of a store that must be globally visible before a subsequent load on the same thread. For these situations, a potentially more efficient alternative is to instead use relaxed operations in combination with a `SeqCst` *fence*, which we'll explore next.

Fences

In addition to operations on atomic variables, there is one more thing that we can apply a memory ordering to: atomic fences.

The `std::sync::atomic::fence` function represents an *atomic fence* and is either a *release fence* (`Release`), an *acquire fence* (`Acquire`), or both (`AcqRel` or `SeqCst`). A `SeqCst` fence additionally also takes part in the sequentially consistent total order.

An atomic fence allows you to separate the memory ordering from the atomic operation. This can be useful if you want to apply a memory ordering to multiple operations, or if you only want to apply it conditionally.

In essence, a release-store can be split into a release fence followed by a (relaxed) store, and an acquire-load can be split into a (relaxed) load followed by an acquire fence:

The store of a release-acquire relationship,
```
    a.store(1, Release);
```
can be substituted by a release fence followed by a relaxed store:
```
    fence(Release);
    a.store(1, Relaxed);
```

The load of a release-acquire relationship,
```
    a.load(Acquire);
```
can be substituted by a relaxed load followed by an acquire fence:
```
    a.load(Relaxed);
    fence(Acquire);
```

Using a separate fence can result in an extra processor instruction, though, which can be slightly less efficient.

More importantly, unlike a release-store or an acquire-load, a fence is not tied to any single atomic variable. This means that a single fence can be used for multiple variables at once.

Formally, a release fence can take the place of a release operation in a happens-before relationship if that release fence is followed (on the same thread) by any atomic operation that stores a value observed by the acquire operation we're synchronizing with. Similarly, an acquire fence can take the place of any acquire operation if that acquire fence is preceded (on the same thread) by any atomic operation that loads a value stored by the release operation.

Putting this together, it means that a happens-before relationship is created between a release fence and an acquire fence if *any* store after the release fence is observed by *any* load before the acquire fence.

For example, suppose we have one thread executing a release fence followed by three atomic store operations to different variables, and another thread executing three load operations from those same variables followed by an acquire fence, as follows:

```
Thread 1:                      Thread 2:
    fence(Release);                A.load(Relaxed);
    A.store(1, Relaxed);           B.load(Relaxed);
    B.store(2, Relaxed);           C.load(Relaxed);
    C.store(3, Relaxed);           fence(Acquire);
```

In this situation, if *any* of the load operations on thread 2 loads the value from the corresponding store operation of thread 1, the release fence on thread 1 happens-before the acquire fence on thread 2.

A fence does not have to directly precede or follow the atomic operations. Anything else can happen in between, including control flow. This can be used to make the fence conditional, similar to how compare-and-swap operations have both a success and a failure ordering.

For example, if we load a pointer from an atomic variable using acquire memory ordering, we could use a fence to apply the acquire ordering only when the pointer is not null:

Using an acquire-load:
```
let p = PTR.load(Acquire);
if p.is_null() {
    println!("no data");
} else {
    println!("data = {}", unsafe { *p });
}
```

Using a conditional acquire fence:
```
let p = PTR.load(Relaxed);
if p.is_null() {
    println!("no data");
} else {
    fence(Acquire);
    println!("data = {}", unsafe { *p });
}
```

This can be beneficial if the pointer is often expected to be null, to avoid acquire memory ordering when not necessary.

Let's take a look at a more complicated use case of release and acquire fences:

```
use std::sync::atomic::fence;

static mut DATA: [u64; 10] = [0; 10];

const ATOMIC_FALSE: AtomicBool = AtomicBool::new(false);
static READY: [AtomicBool; 10] = [ATOMIC_FALSE; 10];

fn main() {
    for i in 0..10 {
        thread::spawn(move || {
            let data = some_calculation(i);
            unsafe { DATA[i] = data };
            READY[i].store(true, Release);
        });
    }
    thread::sleep(Duration::from_millis(500));
    let ready: [bool; 10] = std::array::from_fn(|i| READY[i].load(Relaxed));
    if ready.contains(&true) {
        fence(Acquire);
        for i in 0..10 {
            if ready[i] {
                println!("data{i} = {}", unsafe { DATA[i] });
            }
        }
    }
}
```

`std::array::from_fn` is an easy way to execute something a certain number of times and collect the results into an array.

In this example, 10 threads do some calculations and store their results in a (non-atomic) shared variable. Each thread sets an atomic boolean to indicate that the data is ready to be read by the main thread, using a normal release-store. The main thread waits for half a second, checks all 10 booleans to see which threads are done, and prints whichever results are ready.

Instead of using 10 acquire-load operations to read the booleans, the main thread uses relaxed operations and a single acquire fence. It executes the fence before reading the data, but only if there is data to be read.

While in this particular example it might be completely unnecessary to put any effort into such optimization, this pattern for saving the overhead of additional acquire operations can be important when building highly efficient concurrent data structures.

A SeqCst fence is both a release fence and an acquire fence (just like AcqRel), but also part of the single total order of sequentially consistent operations. However, only the fence is part of the total order, but not necessarily the atomic operations before or after it. This means that unlike a release or acquire operation, a sequentially consistent operation cannot be split into a relaxed operation and a memory fence.

Compiler Fences

In addition to a regular atomic fence, the Rust standard library also provides a *compiler fence*: `std::sync::atomic::compiler_fence`. Its signature is identical to that of the regular `fence()` we discussed above, but its effects are restricted to just the compiler. Unlike a regular atomic fence, it does not prevent the processor from, for example, reordering instructions. In the vast majority of use cases for fences, a compiler fence does not suffice.

A potential use case might arise when implementing a Unix *signal handler*, or an *interrupt* on embedded systems. These are mechanisms that can suddenly interrupt a thread to temporarily execute an unrelated function on the same processor core. Because it happens on the same processor core, the usual ways in which the processor might affect memory ordering don't apply. (More on that in Chapter 7.) In this case, a compiler fence might suffice, potentially saving an instruction and hopefully increasing performance.

Another use case involves *process-wide memory barriers*. This technique falls outside the scope of Rust's memory model and is only supported on some operating systems:

---

on Linux through the `membarrier` syscall, and on Windows using the `FlushProcess WriteBuffers` function. It effectively allows a thread to forcefully inject a (sequentially consistent) atomic fence into all concurrently running threads. This allows us to replace two matching fences with a lightweight compiler fence on one side and a heavyweight process-wide barrier on the other side. If the code on the side of the lightweight fence is executed much more often, this can improve overall performance. (See the documentation of the `membarrier` crate on crates.io for more details and a cross-platform way to use such barriers in Rust.)

A compiler fence can also be an interesting tool for exploring the effect of the processor on memory ordering. In "An Experiment" on page 155, we'll break our code on purpose by replacing a regular fence with a compiler fence. This will let us experience the subtle but potentially disastrous effects of the processor when using the wrong memory ordering.

Common Misconceptions

There are a lot of misconceptions around memory ordering. Before we end this chapter, let's go over the most common ones.

Myth: I need strong memory ordering to make sure changes are "immediately" visible.

A common misunderstanding is that using a weak memory ordering like `Relaxed` means that changes to an atomic variable might never arrive at another thread, or only after a significant delay. The name "relaxed" might make it sound like nothing happens until something forces some part of the hardware to wake up and do what it should've done instead of relaxing.

The truth is that the memory model doesn't say anything about timing at all. It only defines in which order certain things happen; not how long you might have to wait for them. A hypothetical computer in which it takes years to get data from one thread to another is quite unusable, but can perfectly satisfy the memory model.

In real life, memory ordering is about things like reordering instructions, which usually happen at nanosecond scale. Stronger memory ordering does not make your data travel faster; it might even slow your program down.

Myth: Disabling optimization means I don't need to care about memory ordering.

Both the compiler and the processor play a role in making things happen in a different order than we might expect. Disabling compiler optimization does not disable every possible transformation in the compiler, and does not disable the processor features that result in instruction reordering and similar potentially problematic behavior.

Myth: Using a processor that doesn't reorder instructions means I don't need to care about memory ordering.

Some simple processors, such as those in small microcontrollers, have only one core and only ever execute one instruction at a time, all in order. However, while it's true that on such devices there's a significantly lower chance of an incorrect memory ordering resulting in actual issues, it's still possible for the compiler to make invalid assumptions based on incorrect memory ordering, breaking your code. Besides that, it's also important to realize that even when a processor does not execute instructions out of order, it might still have other features that can be relevant for memory ordering.

Myth: Relaxed operations are free.

Whether this is true depends on your definition of "free." It's true that `Relaxed` is the most efficient memory ordering and that it can be significantly faster than the others. It's even true that on all modern platforms, relaxed load and store operations compile down to the same processor instructions as non-atomic reads and writes.

If an atomic variable is only used by a single thread, any difference in speed with a non-atomic variable will most likely be because of the compiler having more freedom and being more effective at optimizing non-atomic operations. (Compilers tend to avoid most types of optimizations for atomic variables.)

However, accessing the same memory from multiple threads is usually significantly slower than accessing it from a single thread. A thread that continuously writes to an atomic variable will likely experience a noticeable slowdown when other threads start repeatedly reading the variable, since the processor cores and their caches now have to start collaborating.

We'll explore this effect in Chapter 7.

Myth: Sequentially consistent memory ordering is a great default and is always correct.

Putting aside performance concerns, sequentially consistent memory ordering is often seen as the perfect type of memory ordering to default to, because of its strong guarantees. It's true that *if* any other memory ordering is correct, `SeqCst` is also correct. This might make it sound like `SeqCst` is always correct. However, it's entirely possible that a concurrent algorithm is simply incorrect, regardless of memory ordering.

More importantly, when reading code, `SeqCst` basically tells the reader: "this operation depends on the total order of every single `SeqCst` operation in the program," which is an incredibly far-reaching claim. The same code would likely be easier to review and verify if it used weaker memory ordering instead, if possible. For example, `Release` effectively tells the reader: "this relates to an acquire operation on the same variable," which involves far fewer considerations when forming an understanding of the code.

It is advisable to see SeqCst as a warning sign. Seeing it in the wild often means that either something complicated is going on, or simply that the author did not take the time to analyze their memory ordering related assumptions, both of which are reasons for extra scrutiny.

Myth: Sequentially consistent memory ordering can be used for a "release-load" or an "acquire-store."

While SeqCst can stand in for Acquire or Release, it is not a way to somehow create an acquire-store or release-load. Those remain nonexistent. Release only applies to store operations, and acquire only to load operations.

For example, a Release-store does not form any release-acquire relationship with a SeqCst-store. If you need them to be part of a globally consistent order, both operations will have to use SeqCst.

Summary

- There might not be a global consistent order of all atomic operations, as things can appear to happen in a different order from different threads.
- However, each individual atomic variable has its own *total modification order*, regardless of memory ordering, which all threads agree on.
- The order of operations is formally defined through *happens-before* relationships.
- Within a single thread, there is a happens-before relationship between every single operation.
- Spawning a thread happens-before everything the spawned thread does.
- Everything a thread does happens-before joining that thread.
- Unlocking a mutex happens-before locking that mutex again.
- Acquire-loading the value from a release-store establishes a happens-before relationship. This value may be modified by any number of fetch-and-modify and compare-and-exchange operations.
- A consume-load would be a lightweight version of an acquire-load, if it existed.
- Sequentially consistent ordering results in a globally consistent order of operations, but is almost never necessary and can make code review more complicated.
- Fences allow you to combine the memory ordering of multiple operations or apply a memory ordering conditionally.

CHAPTER 4

Building Our Own Spin Lock

Locking a regular mutex (see "Locking: Mutexes and RwLocks" on page 18) will put your thread to sleep when the mutex is already locked. This avoids wasting resources while waiting for the lock to be released. If a lock is only ever held for very brief moments and the threads locking it can run in parallel on different processor cores, it might be better for the threads to repeatedly try to lock it without actually going to sleep.

A spin lock is a mutex that does exactly that. Attempting to lock an already locked mutex will result in *busy-looping* or *spinning*: repeatedly trying over and over again until it finally succeeds. This can waste processor cycles, but can sometimes result in lower latency when locking.

 Many real-world implementations of mutexes, including `std::sync::Mutex` on some platforms, briefly behave like a spin lock before asking the operating system to put a thread to sleep. This is an attempt to combine the best of both worlds, although it depends entirely on the specific use case whether this behavior is beneficial or not.

In this chapter, we'll build our own `SpinLock` type, applying what we've learned in Chapters 2 and 3, and see how we can use Rust's type system to provide a safe and useful interface to the user of our `SpinLock`.

A Minimal Implementation

Let's implement such a spin lock from scratch.

The most minimal version is pretty simple, as follows:

```
pub struct SpinLock {
    locked: AtomicBool,
}
```

All we need is a single boolean that indicates whether it is locked or not. We use an *atomic* boolean, since we want more than one thread to be able to interact with it simultaneously.

Then all we need is a constructor function, and the lock and unlock methods:

```
impl SpinLock {
    pub const fn new() -> Self {
        Self { locked: AtomicBool::new(false) }
    }

    pub fn lock(&self) {
        while self.locked.swap(true, Acquire) {
            std::hint::spin_loop();
        }
    }

    pub fn unlock(&self) {
        self.locked.store(false, Release);
    }
}
```

The locked boolean starts at false, the lock swaps that for true and keeps trying if it was already true, and the unlock method just sets it back to false.

> Instead of using a swap operation, we could also have used a compare-and-exchange operation to atomically check if the boolean is false and set it to true if that's the case:
>
> ```
> while self.locked.compare_exchange_weak(
>             false, true, Acquire, Relaxed).is_err()
> ```
>
> It's a bit more verbose, but depending on your tastes this might be easier to follow, as it more clearly captures the concept of an operation that can fail or succeed. It might also result in slightly different instructions, however, as we'll see in Chapter 7.

Within the while loop, we use a *spin loop hint*, which tells the processor that we're spinning while waiting for something to change. On most major platforms, this hint results in a special instruction that causes the processor core to optimize its behavior for such a situation. For example, it might temporarily slow down or prioritize other useful things it can do. Unlike blocking operations such as thread::sleep or thread::park, however, a spin loop hint does not cause the operating system to be called to put your thread to sleep in favor of another thread.

In general, it's good idea to include such a hint in a spin loop. Depending on the situation, it might even be good to execute this hint several times before attempting to access the atomic variable again. If you care about the last few nanoseconds of performance and want to find the optimal strategy, you'll have to benchmark your specific use case. Unfortunately, the conclusions of such benchmarks can be highly dependent on the hardware, as we'll see in Chapter 7.

We use acquire and release memory ordering to make sure that every unlock() call establishes a happens-before relationship with the lock() calls that follow. In other words, to make sure that after locking it, we can safely assume that whatever happened during the last time it was locked has already happened. This is the most classic use case of acquire and release ordering: acquiring and releasing a lock.

Figure 4-1 visualizes a situation where our SpinLock is used to protect access to some shared data, with two threads concurrently attempting to acquire the lock. Note how the unlock operation on the first thread forms a happens-before relationship with the lock operation on the second thread, which makes sure the threads cannot access the data concurrently.

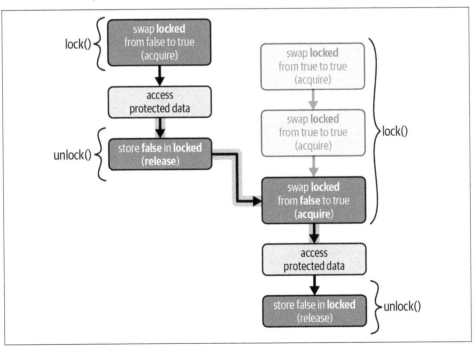

Figure 4-1. The happens-before relationships between two threads using our SpinLock to protect access to some shared data

An Unsafe Spin Lock

Our SpinLock type above has a fully safe interface since, by itself, it doesn't cause any undefined behavior when misused. In most use cases, however, it will be used to protect mutations to a shared variable, which means the user will still have to use unsafe, unchecked code.

To provide an easier interface, we can change the lock method to give us an exclusive reference (&mut T) to the data protected by the lock, since in most use cases, it's the lock operation that guarantees that it's safe to assume exclusive access.

To be able to do that, we have to change the type to be generic over the type of data it protects and add a field to hold that data. Since this data can be mutated (or accessed exclusively) even though the spin lock itself is shared, we need to use interior mutability (see "Interior Mutability" on page 13), for which we'll use an UnsafeCell:

```
use std::cell::UnsafeCell;

pub struct SpinLock<T> {
    locked: AtomicBool,
    value: UnsafeCell<T>,
}
```

As a precaution, UnsafeCell does not implement Sync, which means that our type is now no longer shareable between threads, making it rather useless. To fix that, we need to promise to the compiler that it is actually safe for our type to be shared between threads. However, since the lock can be used to send values of type T from one thread to another, we must limit this promise to types that are safe to send between threads. So, we (unsafely) implement Sync for SpinLock<T> for all T that implement Send, like this:

```
unsafe impl<T> Sync for SpinLock<T> where T: Send {}
```

Note that we don't need to require that T is Sync, because our SpinLock<T> will only allow one thread at a time to access the T it protects. Only if we were to give multiple threads access at once, like a reader-writer lock does for readers, would we (additionally) need to require T: Sync.

Next, our new function now needs to take a value of type T to initialize that Unsafe Cell with:

```
impl<T> SpinLock<T> {
    pub const fn new(value: T) -> Self {
        Self {
            locked: AtomicBool::new(false),
            value: UnsafeCell::new(value),
        }
    }

    …

}
```

And then we get to the interesting part: lock and unlock. The reason we are doing all this, is to be able to return a &mut T from lock(), such that the user isn't required to write unsafe, unchecked code when using our lock to protect their data. This means that we now have to use unsafe code on our side, within the implementation of lock. An UnsafeCell can give us a raw pointer to its contents (*mut T) through its get() method, which we can convert to a reference within an unsafe block, as follows:

```
pub fn lock(&self) -> &mut T {
    while self.locked.swap(true, Acquire) {
        std::hint::spin_loop();
    }
    unsafe { &mut *self.value.get() }
}
```

Since the function signature of lock contains a reference both in its input and output, the lifetimes of the &self and &mut T have been elided and assumed to be identical. (See "Lifetime Elision" in "Chapter 10: Generic Types, Traits, and Lifetimes" of the Rust Book.) We can make the lifetimes explicit by writing them out manually, like this:

```
pub fn lock<'a>(&'a self) -> &'a mut T { … }
```

This clearly shows that the lifetime of the returned reference is the same as that of &self. This means that we have claimed that the returned reference is valid as long as the lock itself exists.

If we pretend unlock() doesn't exist, this would be a perfectly safe and sound interface. A SpinLock can be locked, resulting in a &mut T, and can then never be locked again, which guarantees this exclusive reference is indeed exclusive.

If we try to add the unlock() method back, however, we would need a way to limit the lifetime of the returned reference until the next call to unlock(). If the compiler understood English, perhaps this would work:

```
pub fn lock<'a>(&self) -> &'a mut T
where
    'a ends at the next call to unlock() on self,
    even if that's done by another thread.
    Oh, and it also ends when self is dropped, of course.
    (Thanks!)
{ … }
```

Unfortunately, that's not valid Rust. Instead of trying to explain this limitation to the compiler, we'll have to explain it to the user. To shift the responsibility to the user, we mark the unlock function as unsafe, and leave a note for them explaining what they need to do to keep things sound:

```
/// Safety: The &mut T from lock() must be gone!
/// (And no cheating by keeping reference to fields of that T around!)
pub unsafe fn unlock(&self) {
    self.locked.store(false, Release);
}
```

A Safe Interface Using a Lock Guard

To be able to provide a fully safe interface, we need to tie the unlocking operation to the end of the &mut T. We can do that by wrapping this reference in our own type that behaves like a reference, but also implements the Drop trait to do something when it is dropped.

Such a type is often called a *guard*, as it effectively guards the state of the lock, and stays responsible for that state until it is dropped.

Our Guard type will simply contain a reference to the SpinLock, so that it can both access its UnsafeCell and reset the AtomicBool later:

```
pub struct Guard<T> {
    lock: &SpinLock<T>,
}
```

If we try to compile this, however, the compiler tells us:

```
error[E0106]: missing lifetime specifier
  --> src/lib.rs
   |
   |         lock: &SpinLock<T>,
   |               ^ expected named lifetime parameter
   |
help: consider introducing a named lifetime parameter
   |
 ~         pub struct Guard<'a, T> {
   |                         ^^^
 ~             lock: &'a SpinLock<T>,
   |                   ^^
   |
```

Apparently, this is not a place where lifetimes can be elided. We have to make explicit that the reference has a limited lifetime, exactly as the compiler suggests:

```
pub struct Guard<'a, T> {
    lock: &'a SpinLock<T>,
}
```

This guarantees the Guard cannot outlive the SpinLock.

Next, we change the lock method on our SpinLock to return a Guard:

```
pub fn lock(&self) -> Guard<T> {
    while self.locked.swap(true, Acquire) {
        std::hint::spin_loop();
    }
    Guard { lock: self }
}
```

Our Guard type has no constructor and its field is private, so this is the only way the user can obtain a Guard. Therefore, we can safely assume that the existence of a Guard means that the SpinLock has been locked.

To make Guard<T> behave like an (exclusive) reference, transparently giving access to the T, we have to implement the special Deref and DerefMut traits as follows:

```
use std::ops::{Deref, DerefMut};

impl<T> Deref for Guard<'_, T> {
    type Target = T;
    fn deref(&self) -> &T {
        // Safety: The very existence of this Guard
        // guarantees we've exclusively locked the lock.
        unsafe { &*self.lock.value.get() }
    }
}

impl<T> DerefMut for Guard<'_, T> {
    fn deref_mut(&mut self) -> &mut T {
        // Safety: The very existence of this Guard
        // guarantees we've exclusively locked the lock.
        unsafe { &mut *self.lock.value.get() }
    }
}
```

As the final step, we implement Drop for Guard, allowing us to completely remove the unsafe unlock method:

```
impl<T> Drop for Guard<'_, T> {
    fn drop(&mut self) {
        self.lock.locked.store(false, Release);
    }
}
```

And just like that, through the magic of Drop and Rust's type system, we gave our SpinLock type a fully safe (and useful) interface.

Let's try it out:

```
fn main() {
    let x = SpinLock::new(Vec::new());
    thread::scope(|s| {
        s.spawn(|| x.lock().push(1));
        s.spawn(|| {
            let mut g = x.lock();
            g.push(2);
            g.push(2);
        });
    });
    let g = x.lock();
    assert!(g.as_slice() == [1, 2, 2] || g.as_slice() == [2, 2, 1]);
}
```

The program above demonstrates how easy our SpinLock is to use. Thanks to Deref and DerefMut, we can directly call the Vec::push method on the guard. And thanks to Drop, we don't need to worry about unlocking.

Explicitly unlocking is also possible, by calling drop(g) to drop the guard. If you try to unlock too early, you'll see the guard doing its job through a compiler error. For example, if you insert drop(g); between the two push(2) lines, the second push will not compile, since you've already dropped g at that point:

```
error[E0382]: borrow of moved value: `g`
  --> src/lib.rs
   |
   |         drop(g);
   |              - value moved here
   |         g.push(2);
   |         ^^^^^^^^^ value borrowed here after move
```

Thanks to Rust's type system, we can rest assured that mistakes like this are caught before we can even run our program.

Summary

- A *spin lock* is a mutex that busy-loops, or spins, while waiting.
- Spinning can reduce latency, but can also be a waste of clockcycles and reduce performance.
- A *spin loop hint*, `std::hint::spin_loop()`, can be used to inform the processor of a spin loop, which might increase its efficiency.
- A `SpinLock<T>` can be implement with just an `AtomicBool` and an `Unsafe Cell<T>`, the latter of which is necessary for *interior mutability* (see "Interior Mutability" on page 13).
- A *happens-before relationship* between unlock and lock operations is necessary to prevent a *data race*, which would result in *undefined behavior*.
- *Acquire and release memory ordering* are a perfect fit for this use case.
- When making unchecked assumptions necessary to avoid undefined behavior, the responsibility can be shifted to the caller by making the function `unsafe`.
- The `Deref` and `DerefMut` traits can be used to make a type behave like a reference, transparently providing access to another object.
- The `Drop` trait can be used to do something when an object is dropped, such as when it goes out of scope, or when it is passed to `drop()`.
- A *lock guard* is a useful design pattern of a special type that's used to represent (safe) access to a locked lock. Such a type usually behaves similarly to a reference, thanks to the `Deref` traits, and implements automatic unlocking through the `Drop` trait.

CHAPTER 5

Building Our Own Channels

Channels can be used to send data between threads, and they come in many variants. Some channels can only be used between exactly one sender and one receiver, while others can send from any number of threads, or even allow multiple receivers. Some channels are blocking, meaning that receiving (and sometimes sending) is a blocking operation, making your thread sleep until the operation can be completed. Some channels are optimized for throughput, while others are optimized for low latency.

The variations are endless, and there is no one-size-fits-all version that fits all use cases.

In this chapter, we'll implement a few relatively simple channels to not only explore some more applications of atomics, but also to learn more about how our requirements and assumptions can be captured in Rust's type system.

A Simple Mutex-Based Channel

A basic channel implementation does not require any knowledge of atomics. We can take a VecDeque, which is basically a Vec that allows for efficient adding and removing of elements on both ends, and protect it with a Mutex to allow multiple threads to access it. We then use the VecDeque as a queue of data, often called *messages*, that's been sent but not yet received. Any thread that wants to send a message can simply add it to the back of the queue, and any thread that wants to receive a message just has to remove one from the front of the queue.

There's just one more thing to add, which is used to make the receive operation blocking: a Condvar (see "Condition Variables" on page 26) to notify waiting receivers of a new messsage.

An implementation of this can be quite short and relatively straightforward, as shown below:

```
pub struct Channel<T> {
    queue: Mutex<VecDeque<T>>,
    item_ready: Condvar,
}

impl<T> Channel<T> {
    pub fn new() -> Self {
        Self {
            queue: Mutex::new(VecDeque::new()),
            item_ready: Condvar::new(),
        }
    }

    pub fn send(&self, message: T) {
        self.queue.lock().unwrap().push_back(message);
        self.item_ready.notify_one();
    }

    pub fn receive(&self) -> T {
        let mut b = self.queue.lock().unwrap();
        loop {
            if let Some(message) = b.pop_front() {
                return message;
            }
            b = self.item_ready.wait(b).unwrap();
        }
    }
}
```

Note how we didn't have to use any atomics or unsafe code and didn't have to think about the Send or Sync traits. The compiler understands the interface of Mutex and what guarantees that type provides, and will implicitly understand that if both Mutex<T> and Condvar can safely be shared between threads, so can our Channel<T>.

Our send function locks the mutex to push the new message to the back of the queue, and directly notifies one potentially waiting receiver after unlocking the queue, by using the condition variable.

The receive function also locks the mutex to pop the next message from the front of the queue, but will use the condition variable to wait if there's no message available yet.

 Remember that the Condvar::wait method will unlock the Mutex while waiting and relock it before returning. So, our receive function will not keep the mutex locked while waiting.

While this channel is very flexible in usage, as it allows any number of sending and receiving threads, its implementation can be far from optimal in many situations. Even if there are plenty of messages ready to be received, any send or receive operation will briefly block any other send or receive operation, since they all have to lock the same mutex. If VecDeque::push has to grow the capacity of the VecDeque, all sending and receiving threads will have to wait for that one thread to finish the reallocation, which might be unacceptable in some situations.

Another property which might be undesirable is that this channel's queue might grow without bounds. Nothing is stopping senders from continuously sending new messages at a higher rate than receivers are processing them.

An Unsafe One-Shot Channel

The variety of use cases for channels is virtually endless. However, in the rest of this chapter, we'll focus on a specific type of use case: sending exactly one message from one thread to another. A channel designed for such a use case is often called a *one-shot channel*.

We could take our Mutex<VecDeque> based implementation from above and substitute the VecDeque for an Option, effectively reducing the capacity of the queue to exactly one message. It would avoid allocation, but would still have some of the same downsides of using a Mutex. We can avoid this by building our own one-shot channel from scratch using atomics.

First, let's build a minimal implementation of a one-shot channel without putting much thought into its interface. Later in this chapter, we'll explore ways to improve its interface, and how to team up with Rust's type system to provide users of our channel a pleasant experience.

The tools we need to start with are basically the same as we used for our SpinLock<T> (from Chapter 4): an UnsafeCell for storage and an AtomicBool to indicate its state. In this case, we use the atomic boolean to indicate whether the message is ready for consumption.

Before a message is sent, the channel is "empty" and does not contain any message of type T yet. We could use an Option<T> inside the cell to allow for the absence of a T. However, that could waste valuable space in memory, since our atomic boolean already tells us whether there is a message or not. Instead, we can use a std::mem::MaybeUninit<T>, which is essentially the bare bones unsafe version of Option<T>: it requires its user to manually keep track of whether it has been initialized or not, and almost its entire interface is unsafe, as it can't perform its own checks.

Putting that all together, we start our first attempt with this struct definition:

```
use std::mem::MaybeUninit;

pub struct Channel<T> {
    message: UnsafeCell<MaybeUninit<T>>,
    ready: AtomicBool,
}
```

Just like for our SpinLock<T>, we need to tell the compiler that our channel is safe to share between threads, or at least as long as T is Send:

```
unsafe impl<T> Sync for Channel<T> where T: Send {}
```

A new channel is empty, with ready set to false, and message left uninitialized:

```
impl<T> Channel<T> {
    pub const fn new() -> Self {
        Self {
            message: UnsafeCell::new(MaybeUninit::uninit()),
            ready: AtomicBool::new(false),
        }
    }

    …

}
```

To send a message, it first needs to be stored in the cell, after which we can release it to the receiver by setting the ready flag to true. Attempting to do this more than once would be dangerous, since after setting the ready flag, the receiver might read the message at any point, which could race with a second attempt to send a message. For now, we make this the responsibility of the user by making the method unsafe and leaving a note for them:

```
/// Safety: Only call this once!
pub unsafe fn send(&self, message: T) {
    (*self.message.get()).write(message);
    self.ready.store(true, Release);
}
```

In the snippet above, we use the UnsafeCell::get method to obtain a pointer to the MaybeUninit<T>, and unsafely dereference that to call MaybeUninit::write to initialize it. This could result in undefined behavior when misused, but we've punted that responsibility over to the caller.

For the memory ordering, we need to use release ordering, since the atomic store effectively releases the message to the receiver. This makes sure the initialization of the message will be finished from the perspective of the receiving thread if it loads true from self.ready with acquire ordering.

For receiving, we'll not bother with providing a blocking interface for now. Instead, we'll provide two methods: one to check whether a message is available, and another to receive it. We'll leave it to the user of our channel to use something like thread parking ("Thread Parking" on page 24) if they want to block.

These are the last two methods to complete this version of our channel:

```
pub fn is_ready(&self) -> bool {
    self.ready.load(Acquire)
}

/// Safety: Only call this once,
/// and only after is_ready() returns true!
pub unsafe fn receive(&self) -> T {
    (*self.message.get()).assume_init_read()
}
```

While the `is_ready` method can always be called safely, the `receive` method uses `MaybeUninit::assume_init_read()`, which unsafely assumes it has already been initialized and that it isn't being used to produce multiple copies of non-`Copy` objects. Just like for `send`, we simply make that our user's problem by making the function itself `unsafe`.

The result is a technically usable channel, but one that is unwieldy and generally disappointing. If held right, it does exactly what it is supposed to do, but there are many subtle ways to misuse it.

Calling `send` more than once might result in a data race, since the second sender will be overwriting the data while the receiver might be trying to read the first message. Even if receiving was properly synchronized, calling `send` from multiple threads might result in two threads attempting to concurrently write to the cell, again resulting in a data race. Also, calling `receive` more than once results in two copies of the message, even if `T` does not implement `Copy` and thus cannot safely be copied.

A more subtle issue is the lack of a `Drop` implementation for our channel. The `MaybeUninit` type does not track whether it has been initialized or not, and will therefore not automatically drop its contents when dropped. This means that if a message is sent but never received, the message will never be dropped. This is not unsound, but it's still something to avoid. While leaking is universally considered safe in Rust, it's generally only acceptable as a consequence of another leak. For example, leaking a `Vec` also leaks its contents, but regular usage of a `Vec` does not result in any leaks.

Since we made the user responsible for everything, it's only a matter of time before this results in an unfortunate accident.

Safety Through Runtime Checks

To allow for a safer interface, we can add some checks to make misuse result in a panic with a clear message, which is much preferable to undefined behavior.

Let's start with the issue of calling `receive` before a message is ready. This one is simple to handle, as all we have to do is make the `receive` method validate the `ready` flag before attempting to read a message:

```
/// Panics if no message is available yet.
///
/// Tip: Use `is_ready` to check first.
///
/// Safety: Only call this once!
pub unsafe fn receive(&self) -> T {
    if !self.ready.load(Acquire) {
        panic!("no message available!");
    }
    (*self.message.get()).assume_init_read()
}
```

The function is still unsafe, as the user is still responsible for not calling this function more than once, but failing to check `is_ready()` first no longer results in undefined behavior.

Since we now have an acquire-load of the ready flag inside the `receive` method providing the necessary synchronization, we can lower the memory ordering of the load in `is_ready` to `Relaxed`, since that one is now only used for indicative purposes:

```
pub fn is_ready(&self) -> bool {
    self.ready.load(Relaxed)
}
```

 Remember that the *total modification order* (see "Relaxed Ordering" on page 54) on `ready` guarantees that after `is_ready` loads `true` from it, `receive` will also see `true`. There is no possibility of `is_ready` returning `true` and `receive()` still panicking, regardless of the memory ordering used in `is_ready`.

The next issue to address is what happens when calling `receive` more than once. We can easily make that result in a panic as well by setting the `ready` flag back to `false` in our `receive` method, like this:

```
/// Panics if no message is available yet,
/// or if the message was already consumed.
///
/// Tip: Use `is_ready` to check first.
pub fn receive(&self) -> T {
    if !self.ready.swap(false, Acquire) {
```

```
        panic!("no message available!");
    }
    // Safety: We've just checked (and reset) the ready flag.
    unsafe { (*self.message.get()).assume_init_read() }
}
```

We've simply changed the load for a swap to false, and suddenly the receive method is fully safe to call in any condition. The function is no longer marked as unsafe. Instead of making the user responsible for everything, we now take responsibility for the unsafe code, resulting in less stress for our user.

For send, things are slightly more complicated. To prevent multiple send calls from accessing the cell at the same time, we need to know whether another send call has already started. The ready flag only tells us whether another send call has already finished, so that won't suffice.

Let's add a second flag, named in_use, to indicate whether the channel has been taken in use:

```
pub struct Channel<T> {
    message: UnsafeCell<MaybeUninit<T>>,
    in_use: AtomicBool, // New!
    ready: AtomicBool,
}

impl<T> Channel<T> {
    pub const fn new() -> Self {
        Self {
            message: UnsafeCell::new(MaybeUninit::uninit()),
            in_use: AtomicBool::new(false), // New!
            ready: AtomicBool::new(false),
        }
    }

    …

}
```

Now all we need to do is set in_use to true in the send method before accessing the cell and panic if it was already set by another call:

```
/// Panics when trying to send more than one message.
pub fn send(&self, message: T) {
    if self.in_use.swap(true, Relaxed) {
        panic!("can't send more than one message!");
    }
    unsafe { (*self.message.get()).write(message) };
    self.ready.store(true, Release);
}
```

We can use relaxed memory ordering for the atomic swap operation, because the *total modification order* (see "Relaxed Ordering" on page 54) of in_use guarantees that there will only be a single swap operation on in_use that will return false, which is the only case in which send will attempt to access the cell.

We now have a fully safe interface, though there is still one problem left. The last remaining issue occurs when sending a message that's never received: it will never be dropped. While this does not result in undefined behavior and is allowed in safe code, it's definitely something to avoid.

Since we reset the ready flag in the receive method, fixing this is easy: the ready flag indicates whether there's a not-yet-received message in the cell that needs to be dropped.

In the Drop implementation of our Channel, we don't need to use an atomic operation to check the atomic ready flag, because an object can only be dropped if it is fully owned by whichever thread is dropping it, with no outstanding borrows. This means we can use the AtomicBool::get_mut method, which takes an exclusive reference (&mut self), proving that atomic access is unnecessary. The same holds for Unsafe Cell, through UnsafeCell::get_mut.

Using that, here's the final piece of our fully safe and non-leaking channel:

```
impl<T> Drop for Channel<T> {
    fn drop(&mut self) {
        if *self.ready.get_mut() {
            unsafe { self.message.get_mut().assume_init_drop() }
        }
    }
}
```

Let's try it out!

Since our Channel doesn't provide a blocking interface (yet), we'll manually use thread parking to wait on a message. The receiving thread will park() itself as long as there's no message ready, and the sending thread will unpark() the receiver once it has sent something.

Here's a complete test program, sending the string literal "hello world!" through our Channel from a second thread back to the main thread:

```
fn main() {
    let channel = Channel::new();
    let t = thread::current();
    thread::scope(|s| {
        s.spawn(|| {
            channel.send("hello world!");
            t.unpark();
        });
        while !channel.is_ready() {
            thread::park();
        }
```

```
        assert_eq!(channel.receive(), "hello world!");
    });
}
```

This program compiles, runs, and exits cleanly, showing that our `Channel` works as it should.

If we duplicate the `send` line, we can also see one of our safety checks in action, producing the following panic message when the program is run:

```
thread '<unnamed>' panicked at 'can't send more than one message!', src/main.rs
```

While a panicking program isn't great, it's far better for a program to reliably panic than to get anywhere near the potential horrors of undefined behavior.

Using a Single Atomic for the Channel State

In case you can't get enough of implementing channels, here's a subtle variation that can save one byte of memory.

Instead of using two separate atomic booleans to represent the state of the channel, we instead use a single `AtomicU8` to represent all four states. Rather than atomically swapping booleans, we'll have to use `compare_exchange` to atomically check if the channel is in the expected state and change it to another state.

```
const EMPTY: u8 = 0;
const WRITING: u8 = 1;
const READY: u8 = 2;
const READING: u8 = 3;

pub struct Channel<T> {
    message: UnsafeCell<MaybeUninit<T>>,
    state: AtomicU8,
}

unsafe impl<T: Send> Sync for Channel<T> {}

impl<T> Channel<T> {
    pub const fn new() -> Self {
        Self {
            message: UnsafeCell::new(MaybeUninit::uninit()),
            state: AtomicU8::new(EMPTY),
        }
    }

    pub fn send(&self, message: T) {
        if self.state.compare_exchange(
            EMPTY, WRITING, Relaxed, Relaxed
        ).is_err() {
            panic!("can't send more than one message!");
        }
```

```
            unsafe { (*self.message.get()).write(message) };
            self.state.store(READY, Release);
        }

        pub fn is_ready(&self) -> bool {
            self.state.load(Relaxed) == READY
        }

        pub fn receive(&self) -> T {
            if self.state.compare_exchange(
                READY, READING, Acquire, Relaxed
            ).is_err() {
                panic!("no message available!");
            }
            unsafe { (*self.message.get()).assume_init_read() }
        }
    }

    impl<T> Drop for Channel<T> {
        fn drop(&mut self) {
            if *self.state.get_mut() == READY {
                unsafe { self.message.get_mut().assume_init_drop() }
            }
        }
    }
```

Safety Through Types

While we've successfully protected users of our `Channel` from undefined behavior, they still risk a panic if they accidentally use it incorrectly. Ideally, the compiler would check correct usage and point out misuse before the program is even run.

Let's take a look at the issue of calling `send` or `receive` more than once.

To prevent a function from being called more than once, we can let it take an argument *by value*, which—for non-Copy types—will consume the object. After an object is consumed, or moved, it's gone from the caller, preventing it from being used another time.

By representing the ability to call `send` or `receive` each as a separate (non-Copy) type, and consuming that object when performing the operation, we can make sure each can only happen once.

This brings us to the following interface design, where instead of a single `Channel` type, a channel is represented by a pair of a `Sender` and a `Receiver`, which each have a method that takes `self` by value:

```
pub fn channel<T>() -> (Sender<T>, Receiver<T>) { … }

pub struct Sender<T> { … }
pub struct Receiver<T> { … }

impl<T> Sender<T> {
    pub fn send(self, message: T) { … }
}

impl<T> Receiver<T> {
    pub fn is_ready(&self) -> bool { … }
    pub fn receive(self) -> T { … }
}
```

The user can create a channel by calling channel(), which will give them one Sender and one Receiver. They can freely pass each of these objects around, move them to another thread, and so on. However, they cannot end up with multiple copies of either of them, guaranteeing that send and receive can each only be called once.

To implement this, we need to find a place for our UnsafeCell and AtomicBool. Previously, we just had a single struct with those fields, but now we have two separate structs, each of which could outlive the other.

Since the sender and receiver will need to share the ownership of those variables, we'll use an Arc ("Reference Counting" on page 8) to provide us with a reference-counted shared allocation, in which we store the shared Channel object. As shown below, the Channel type does not have to be public, as its existence is just an implementation detail irrelevant to the user.

```
pub struct Sender<T> {
    channel: Arc<Channel<T>>,
}

pub struct Receiver<T> {
    channel: Arc<Channel<T>>,
}

struct Channel<T> { // no longer `pub`
    message: UnsafeCell<MaybeUninit<T>>,
    ready: AtomicBool,
}

unsafe impl<T> Sync for Channel<T> where T: Send {}
```

Just like before, we implement Sync for Channel<T> on the condition that T is Send, to allow it to be used across threads.

Note how we no longer need the in_use atomic boolean like we did in our previous channel implementation. It was only used by send to check that it hadn't been called more than once, which is now statically guaranteed through the type system.

The `channel` function to create a channel and sender-receiver pair looks similar to the `Channel::new` function we had previously, except it wraps the `Channel` in an `Arc`, and wraps that `Arc` and a clone of it in the `Sender` and `Receiver` types:

```
pub fn channel<T>() -> (Sender<T>, Receiver<T>) {
    let a = Arc::new(Channel {
        message: UnsafeCell::new(MaybeUninit::uninit()),
        ready: AtomicBool::new(false),
    });
    (Sender { channel: a.clone() }, Receiver { channel: a })
}
```

The `send`, `is_ready`, and `receive` methods are basically identical to the ones we implemented before, with a few differences:

- They are now moved to their respective type, such that only the (one single) sender can send, and only the (one single) receiver can receive.

- `send` and `receive` now take `self` by value rather than by reference, to make sure they can each only be called once.

- `send` can no longer panic, as its precondition (only being called once) is now statically guaranteed.

So, they now look like this:

```
impl<T> Sender<T> {
    /// This never panics. :)
    pub fn send(self, message: T) {
        unsafe { (*self.channel.message.get()).write(message) };
        self.channel.ready.store(true, Release);
    }
}

impl<T> Receiver<T> {
    pub fn is_ready(&self) -> bool {
        self.channel.ready.load(Relaxed)
    }

    pub fn receive(self) -> T {
        if !self.channel.ready.swap(false, Acquire) {
            panic!("no message available!");
        }
        unsafe { (*self.channel.message.get()).assume_init_read() }
    }
}
```

The `receive` function can still panic, since the user might still call it before `is_ready()` returns `true`. It also still uses `swap` to set the `ready` flag back to `false` (instead of just `load`), so that the `Drop` implementation of `Channel` knows whether there's an unread message that needs to be dropped.

That `Drop` implementation is exactly the same as the one we implemented before:

```
impl<T> Drop for Channel<T> {
    fn drop(&mut self) {
        if *self.ready.get_mut() {
            unsafe { self.message.get_mut().assume_init_drop() }
        }
    }
}
```

The `Drop` implementation of `Arc<Channel<T>>` will decrement the reference counter of the allocation when either the `Sender<T>` or `Receiver<T>` is dropped. When dropping the second one, that counter reaches zero, and the `Channel<T>` itself is dropped. That will invoke our `Drop` implementation above, where we get to drop the message if one was sent but not received.

Let's try it out:

```
fn main() {
    thread::scope(|s| {
        let (sender, receiver) = channel();
        let t = thread::current();
        s.spawn(move || {
            sender.send("hello world!");
            t.unpark();
        });
        while !receiver.is_ready() {
            thread::park();
        }
        assert_eq!(receiver.receive(), "hello world!");
    });
}
```

It's a bit inconvenient that we still have to manually use thread parking to wait on a message, but we'll deal with that problem later.

Our goal, for now, was to make at least one form of misuse impossible at compile time. Unlike last time, attempting to send twice does not result in a program that panics, but instead does not result in a valid program at all. If we add another send call to the working program above, the compiler now catches the issue and patiently informs us of our mistake:

```
error[E0382]: use of moved value: `sender`
  --> src/main.rs
   |
   |                 sender.send("hello world!");
   |                 --------------------
   |                     `sender` moved due to this method call
   |
   |                 sender.send("second message");
   |                 ^^^^^^ value used here after move
   |
```

```
note: this function takes ownership of the receiver `self`, which moves `sender`
  --> src/lib.rs
   |
   |        pub fn send(self, message: T) {
   |                    ^^^^
   = note: move occurs because `sender` has type `Sender<&str>`,
           which does not implement the `Copy` trait
```

Depending on the situation, it can be extremely tricky to design an interface that catches mistakes at compile time. If the situation does lend itself to such an interface, it can result not only in more convenience for the user, but also in a reduced number of runtime checks for things that are now statically guaranteed. We no longer needed the in_use flag, and removed the swap and check from the send method, for example.

Unfortunately, new problems may arise that could lead to more runtime overhead. In this case, the problem was the split ownership, for which we had to reach for an Arc and pay the cost of an allocation.

Having to make trade-offs between safety, convenience, flexibility, simplicity, and performance is unfortunate, but sometimes unavoidable. Rust generally strives to make it easy to excel at all of these, but sometimes makes you trade a bit of one to maximize another.

Borrowing to Avoid Allocation

The Arc-based channel implementation we just designed is very convenient to use—at the cost of some performance, since it has to allocate memory. If we want to optimize for efficiency, we can trade some convenience for performance by making the user responsible for the shared Channel object. Instead of taking care of the allocation and ownership of the Channel behind the scenes, we can force the user to create a Channel that can be *borrowed* by the Sender and Receiver. That way, they can choose to simply put that Channel in a local variable, avoiding the overhead of allocating memory.

We will also have to trade in some simplicity, since we will now have to deal with borrowing and lifetimes.

So, the three types will now look as follows, with Channel public again, and Sender and Receiver borrowing it for a certain lifetime.

```
pub struct Channel<T> {
    message: UnsafeCell<MaybeUninit<T>>,
    ready: AtomicBool,
}

unsafe impl<T> Sync for Channel<T> where T: Send {}

pub struct Sender<'a, T> {
```

```
        channel: &'a Channel<T>,
    }

    pub struct Receiver<'a, T> {
        channel: &'a Channel<T>,
    }
```

Instead of a `channel()` function to create a (`Sender`, `Receiver`) pair, we move back to the `Channel::new` we had earlier in this chapter, allowing the user to create such an object as a local variable.

In addition, we need a way for the user to create a `Sender` and `Receiver` object that will borrow the `Channel`. This will need to be an exclusive borrow (`&mut Channel`), to make sure there can't be multiple senders or receivers for the same channel. By providing both the `Sender` and the `Receiver` at the same time, we can *split* the exclusive borrow into two shared borrows, such that both the sender and receiver can reference the channel, while preventing anything else from touching the channel.

This leads us to the following implementation:

```
    impl<T> Channel<T> {
        pub const fn new() -> Self {
            Self {
                message: UnsafeCell::new(MaybeUninit::uninit()),
                ready: AtomicBool::new(false),
            }
        }

        pub fn split<'a>(&'a mut self) -> (Sender<'a, T>, Receiver<'a, T>) {
            *self = Self::new();
            (Sender { channel: self }, Receiver { channel: self })
        }
    }
```

The `split` method, with its somewhat complicated signature, warrants a closer look. It exclusively borrows `self` through an exclusive reference, but it splits that into two shared references, wrapped in the `Sender` and `Receiver` types. The `'a` lifetime makes it clear that both of those objects borrow something with a limited lifetime; in this case, the `Channel` itself. Since the `Channel` is exclusively borrowed, the caller will not be able to borrow or move it as long as the `Sender` or `Receiver` object exists.

Once those objects both cease to exist, however, the mutable borrow expires and the compiler happily lets the `Channel` object be borrowed again by a second call to `split()`. While we can assume `split()` cannot be called again while the `Sender` and `Receiver` still exist, we cannot prevent a second call to `split()` after those objects are dropped or forgotten. We need to make sure we don't accidentally create a new `Sender` or `Receiver` object for a channel that already has its `ready` flag set, since that would break the assumptions that prevent undefined behavior.

By overwriting *self with a new empty channel in split(), we make sure it's in the expected state when creating the Sender and Receiver states. This also invokes the Drop implementation on the old *self, which will take care of dropping a message that was previously sent but not received.

 Since the lifetime in the signature of split comes from self, it can be elided. The signature of split in the snippet above is identical to this less verbose version:

```
pub fn split(&mut self) -> (Sender<T>, Receiver<T>) { … }
```

While this version doesn't explicitly show that the returned objects borrow self, the compiler still checks correct usage of the lifetime exactly the same as it does with the more verbose version.

The remaining methods and Drop implementation are the same as in our Arc-based implementation, except for an additional '_ lifetime argument to the Sender and Receiver types. (If you forget those, the compiler will helpfully suggest adding them.)

For completeness, here's the remaining code:

```rust
impl<T> Sender<'_, T> {
    pub fn send(self, message: T) {
        unsafe { (*self.channel.message.get()).write(message) };
        self.channel.ready.store(true, Release);
    }
}

impl<T> Receiver<'_, T> {
    pub fn is_ready(&self) -> bool {
        self.channel.ready.load(Relaxed)
    }

    pub fn receive(self) -> T {
        if !self.channel.ready.swap(false, Acquire) {
            panic!("no message available!");
        }
        unsafe { (*self.channel.message.get()).assume_init_read() }
    }
}

impl<T> Drop for Channel<T> {
    fn drop(&mut self) {
        if *self.ready.get_mut() {
            unsafe { self.message.get_mut().assume_init_drop() }
        }
    }
}
```

Let's test it!

```
fn main() {
    let mut channel = Channel::new();
    thread::scope(|s| {
        let (sender, receiver) = channel.split();
        let t = thread::current();
        s.spawn(move || {
            sender.send("hello world!");
            t.unpark();
        });
        while !receiver.is_ready() {
            thread::park();
        }
        assert_eq!(receiver.receive(), "hello world!");
    });
}
```

The reduction in convenience compared to the Arc-based version is quite minimal: we only needed one more line to manually create a Channel object. Note, however, how the channel has to be created before the scope, to prove to the compiler that its existence will outlast both the sender and receiver.

To see the compiler's borrow checker in action, try adding a second call to chan nel.split() in various places. You'll see that calling it a second time within the thread scope results in an error, while calling it after the scope is acceptable. Even calling split() before the scope is fine, as long as you stop using the returned Sender and Receiver before the scope starts.

Blocking

Let's finally deal with the last remaining major inconvenience of our Channel, the lack of a blocking interface. We've already used thread parking every time we tested a new variant of our channel. It shouldn't be too hard to integrate that pattern into the channel itself.

To be able to unpark the receiver, the sender needs to know which thread to unpark. The std::thread::Thread type represents a handle to a thread and is exactly what we need for calling unpark(). We'll store the handle to the receiving thread inside the Sender object, as follows:

```
use std::thread::Thread;

pub struct Sender<'a, T> {
    channel: &'a Channel<T>,
    receiving_thread: Thread, // New!
}
```

This handle would refer to the wrong thread, however, if the Receiver object is sent between threads. The Sender would be unaware of that and would still refer to the thread that originally held the Receiver.

We can handle that problem by making the Receiver a bit more restrictive, by not allowing it to be sent between threads anymore. As discussed in "Thread Safety: Send and Sync" on page 16, we can use the special PhantomData marker type to add this restriction to our struct. A PhantomData<*const ()> does the job, since a raw pointer, such as *const (), does not implement Send:

```rust
pub struct Receiver<'a, T> {
    channel: &'a Channel<T>,
    _no_send: PhantomData<*const ()>, // New!
}
```

Next, we'll have to modify the Channel::split method to fill in the new fields, like this:

```rust
pub fn split<'a>(&'a mut self) -> (Sender<'a, T>, Receiver<'a, T>) {
    *self = Self::new();
    (
        Sender {
            channel: self,
            receiving_thread: thread::current(), // New!
        },
        Receiver {
            channel: self,
            _no_send: PhantomData, // New!
        }
    )
}
```

We use the handle to the current thread for the receiving_thread field, since the Receiver object we return will stay on the current thread.

The send method doesn't change much, as shown below. We only have to call unpark() on the receiving_thread to wake up the receiver in case it is waiting:

```rust
impl<T> Sender<'_, T> {
    pub fn send(self, message: T) {
        unsafe { (*self.channel.message.get()).write(message) };
        self.channel.ready.store(true, Release);
        self.receiving_thread.unpark(); // New!
    }
}
```

The receive function undergoes a slightly larger change. The new version won't panic if there's no message yet, but will instead patiently wait for a message using thread::park() and try again, as many times as necessary.

```
impl<T> Receiver<'_, T> {
    pub fn receive(self) -> T {
        while !self.channel.ready.swap(false, Acquire) {
            thread::park();
        }
        unsafe { (*self.channel.message.get()).assume_init_read() }
    }
}
```

 Remember that thread::park() might return spuriously. (Or
because something other than our send method called unpark().)
This means that we cannot assume that the ready flag has been set
when park() returns. So, we need to use a loop to check the flag
again after getting unparked.

The Channel<T> struct, its Sync implementation, its new function, and its Drop implementation remain unchanged.

Let's try it out!

```
fn main() {
    let mut channel = Channel::new();
    thread::scope(|s| {
        let (sender, receiver) = channel.split();
        s.spawn(move || {
            sender.send("hello world!");
        });
        assert_eq!(receiver.receive(), "hello world!");
    });
}
```

Clearly, this Channel is more convenient to use than the last one, at least in this
simple test program. We've had to pay for this convenience by trading in some
flexibility: only the thread that calls split() may call receive(). If you swap the
send and receive lines, this program will no longer compile. Depending on the use
case, that might be entirely fine, useful, or very inconvenient.

There are a number of ways to address that issue, many of which will cost us some
additional complexity and affect performance. In general, the number of variations
and trade-offs we can continue to explore are virtually endless.

We could easily spend an unhealthy number of hours implementing another twenty
variants of a one-shot channel, each with slightly different properties, for every
imaginable use case and more. While that might sound like lots of fun, we should
probably avoid that rabbit hole and end this chapter before things get out of hand.

Summary

- A *channel* is used to send *messages* between threads.

- A simple and flexible, but potentially inefficient, channel is relatively easy to implement with just a `Mutex` and a `Condvar`.

- A *one-shot channel* is a channel designed to send only one message.

- The `MaybeUninit<T>` type can be used to represent a potentially not-yet-initialized `T`. Its interface is mostly unsafe, making its user responsible for tracking whether it has been initialized, not duplicating `Copy` data, and dropping its contents if necessary.

- Not dropping objects (also called *leaking* or *forgetting*) is safe, but frowned upon when done without good reason.

- Panicking is an important tool for creating a safe interface.

- Taking a non-`Copy` object by value can be used to prevent something to be done more than once.

- Exclusively borrowing and splitting borrows can be a powerful tool for forcing correctness.

- We can make sure an object stays on the same thread by making sure its type does not implement `Send`, which can be achieved with the `PhantomData` marker type.

- Every design and implementation decision involves a trade-off and can best be made with a specific use case in mind.

- Designing something without a use case can be fun and educational, but can turn out to be an endless task.

CHAPTER 6

Building Our Own "Arc"

In "Reference Counting" on page 8, we saw the std::sync::Arc<T> type that allows for shared ownership through reference counting. The Arc::new function creates a new allocation, just like Box::new. However, unlike a Box, a cloned Arc will share the original allocation, without creating a new one. The shared allocation will only be dropped once the Arc and all its clones are dropped.

The memory ordering considerations involved in an implementation of this type can get quite interesting. In this chapter, we'll put more of the theory to practice by implementing our own Arc<T>. We'll start with a basic version, then extend it to support *weak pointers* for cyclic structures, and finish the chapter with an optimized version that's nearly identical to the implementation in the standard library.

Basic Reference Counting

Our first version will use a single AtomicUsize to count the number of Arc objects that share an allocation. Let's start with a struct that holds this counter and the T object:

```
struct ArcData<T> {
    ref_count: AtomicUsize,
    data: T,
}
```

Note that this struct is not public. It's an internal implementation detail of our Arc implementation.

Next is the Arc<T> struct itself, which is effectively just a pointer to a (shared) ArcData<T> object.

It might be tempting to make it a wrapper for a Box<ArcData<T>>, using a standard Box to handle the allocation of the ArcData<T>. However, a Box represents exclusive ownership, not shared ownership. We can't use a reference either, because we're not just borrowing the data owned by something else, and its lifetime ("until the last clone of this Arc is dropped") is not directly representable with a Rust lifetime.

Instead, we'll have to resort to using a pointer and handle allocation and the concept of ownership manually. Instead of a *mut T or *const T, we'll use a std::ptr::NonNull<T>, which represents a pointer to T that is never null. That way, an Option<Arc<T>> will be the same size as an Arc<T>, using the null pointer representation for None.

```
use std::ptr::NonNull;

pub struct Arc<T> {
    ptr: NonNull<ArcData<T>>,
}
```

With a reference or a Box, the compiler automatically understands for which T it should make your struct Send or Sync. When using a raw pointer or NonNull, however, it'll conservatively assume it's never Send or Sync unless we explicitly tell it otherwise.

Sending an Arc<T> across threads results in a T object being shared, requiring T to be Sync. Similarly, sending an Arc<T> across threads could result in another thread dropping that T, effectively transferring it to the other thread, requiring T to be Send. In other words, Arc<T> should be Send if and only if T is both Send and Sync. The exact same holds for Sync, since a shared &Arc<T> can be cloned into a new Arc<T>.

```
unsafe impl<T: Send + Sync> Send for Arc<T> {}
unsafe impl<T: Send + Sync> Sync for Arc<T> {}
```

For Arc<T>::new, we'll have to create a new allocation with an ArcData<T> with a reference count of one. We'll use Box::new to create a new allocation, Box::leak to give up our exclusive ownership of this allocation, and NonNull::from to turn it into a pointer:

```
impl<T> Arc<T> {
    pub fn new(data: T) -> Arc<T> {
        Arc {
            ptr: NonNull::from(Box::leak(Box::new(ArcData {
                ref_count: AtomicUsize::new(1),
                data,
            }))),
        }
    }

    …
}
```

We know the pointer will always point to a valid ArcData<T> as long as the Arc object exists. However, this is not something the compiler knows or checks for us, so accessing the ArcData through the pointer requires unsafe code. We'll add a private helper function to get from the Arc to the ArcData, since this is something we'll have to do several times:

```
fn data(&self) -> &ArcData<T> {
    unsafe { self.ptr.as_ref() }
}
```

Using that, we can now implement the Deref trait to make our Arc<T> transparently behave like a reference to a T:

```
impl<T> Deref for Arc<T> {
    type Target = T;

    fn deref(&self) -> &T {
        &self.data().data
    }
}
```

Note that we don't implement DerefMut. Since an Arc<T> represents shared ownership, we can't unconditionally provide a &mut T.

Next: the Clone implementation. The cloned Arc will use the same pointer, after incrementing the reference counter:

```
impl<T> Clone for Arc<T> {
    fn clone(&self) -> Self {
        // TODO: Handle overflows.
        self.data().ref_count.fetch_add(1, Relaxed);
        Arc {
            ptr: self.ptr,
        }
    }
}
```

We can use Relaxed memory ordering to increment the reference counter, since there are no operations on other variables that need to strictly happen before or after this atomic operation. We already had access to the contained T before this operation (through the original Arc), and that remains unchanged afterwards (but now through at least two Arc objects).

An Arc would need to be cloned many times before the counter has any chance of overflowing, but running std::mem::forget(arc.clone()) in a loop can make it happen. We can use any of the techniques discussed in "Example: ID Allocation" on page 41 and "Example: ID Allocation Without Overflow" on page 44 to handle this issue.

To keep things as efficient as possible in the normal (non-overflowing) case, we'll keep the original `fetch_add` and simply abort the whole process if we get uncomfortably close to overflowing:

```
if self.data().ref_count.fetch_add(1, Relaxed) > usize::MAX / 2 {
    std::process::abort();
}
```

 Aborting the process is not instant, leaving for some time during which another thread can also call `Arc::clone`, incrementing the reference counter further. Therefore, just checking for `usize::MAX - 1` would not suffice. However, using `usize::MAX / 2` as the limit works fine: assuming every thread takes at least a few bytes of space in memory, it's impossible for `usize::MAX / 2` threads to exist concurrently.

Just like we increment the counter when cloning, we need to decrement it when dropping an `Arc`. The thread that sees the counter go from one to zero knows it dropped the last `Arc<T>`, and is responsible for dropping and deallocating the `ArcData<T>`.

We'll use `Box::from_raw` to reclaim exclusive ownership of the allocation, and then drop it right away using `drop()`:

```
impl<T> Drop for Arc<T> {
    fn drop(&mut self) {
        // TODO: Memory ordering.
        if self.data().ref_count.fetch_sub(1, …) == 1 {
            unsafe {
                drop(Box::from_raw(self.ptr.as_ptr()));
            }
        }
    }
}
```

For this operation, we can't use `Relaxed` ordering, since we need to make sure that nothing is still accessing the data when we drop it. In other words, every single drop of one of the former `Arc` clones must have happened before the final drop. So, the final `fetch_sub` must establish a happens-before relationship with every previous `fetch_sub` operation, which we can do using release and acquire ordering: decrementing it from, for example, two to one effectively "releases" the data, while decrementing it from one to zero "acquires" ownership of it.

We could use `AcqRel` memory ordering to cover both cases, but only the final decrement to zero needs `Acquire`, while the others only need `Release`. For efficiency, we'll use only `Release` for the `fetch_sub` operation and a separate `Acquire` fence only when necessary:

```
        if self.data().ref_count.fetch_sub(1, Release) == 1 {
            fence(Acquire);
            unsafe {
                drop(Box::from_raw(self.ptr.as_ptr()));
            }
        }
    }
```

Testing It

To test that our Arc is behaving as intended, we can write a unit test that creates an
Arc containing a special object that lets us know when it gets dropped:

```
#[test]
fn test() {
    static NUM_DROPS: AtomicUsize = AtomicUsize::new(0);

    struct DetectDrop;

    impl Drop for DetectDrop {
        fn drop(&mut self) {
            NUM_DROPS.fetch_add(1, Relaxed);
        }
    }

    // Create two Arcs sharing an object containing a string
    // and a DetectDrop, to detect when it's dropped.
    let x = Arc::new(("hello", DetectDrop));
    let y = x.clone();

    // Send x to another thread, and use it there.
    let t = std::thread::spawn(move || {
        assert_eq!(x.0, "hello");
    });

    // In parallel, y should still be usable here.
    assert_eq!(y.0, "hello");

    // Wait for the thread to finish.
    t.join().unwrap();

    // One Arc, x, should be dropped by now.
    // We still have y, so the object shouldn't have been dropped yet.
    assert_eq!(NUM_DROPS.load(Relaxed), 0);

    // Drop the remaining `Arc`.
    drop(y);

    // Now that `y` is dropped too,
    // the object should've been dropped.
    assert_eq!(NUM_DROPS.load(Relaxed), 1);
}
```

This compiles and runs fine, so it seems our Arc is behaving as intended! While this is encouraging, it doesn't prove that the implementation is fully correct. It's advisable to use a long stress test involving many threads to gain more confidence.

Miri

It can also be very useful to run tests using Miri. Miri is an experimental but very useful and powerful tool to check unsafe code for various forms of undefined behavior.

Miri is an interpreter for the Rust compiler's mid-level intermediate representation. This means that it runs your code not by compiling it to native processor instructions, but instead by interpreting it at a point when information like types and lifetimes are still available. Because of this, Miri runs programs significantly slower than when they are compiled and run normally, but is able to detect many mistakes that would result in undefined behavior.

It includes experimental support for detecting data races, which allows it to detect memory ordering problems.

For more details and a guide on how to use Miri, see its GitHub page (*https://oreil.ly/ 4VORa*).

Mutation

As mentioned before, we can't implement DerefMut for our Arc. We can't unconditionally promise exclusive access (&mut T) to the data, because it might be accessed through other Arc objects.

However, what we can do is to allow it conditionally. We can make a method that only gives out a &mut T if the reference counter is one, proving that there's no other Arc object that could be used to access the same data.

This function, which we'll call get_mut, will have to take a &mut Self to make sure nothing else can use this same Arc to access the T. Knowing that there's only one Arc would be meaningless if that one Arc can still be shared.

We'll need to use acquire memory ordering to make sure that threads that previously owned a clone of the Arc are no longer accessing the data. We need to establish a happens-before relationship with every single drop that led to the reference counter being one.

This only matters when the reference counter is actually one; if it's higher, we'll not provide a &mut T, and the memory ordering is irrelevant. So, we can use a relaxed load, followed by a conditional acquire fence, as follows:

```
pub fn get_mut(arc: &mut Self) -> Option<&mut T> {
    if arc.data().ref_count.load(Relaxed) == 1 {
        fence(Acquire);
        // Safety: Nothing else can access the data, since
        // there's only one Arc, to which we have exclusive access.
        unsafe { Some(&mut arc.ptr.as_mut().data) }
    } else {
        None
    }
}
```

This function does not take a `self` argument, but takes a regular argument (named arc) instead. This means it can only be called as `Arc::get_mut(&mut a)`, and not as `a.get_mut()`. This is advisable for types that implement `Deref`, to avoid ambiguity with a similarly named method on the underlying `T`.

The returned mutable reference implicitly borrows the lifetime from the argument, meaning that nothing can use the original `Arc` as long as the returned `&mut T` is still around, allowing for safe mutation.

When the lifetime of the `&mut T` expires, the `Arc` can be used and shared with other threads again. One might wonder whether we need to worry about memory ordering for threads accessing the data afterwards. However, that's the responsibility of whatever mechanism is used for sharing the `Arc` (or a new clone of it) with another thread. (For example, a mutex, a channel, or spawning a new thread.)

Weak Pointers

Reference counting can be very useful when representing structures in memory consisting of multiple objects. For example, every node in a tree structure could contain an `Arc` to each of its child nodes. That way, when a node is dropped, its child nodes that are no longer in use are all (recursively) dropped as well.

This breaks down for *cyclic structures*, however. If a child node also contains an `Arc` to its parent node, neither will be dropped since there's always at least one `Arc` that still refers to it.

The standard library's `Arc` comes with a solution for that problem: `Weak<T>`. A `Weak<T>`, also called a *weak pointer*, behaves a bit like an `Arc<T>`, but does not prevent an object from getting dropped. A `T` can be shared between several `Arc<T>` and `Weak<T>` objects, but when all `Arc<T>` objects are gone, the `T` is dropped, regardless of whether there are any `Weak<T>` objects left.

This means that a `Weak<T>` can exist without a `T`, and thus cannot provide a `&T` unconditionally, like an `Arc<T>` can. However, to access the `T` given a `Weak<T>`, it can be *upgraded* to an Arc<T> through its upgrade() method. This method returns an Option<Arc<T>>, returning None if the T has already been dropped.

In an Arc-based structure, Weak can be used to break cycles. For example, child nodes in a tree structure could use Weak rather than Arc for their parent node. Then, dropping of a parent node is not prevented through the existence of its child nodes.

Let's implement this.

Just like before, when the number of Arc objects reaches zero, we can drop the contained T object. However, we can't drop and deallocate the ArcData yet, since there might still be weak pointers referencing it. Only once the last Weak pointer is also gone can we drop and deallocate the ArcData.

So, we'll use two counters: one for "the number of things that reference the T," and another for "the number of things that reference the ArcData<T>." In other words, the first counter is the same as before: it counts Arc objects, while the second counter counts both Arc and Weak objects.

We also need something that allows us to drop the contained object (T) while the ArcData<T> is still in use by the weak pointers. We'll use an Option<T> so we can use None for when the data is dropped, and wrap that in an UnsafeCell for *interior mutability* ("Interior Mutability" on page 13), to allow that to happen when the ArcData<T> isn't exclusively owned:

```
struct ArcData<T> {
    /// Number of `Arc`s.
    data_ref_count: AtomicUsize,
    /// Number of `Arc`s and `Weak`s combined.
    alloc_ref_count: AtomicUsize,
    /// The data. `None` if there's only weak pointers left.
    data: UnsafeCell<Option<T>>,
}
```

If we think of a Weak<T> as an object responsible for keeping an ArcData<T> alive, it can make sense to implement Arc<T> as a struct containing a Weak<T>, since an Arc<T> needs to do the same, and more.

```
pub struct Arc<T> {
    weak: Weak<T>,
}

pub struct Weak<T> {
    ptr: NonNull<ArcData<T>>,
}

unsafe impl<T: Sync + Send> Send for Weak<T> {}
unsafe impl<T: Sync + Send> Sync for Weak<T> {}
```

The new function is mostly the same as before, except it now has two counters to initialize at once:

```
impl<T> Arc<T> {
    pub fn new(data: T) -> Arc<T> {
        Arc {
            weak: Weak {
                ptr: NonNull::from(Box::leak(Box::new(ArcData {
                    alloc_ref_count: AtomicUsize::new(1),
                    data_ref_count: AtomicUsize::new(1),
                    data: UnsafeCell::new(Some(data)),
                }))),
            },
        }
    }

    ...
}
```

Just like before, we assume that the ptr field always points at a valid ArcData<T>. This time, we'll encode that assumption as a private data() helper method on Weak<T>:

```
impl<T> Weak<T> {
    fn data(&self) -> &ArcData<T> {
        unsafe { self.ptr.as_ref() }
    }

    ...
}
```

In the Deref implementation for Arc<T>, we now have to use UnsafeCell::get() to get a pointer to the contents of the cell, and use unsafe code to promise it can safely be shared at this point. We also need as_ref().unwrap() to get a reference into the Option<T>. We don't have to worry about this panicking, since the Option will only be None when there are no Arc objects left.

```
impl<T> Deref for Arc<T> {
    type Target = T;

    fn deref(&self) -> &T {
        let ptr = self.weak.data().data.get();
        // Safety: Since there's an Arc to the data,
        // the data exists and may be shared.
        unsafe { (*ptr).as_ref().unwrap() }
    }
}
```

The Clone implementation for Weak<T> is quite straightforward; it's pretty much identical to our previous Clone implementation for Arc<T>:

```
impl<T> Clone for Weak<T> {
    fn clone(&self) -> Self {
        if self.data().alloc_ref_count.fetch_add(1, Relaxed) > usize::MAX / 2 {
            std::process::abort();
        }
        Weak { ptr: self.ptr }
    }
}
```

In the Clone implementation for our new Arc<T>, we need to increment both counters. We'll simply use self.weak.clone() to reuse the code above for the first counter, so we only have to manually increment the second counter:

```
impl<T> Clone for Arc<T> {
    fn clone(&self) -> Self {
        let weak = self.weak.clone();
        if weak.data().data_ref_count.fetch_add(1, Relaxed) > usize::MAX / 2 {
            std::process::abort();
        }
        Arc { weak }
    }
}
```

Dropping a Weak should decrement its counter and drop and deallocate the ArcData when the counter goes from one to zero. This is identical to what the Drop implementation of our previous Arc did.

```
impl<T> Drop for Weak<T> {
    fn drop(&mut self) {
        if self.data().alloc_ref_count.fetch_sub(1, Release) == 1 {
            fence(Acquire);
            unsafe {
                drop(Box::from_raw(self.ptr.as_ptr()));
            }
        }
    }
}
```

Dropping an Arc should decrement both counters. Note that one of these is already automatically taken care of, since every Arc contains a Weak, such that dropping an Arc will also result in dropping a Weak. We only have to take care of the other counter:

```
impl<T> Drop for Arc<T> {
    fn drop(&mut self) {
        if self.weak.data().data_ref_count.fetch_sub(1, Release) == 1 {
            fence(Acquire);
            let ptr = self.weak.data().data.get();
            // Safety: The data reference counter is zero,
            // so nothing will access it.
            unsafe {
                (*ptr) = None;
            }
        }
    }
}
```

 Dropping an object in Rust will first run its Drop::drop function
(if it implements Drop), and then drop all of its fields, one by
one, recursively.

The check in the get_mut method remains mostly unchanged, except it now needs
to take weak pointers into account. It might seem like it could ignore weak pointers
when checking for exclusivity, but a Weak<T> can be upgraded to an Arc<T> at any
time. So, get_mut will have to check that there are no other Arc<T> or Weak<T>
pointers before it can give out a &mut T:

```
impl<T> Arc<T> {
    ...

    pub fn get_mut(arc: &mut Self) -> Option<&mut T> {
        if arc.weak.data().alloc_ref_count.load(Relaxed) == 1 {
            fence(Acquire);
            // Safety: Nothing else can access the data, since
            // there's only one Arc, to which we have exclusive access,
            // and no Weak pointers.
            let arcdata = unsafe { arc.weak.ptr.as_mut() };
            let option = arcdata.data.get_mut();
            // We know the data is still available since we
            // have an Arc to it, so this won't panic.
            let data = option.as_mut().unwrap();
            Some(data)
        } else {
            None
        }
    }

    ...
}
```

Next up: upgrading a weak pointer. Upgrading a Weak to an Arc is only possible when the data still exists. If there are only weak pointers left, there's no data left that can be shared through an Arc. So, we'll have to increase the Arc counter, but can only do so if it isn't already zero. We'll use a compare-and-exchange loop ("Compare-and-Exchange Operations" on page 42) to do this.

Just like before, relaxed memory ordering is fine for incrementing a reference counter. There are no operations on other variables that need to strictly happen before or after this atomic operation.

```
impl<T> Weak<T> {
    ...

    pub fn upgrade(&self) -> Option<Arc<T>> {
        let mut n = self.data().data_ref_count.load(Relaxed);
        loop {
            if n == 0 {
                return None;
            }
            assert!(n < usize::MAX);
            if let Err(e) =
                self.data()
                    .data_ref_count
                    .compare_exchange_weak(n, n + 1, Relaxed, Relaxed)
            {
                n = e;
                continue;
            }
            return Some(Arc { weak: self.clone() });
        }
    }
}
```

Note how this time we can check for n < usize::MAX, since that assertion would panic *before* we modify data_ref_count.

The opposite, getting a Weak<T> from an Arc<T>, is much simpler:

```
impl<T> Arc<T> {
    ...

    pub fn downgrade(arc: &Self) -> Weak<T> {
        arc.weak.clone()
    }
}
```

Testing It

To quickly test our creation, we'll modify our previous unit test to use weak pointers and verify that they can be upgraded when expected:

```
#[test]
fn test() {
    static NUM_DROPS: AtomicUsize = AtomicUsize::new(0);

    struct DetectDrop;

    impl Drop for DetectDrop {
        fn drop(&mut self) {
            NUM_DROPS.fetch_add(1, Relaxed);
        }
    }

    // Create an Arc with two weak pointers.
    let x = Arc::new(("hello", DetectDrop));
    let y = Arc::downgrade(&x);
    let z = Arc::downgrade(&x);

    let t = std::thread::spawn(move || {
        // Weak pointer should be upgradable at this point.
        let y = y.upgrade().unwrap();
        assert_eq!(y.0, "hello");
    });
    assert_eq!(x.0, "hello");
    t.join().unwrap();

    // The data shouldn't be dropped yet,
    // and the weak pointer should be upgradable.
    assert_eq!(NUM_DROPS.load(Relaxed), 0);
    assert!(z.upgrade().is_some());

    drop(x);

    // Now, the data should be dropped, and the
    // weak pointer should no longer be upgradable.
    assert_eq!(NUM_DROPS.load(Relaxed), 1);
    assert!(z.upgrade().is_none());
}
```

This also compiles and runs without problems, which leaves us with a very usable handmade Arc implementation.

Optimizing

While weak pointers can be useful, the Arc type is often used without any weak pointers. A downside of our last implementation is that cloning and dropping an Arc now both take two atomic operations each, as they have to increment or decrement both counters. This makes all Arc users "pay" for the cost of weak pointers, even when they are not using them.

It might seem like the solution is to count Arc<T> and Weak<T> pointers separately, but then we wouldn't be able to atomically check that both counters are zero. To understand how that's a problem, imagine we have a thread executing the following annoying function:

```
fn annoying(mut arc: Arc<Something>) {
    loop {
        let weak = Arc::downgrade(&arc);
        drop(arc);
        println!("I have no Arc!"); ❶
        arc = weak.upgrade().unwrap();
        drop(weak);
        println!("I have no Weak!"); ❷
    }
}
```

This thread continuously downgrades and upgrades an Arc, such that it repeatedly cycles through moments where it holds no Arc (❶), and moments where it holds no Weak (❷). If we check both counters to see if there are any threads still using the allocation, this thread might be able to hide its existence if we are unlucky and check the Arc counter during its first print statement (❶), but check the Weak counter during its second print statement (❷).

In our last implementation, we solved this by counting every Arc also as a Weak. A more subtle way of solving this is to count all Arc pointers combined as one single Weak pointer. That way, the weak pointer counter (alloc_ref_count) never reaches zero as long as there is still at least one Arc object around, just like in our last implementation, but cloning an Arc doesn't need to touch that counter at all. Only dropping the very last Arc will decrement the weak pointer counter too.

Let's try that.

This time, we can't just implement Arc<T> as a wrapper around Weak<T>, so both will wrap a non-null pointer to the allocation:

```
pub struct Arc<T> {
    ptr: NonNull<ArcData<T>>,
}

unsafe impl<T: Sync + Send> Send for Arc<T> {}
```

```
unsafe impl<T: Sync + Send> Sync for Arc<T> {}

pub struct Weak<T> {
    ptr: NonNull<ArcData<T>>,
}

unsafe impl<T: Sync + Send> Send for Weak<T> {}
unsafe impl<T: Sync + Send> Sync for Weak<T> {}
```

Since we're optimizing our implementation, we might as well make ArcData<T> slightly smaller by using a std::mem::ManuallyDrop<T> instead of an Option<T>. We used an Option<T> to be able to replace a Some(T) by None when dropping the data, but we don't actually need a separate None state to tell us the data is gone, since the existence or absence of Arc<T> already tells us that. A ManuallyDrop<T> takes the exact same amount of space as a T, but allows us to manually drop it at any point by using an unsafe call to ManuallyDrop::drop():

```
use std::mem::ManuallyDrop;

struct ArcData<T> {
    /// Number of `Arc`s.
    data_ref_count: AtomicUsize,
    /// Number of `Weak`s, plus one if there are any `Arc`s.
    alloc_ref_count: AtomicUsize,
    /// The data. Dropped if there are only weak pointers left.
    data: UnsafeCell<ManuallyDrop<T>>,
}
```

The Arc::new function remains almost unchanged, initializing both counters at one like before, but now using ManuallyDrop::new() instead of Some():

```
impl<T> Arc<T> {
    pub fn new(data: T) -> Arc<T> {
        Arc {
            ptr: NonNull::from(Box::leak(Box::new(ArcData {
                alloc_ref_count: AtomicUsize::new(1),
                data_ref_count: AtomicUsize::new(1),
                data: UnsafeCell::new(ManuallyDrop::new(data)),
            }))),
        }
    }

    ...

}
```

The Deref implementation can no longer make use of the private data method on the Weak type, so we'll add the same private helper function on Arc<T>:

```
impl<T> Arc<T> {

    …

    fn data(&self) -> &ArcData<T> {
        unsafe { self.ptr.as_ref() }
    }

    …

}

impl<T> Deref for Arc<T> {
    type Target = T;

    fn deref(&self) -> &T {
        // Safety: Since there's an Arc to the data,
        // the data exists and may be shared.
        unsafe { &*self.data().data.get() }
    }
}
```

The Clone and Drop implementations for Weak<T> remain exactly the same as for our last implementation. Here they are for completeness, including the private Weak::data helper function:

```
impl<T> Weak<T> {
    fn data(&self) -> &ArcData<T> {
        unsafe { self.ptr.as_ref() }
    }

    …

}

impl<T> Clone for Weak<T> {
    fn clone(&self) -> Self {
        if self.data().alloc_ref_count.fetch_add(1, Relaxed) > usize::MAX / 2 {
            std::process::abort();
        }
        Weak { ptr: self.ptr }
    }
}

impl<T> Drop for Weak<T> {
    fn drop(&mut self) {
        if self.data().alloc_ref_count.fetch_sub(1, Release) == 1 {
            fence(Acquire);
            unsafe {
                drop(Box::from_raw(self.ptr.as_ptr()));
            }
        }
    }
}
```

And now we get to the part that this new optimized implementation was all about—cloning an Arc<T> now needs to touch only one counter:

```
impl<T> Clone for Arc<T> {
    fn clone(&self) -> Self {
        if self.data().data_ref_count.fetch_add(1, Relaxed) > usize::MAX / 2 {
            std::process::abort();
        }
        Arc { ptr: self.ptr }
    }
}
```

Similarly, dropping an Arc<T> now needs to decrement only one counter, except for the last drop that sees that counter go from one to zero. In that case, the weak pointer counter also needs to be decremented, such that it can reach zero once there are no weak pointers left. We do this by simply creating a Weak<T> out of thin air and immediately dropping it:

```
impl<T> Drop for Arc<T> {
    fn drop(&mut self) {
        if self.data().data_ref_count.fetch_sub(1, Release) == 1 {
            fence(Acquire);
            // Safety: The data reference counter is zero,
            // so nothing will access the data anymore.
            unsafe {
                ManuallyDrop::drop(&mut *self.data().data.get());
            }
            // Now that there's no `Arc<T>`s left,
            // drop the implicit weak pointer that represented all `Arc<T>`s.
            drop(Weak { ptr: self.ptr });
        }
    }
}
```

The upgrade method on Weak<T> remains mostly the same, except it no longer clones a weak pointer, since it doesn't need to increment the weak pointer counter anymore. Upgrading only succeeds if there is already at least one Arc<T> to the allocation, which means that Arcs are already accounted for in the weak pointer counter.

```
impl<T> Weak<T> {
    …

    pub fn upgrade(&self) -> Option<Arc<T>> {
        let mut n = self.data().data_ref_count.load(Relaxed);
        loop {
            if n == 0 {
                return None;
            }
            assert!(n < usize::MAX);
            if let Err(e) =
                self.data()
```

```
                    .data_ref_count
                    .compare_exchange_weak(n, n + 1, Relaxed, Relaxed)
                {
                    n = e;
                    continue;
                }
                return Some(Arc { ptr: self.ptr });
            }
        }
    }
```

So far the differences between this and our previous implementation are very minimal. Where things get tricky, though, is with the last two methods we still need to implement: downgrade and get_mut.

Unlike before, the get_mut method now needs to check if both counters are set to one to be able to determine whether there's only one Arc<T> and no Weak<T> left, since a weak pointer counter of one can now represent multiple Arc<T> pointers. Reading the counters are two separate operations that happen at (slightly) different times, so we have to be very careful to not miss any concurrent downgrades, such as in the example case we saw at the start of "Optimizing" on page 118.

If we first check that data_ref_count is one, then we could miss a subsequent upgrade() before we check the other counter. But, if we first check that alloc_ref_count is one, then we could miss a subsequent downgrade() before we check the other counter.

A way out of this dilemma is to briefly block the downgrade() operation by "locking" the weak pointer counter. To do that, we don't need anything like a mutex. We can use a special value, like usize::MAX, to represent a special "locked" state of the weak pointer counter. It'll only be locked very briefly, only to load the other counter, so the downgrade method could just spin until it's unlocked, in the unlikely situation it runs at the exact same moment as get_mut.

So, in get_mut we'll first have to check if alloc_ref_count is one and at the same time replace it by usize::MAX, if it was indeed one. That's a job for com pare_exchange.

Then we'll have to check if the other counter is also one, after which we can immediately unlock the weak pointer counter. If the second counter is also one, we know we have exclusive access to the allocation and the data, such that we can return a &mut T.

```
            pub fn get_mut(arc: &mut Self) -> Option<&mut T> {
                // Acquire matches Weak::drop's Release decrement, to make sure any
                // upgraded pointers are visible in the next data_ref_count.load.
                if arc.data().alloc_ref_count.compare_exchange(
                    1, usize::MAX, Acquire, Relaxed
                ).is_err() {
```

```
        return None;
    }
    let is_unique = arc.data().data_ref_count.load(Relaxed) == 1;
    // Release matches Acquire increment in `downgrade`, to make sure any
    // changes to the data_ref_count that come after `downgrade` don't
    // change the is_unique result above.
    arc.data().alloc_ref_count.store(1, Release);
    if !is_unique {
        return None;
    }
    // Acquire to match Arc::drop's Release decrement, to make sure nothing
    // else is accessing the data.
    fence(Acquire);
    unsafe { Some(&mut *arc.data().data.get()) }
}
```

As you might have expected, the locking operation (the `compare_exchange`) will have to use `Acquire` memory ordering, and the unlocking operation (the `store`) will have to use `Release` memory ordering.

If we had used `Relaxed` for the `compare_exchange` instead, it would have been possible for the subsequent `load` from `data_ref_count` to not see the new value of a freshly upgraded `Weak` pointer, even though the `compare_exchange` had already confirmed that every `Weak` pointer had been dropped.

If we had used `Relaxed` for the `store`, it would have been possible for the preceding `load` to observe the result of a future `Arc::drop` for an `Arc` that can still be downgraded.

The acquire fence is the same as before: it synchronizes with the release-decrement operation in `Arc::Drop` to make sure every access through former `Arc` clones has happened before the new exclusive access.

The last piece of the puzzle is the `downgrade` method, which will have to check for the special `usize::MAX` value to see if the weak pointer counter is locked, and spin until it is unlocked. Just like in the `upgrade` implementation, we'll use a compare-and-exchange loop to check for the special value and overflow before incrementing the counter:

```
pub fn downgrade(arc: &Self) -> Weak<T> {
    let mut n = arc.data().alloc_ref_count.load(Relaxed);
    loop {
        if n == usize::MAX {
            std::hint::spin_loop();
            n = arc.data().alloc_ref_count.load(Relaxed);
            continue;
        }
        assert!(n < usize::MAX - 1);
        // Acquire synchronises with get_mut's release-store.
        if let Err(e) =
```

```
                arc.data()
                    .alloc_ref_count
                    .compare_exchange_weak(n, n + 1, Acquire, Relaxed)
            {
                n = e;
                continue;
            }
            return Weak { ptr: arc.ptr };
        }
    }
```

We use acquire memory ordering for `compare_exchange_weak`, which synchronizes with the release-store in the `get_mut` function. Otherwise, it would be possible for the effect of a subsequent `Arc::drop` to be visible to a thread running `get_mut` before it unlocks the counter.

In other words, the acquire compare-and-exchange operation here effectively "locks" `get_mut`, preventing it from succeeding. It can be "unlocked" again by a later `Weak::drop` that decrements the counter back to one, using release memory ordering.

The optimized implementation of `Arc<T>` and `Weak<T>` that we just made is nearly identical to the one included in the Rust standard library.

If we run the exact same test as before ("Testing It" on page 117), we see that this optimized implementation also compiles and passes our tests.

If you feel that getting the memory ordering decisions right for this optimized implementation was difficult, don't worry. Many concurrent data structures are simpler to implement correctly than this one. This `Arc` implementation is included in this chapter specifically because of its tricky subtleties around memory ordering.

Summary

- `Arc<T>` provides shared ownership of a reference-counted allocation.
- By checking if the reference counter is exactly one, an `Arc<T>` can conditionally provide exclusive access (`&mut T`).
- Incrementing the atomic reference counter can be done using a relaxed operation, but the final decrement must synchronize with all previous decrements.
- A *weak pointer* (`Weak<T>`) can be used to avoid cycles.
- The `NonNull<T>` type represents a pointer to T that is never null.
- The `ManuallyDrop<T>` type can be used to manually decide, using `unsafe` code, when to drop a T.
- As soon as more than one atomic variable is involved, things get more complicated.
- Implementing an ad hoc (spin) lock can sometimes be a valid strategy for operating on multiple atomic variables at once.

CHAPTER 7

Understanding the Processor

While the theory from Chapters 2 and 3 is all we need to write correct concurrent code, it can additionally be very useful to develop an approximate understanding of what goes on in practice at the processor level. In this chapter, we'll explore the machine instructions that atomic operations compile down to, how different processor architectures differ, why a weak version of compare_exchange exists, what memory ordering means at the lowest level of individual instructions, and how caching relates to it all.

The goal of this chapter is not to understand every relevant detail of every single processor architecture. That would take many bookshelves full of books, many of which have probably not been written or are not publicly available. Instead, the goal of this chapter is to develop a general idea of how atomics work at the processor level, to be able to make more informed decisions when implementing and optimizing code involving atomics. And, of course, to simply satisfy our curiosity about what goes on behind the scenes—taking a break from all the abstract theory.

To make things as concrete as possible, we'll focus on two specific processor architectures:

x86-64:
> The 64-bit version of the x86 architecture implemented by Intel and AMD processors used in the majority of laptops, desktops, servers, and some game consoles. While the originally 16-bit x86 architecture and its very popular 32-bit extension were developed by Intel, the 64-bit version that we now call x86-64 was initially an extension developed by AMD, often referred to as AMD64. Intel also developed its own 64-bit architecture, IA-64, but ended up adopting AMD's more popular x86 extension instead (under the names IA-32e, EM64T, and later Intel 64).

ARM64:

> The 64-bit version of the ARM architecture used by nearly all modern mobile devices, high performance embedded systems, and also increasingly in recent laptops and desktops. It is also known as AArch64 and was introduced as part of ARMv8. Earlier (32-bit) versions of ARM, which are similar in many ways, are used in an even wider variety of applications. Many popular microcontrollers in every kind of embedded system imaginable, from cars to electronic COVID tests, are based on ARMv6 and ARMv7.

These two architectures are unalike in many ways. Most importantly, they take different approaches to atomics. Understanding how atomics work on both of them provides us with a more general understanding that is transferable to many other architectures.

Processor Instructions

We can develop an approximate understanding of how things work at the processor level by taking a close look at the output of the compiler, the exact instructions that the processor will execute.

Brief Introduction to Assembly

When compiling software written in any compiled language like Rust or C, your code gets translated into *machine instructions* that can be executed by the processor that will eventually run your program. These instructions are highly specific to the processor architecture you're compiling your program for.

These instructions, also called *machine code*, are encoded in binary form, which is quite unreadable to us humans. *Assembly* is the human-readable representation of these instructions. Every instruction is represented by one line of text, usually starting with a single word or acronym to identify the instruction, followed by its arguments or operands. An *assembler* converts the text representation to binary representation, and a *disassembler* does the opposite.

After compiling from a language like Rust, most of the structure of the original source code is gone. Depending on optimization level, functions and function calls might still be recognizable. However, types such as structs or enums have been reduced to bytes and addresses, and loops and conditionals have been reduced to a flat structure with basic jump or branch instructions.

Here's an example of what a snippet of assembly for a small part of a program might look like, for some made-up architecture:

```
ldr x, 1234 // load from memory address 1234 into x
li y, 0     // set y to zero
inc x       // increment x
add y, x    // add x to y
mul x, 3    // multiply x by 3
cmp y, 10   // compare y to 10
jne -5      // jump five instructions back if not equal
str 1234, x // store x to memory address 1234
```

In this example, x and y are names of *registers*. Registers are part of the processor, not of the main memory, and usually hold a single integer or memory address. On 64-bit architectures, they are generally 64 bits in size. The number of registers varies per architecture, but is usually very limited. Registers are basically used as a temporary scratchpad in calculations, a place to keep intermediary results before storing things back to memory.

Constants that refer to specific memory addresses, such as 1234 and -5 in the example above, are often replaced with more human-readable *labels*. The assembler will automatically replace them with the actual address when converting assembly to binary machine code.

Using labels, the previous example might look like this instead:

```
          ldr x, SOME_VAR
          li y, 0
my_loop: inc x
          add y, x
          mul x, 3
          cmp y, 10
          jne my_loop
          str SOME_VAR, x
```

Since the names of the labels are only part of the assembly, but not of the binary machine code, a disassembler will not know what labels were originally used and will most likely just use meaningless generated names like label1 and var2.

A full course on assembly for all the different architectures falls outside the scope of this book, but is not a prerequisite for reading this chapter. A very general understanding is more than enough to understand the examples, as we'll only be reading assembly, not writing it. The relevant instructions in each example will be explained in enough detail to be able to follow along with no prior experience with assembly.

To look at the exact machine code that the Rust compiler produces, we have several options. We could compile our code as usual, and then use a disassembler (such as `objdump`) to turn the produced binary file back into assembly. Using the debug information the compiler produces as part of the compilation process, the disassembler can produce labels that correspond to the original function names of the Rust source code. A downside of this method is that you need a disassembler that supports the specific processor architecture you're compiling for. While the Rust compiler supports many architectures, many disassemblers only support the one architecture that they were compiled for.

A more direct option is to ask the compiler to produce assembly instead a binary by using the `--emit=asm` flag to `rustc`. A downside of this method is that the produced output contains a lot of irrelevant lines, containing information for the assembler and debug tools that we don't need.

There are great tools such as `cargo-show-asm` (*https://oreil.ly/ePDzj*) that integrate with `cargo` and automate the process of compiling your crate with the right flags, finding the relevant assembly for the function you're interested in, and highlighting the relevant lines containing the actual instructions.

For relatively small snippets, the easiest and most recommended way is to use a web service like the excellent Compiler Explorer by Matt Godbolt (*https://godbolt.org/*). This website allows you to write code in a number of languages, including Rust, and directly see corresponding compiled assembly using the selected compiler version. It even uses coloring to show which lines of Rust correspond to which lines of assembly, as far as such a correspondence still exists after optimization.

Since we want to look at the assembly for different architectures, we'll need to specify an exact target for the Rust compiler to compile to. We'll use `x86_64-unknown-linux-musl` for x86-64 and `aarch64-unknown-linux-musl` for ARM64. These are already supported directly in Compiler Explorer. If you're compiling locally, for example using `cargo-show-asm` or the other methods mentioned above, you'll need to make sure you've installed the Rust standard library for these targets, which is usually done using `rustup target add`.

In all cases, the target to compile for is selected using the `--target` compiler flag. For example, `--target=aarch64-unknown-linux-musl`. If you don't specify any target, it'll automatically pick the platform you're currently on. (Or, in the case of Compiler Explorer, the platform that it is hosted on, which is currently `x86_64-unknown-linux-gnu`.)

In addition, it's advisable to enable the `-O` flag to enable optimization (or `--release` when using Cargo), as that will enable optimization and disable overflow checking, which can significantly reduce the amount of produced assembly for the small functions we'll be looking at.

To try it out, let's look at the assembly for x86-64 and ARM64 for the following function:

```
pub fn add_ten(num: &mut i32) {
    *num += 10;
}
```

Using `-O --target=aarch64-unknown-linux-musl` as the compiler flags with any of the methods described above, we'll get something like the following assembly output for ARM64:

```
add_ten:
    ldr w8, [x0]
    add w8, w8, #10
    str w8, [x0]
    ret
```

The `x0` register contains the argument to our function, `num`, the address of the `i32` to increment by ten. First, the `ldr` instruction loads the 32-bit value from that memory address into the `w8` register. Then, the `add` instruction adds ten to `w8` and stores the result back into `w8`. And afterwards, the `str` instruction stores the `w8` register back into the same memory address. Finally, the `ret` instruction marks the end of the function and causes the processor to jump back and continue with the function that called `add_ten`.

If we compile the exact same code for `x86_64-unknown-linux-musl`, we'll get something like this instead:

```
add_ten:
    add dword ptr [rdi], 10
    ret
```

This time, a register called `rdi` is used for the `num` argument. More interestingly, on x86-64, a single `add` instruction can do what takes three instructions on ARM64: loading, incrementing, and storing a value.

This is usually the case on a *complex instruction set computer* (CISC) architecture, such as x86. Instructions on such an architecture often have many variants, for example to operate on a register or to directly operate on memory of certain size. (The `dword` in the assembly specifies a 32-bit operation.)

In contrast, a *reduced instruction set computer* (RISC) architecture, like ARM, usually has a simpler set of instructions with very few variants. Most instructions can only operate on registers, and loading and storing to memory takes a separate instruction. This allows for a simpler processor, which can result in a reduction in cost or sometimes higher performance.

This difference is especially relevant for atomic fetch-and-modify instructions, as we'll see momentarily.

While compilers are generally pretty smart, they don't always generate the most optimal assembly, especially when atomic operations are involved. If you're experimenting and find cases where you feel confused by a seemingly needless complexity in the assembly, that often just means there's more optimization opportunities for a future version of the compiler.

Load and Store

Before we dive into anything more advanced, let's first look at the instructions used for the most basic atomic operations: load and store.

A regular non-atomic store through a &mut i32 takes just a single instruction on both x86-64 and ARM64, as shown below:

Rust source	Compiled x86-64	Compiled ARM64
```pub fn a(x: &mut i32) { *x = 0; }```	```a: mov dword ptr [rdi], 0 ret```	```a: str wzr, [x0] ret```

On x86-64, the very versatile mov instruction is used to copy ("move") data from one place to another; in this case, from a zero constant to memory. On ARM64, the str (store register) instruction is used to store a 32-bit register into memory. In this case, the special wzr register is used, which always contains zero.

If we change the code to instead use a relaxed atomic store to an AtomicI32, we get:

Rust source	Compiled x86-64	Compiled ARM64
```pub fn a(x: &AtomicI32) { x.store(0, Relaxed); }```	```a: mov dword ptr [rdi], 0 ret```	```a: str wzr, [x0] ret```

Perhaps somewhat surprisingly, the assembly is identical to the non-atomic version. As it turns out, the mov and str instructions were already atomic. They either happened, or they didn't happen at all. Apparently, any difference between &mut i32 and &AtomicI32 here is only relevant for the compiler checks and optimizations, but is meaningless for the processor—at least for relaxed store operations on these two architectures.

The same thing happens when we look at relaxed load operations:

Rust source	Compiled x86-64	Compiled ARM64

``
pub fn a(x: &i32) -> i32 {
    *x
}
``
	``
	a:
	    mov eax, dword ptr [rdi]
	    ret
	``
		``
		a:
		    ldr w0, [x0]
		    ret
		``

``
pub fn a(x: &AtomicI32) -> i32 {
    x.load(Relaxed)
}
``
	``
	a:
	    mov eax, dword ptr [rdi]
	    ret
	``
		``
		a:
		    ldr w0, [x0]
		    ret
		``

On x86-64 the mov instruction is used again, this time to copy from memory into the 32-bit eax register. On ARM64, the ldr (load register) instruction is used to load the value from memory into the w0 register.

> The 32-bit eax and w0 registers are used for passing back a 32-bit return value of a function. (For 64-bit values, the 64-bit rax and x0 registers are used.)

While the processor apparently does not differentiate between atomic and non-atomic stores and loads, we cannot safely ignore the difference in our Rust code. If we use a &mut i32, the Rust compiler may assume that no other thread can concurrently access the same i32, and might decide to transform or optimize the code in such a way that a store operation no longer results in a single corresponding store instruction. For example, it would be perfectly correct, although somewhat unusual, for a non-atomic 32-bit load or store to happen with two separate 16-bit instructions.

Read-Modify-Write Operations

Things get far more interesting for *read-modify-write operations* such as addition. As discussed earlier in this chapter, a non-atomic read-modify-write operation usually compiles to three separate instructions (read, modify, and write) on a RISC architecture like ARM64, but can often be done in a single instruction on a CISC architecture like x86-64. This short example demonstrates that:

Rust source	Compiled x86-64	Compiled ARM64

``
pub fn a(x: &mut i32) {
    *x += 10;
}
``
	``
	a:
	    add dword ptr [rdi], 10
	    ret
	``
		``
		a:
		    ldr w8, [x0]
		    add w8, w8, #10
		    str w8, [x0]
		    ret
		``

Before we even look at the corresponding atomic operation, we can reasonably assume that this time we will see a difference between the non-atomic and atomic versions. The ARM64 version here is clearly not atomic, as loading and storing happens in separate steps.

While not directly obvious from the assembly itself, the x86-64 version is not atomic. The add instruction will be split by the processor into several *microinstructions* behind the scenes, with separate steps for loading the value and storing the result. This would be irrelevant on a single-core computer, as switching a processor core between threads generally only happens between instructions. However, when multiple cores are executing instructions in parallel, we can no longer assume instructions all happen atomically without considering the multiple steps involved in executing a single instruction.

x86 lock prefix

To support multi-core systems, Intel introduced an instruction prefix called lock. It is used as a modifier to instructions like add to make their operation atomic.

The lock prefix originally caused the processor to temporarily block all other cores from accessing memory for the duration of the instruction. While this is a simple and effective way to make something appear as atomic to the other cores, it can be quite inefficient to stop the world for every atomic operation. Newer processors have a much more advanced implementation of the lock prefix, which doesn't stop other cores from operating on unrelated memory, and allows cores to do useful things while waiting for a certain piece of memory to become available.

The lock prefix can only be applied to a very limited number of instructions, including add, sub, and, not, or, and xor, which are all very useful operations to be able to do atomically. The xchg (exchange) instruction, which corresponds to the atomic swap operation, has an implicit lock prefix: it behaves like lock xchg regardless of the lock prefix.

Let's see lock add in action by changing our last example to operate on an AtomicI32:

Rust source	Compiled x86-64
```pub fn a(x: &AtomicI32) { x.fetch_add(10, Relaxed); }```	```a: lock add dword ptr [rdi], 10 ret```

As expected, the only difference with the non-atomic version is the lock prefix.

In the example above, we ignore the return value from fetch_add, the value of x before the operation. However, if we use that value, the add instruction no longer suffices. The add instruction can provide a little bit of useful information to next instructions, such as whether the updated value was zero or negative, but it does not provide the full (original or updated) value. Instead, another instruction can be used: xadd ("exchange and add"), which puts the originally loaded value into a register.

We can see it in action by making a small modification to our code to return the value that fetch_add returns:

Rust source	Compiled x86-64
```pub fn a(x: &AtomicI32) -> i32 { x.fetch_add(10, Relaxed) }```	```a: mov eax, 10 lock xadd dword ptr [rdi], eax ret```

Instead of a constant 10, a register containing the value 10 is now used instead. The xadd instruction will reuse that register to store the old value.

Unfortunately, other than xadd and xchg, none of the other lock-prefixable instructions, like sub, and, and or, have such a variant. For example, there is no xsub instruction. For subtraction that's no issue, as xadd can be used with a negative value. For and and or, however, there's no such alternative.

For and, or, and xor operations that affect only a single bit, such as fetch_or(1) or fetch_and(!1), it's be possible to use the bts (bit test and set), btr (bit test and reset), and btc (bit test and complement) instructions. These instructions also allow a lock prefix, change only a single bit, and make the previous value of that one bit available for an instruction that follows, such as a conditional jump.

When these operations affect more than one bit, they cannot be represented by a single x86-64 instruction. Similarly, the fetch_max and fetch_min operations also have no corresponding x86-64 instruction. For these operations, we need a different strategy than a simple lock prefix.

x86 compare-and-exchange instruction

In "Compare-and-Exchange Operations" on page 42, we saw how any atomic fetch-and-modify operation can be implemented as a compare-and-exchange loop. This is exactly what the compiler will use for operations that cannot be represented by a single x86-64 instruction, since this architecture does include a (lock-prefixable) cmpxchg (compare and exchange) instruction.

We can see this in action by changing our last example from `fetch_add` to `fetch_or`:

Rust source	Compiled x86-64
```pub fn a(x: &AtomicI32) -> i32 { x.fetch_or(10, Relaxed) }```	```a: mov eax, dword ptr [rdi] .L1: mov ecx, eax or ecx, 10 lock cmpxchg dword ptr [rdi], ecx jne .L1 ret```

The first `mov` instruction loads the value from the atomic variable into the `eax` register. The following `mov` and `or` instructions copy that value into `ecx` and apply the binary `or` operation, such that `eax` contains the old value and `ecx` the new value. The `cmpxchg` instruction afterwards behaves exactly like the `compare_exchange` method in Rust. Its first argument is the memory address on which to operate (the atomic variable), the second argument (`ecx`) is the new value, the expected value is implicitly taken from `eax`, and the return value is implicitly stored in `eax`. It also sets a status flag that a subsequent instruction can use to conditionally branch based on whether the operation succeeded or not. In this case, a `jne` (jump if not equal) instruction is used to jump back to the `.L1` label to try again on failure.

Here's what the equivalent compare-and-exchange loop looks like in Rust, just like we saw in "Compare-and-Exchange Operations" on page 42:

```
pub fn a(x: &AtomicI32) -> i32 {
    let mut current = x.load(Relaxed);
    loop {
        let new = current | 10;
        match x.compare_exchange(current, new, Relaxed, Relaxed) {
            Ok(v) => return v,
            Err(v) => current = v,
        }
    }
}
```

Compiling this code results in the exact same assembly as the `fetch_or` version. This shows that, at least on x86-64, they are indeed equivalent in every way.

 On x86-64, there is no difference between `compare_exchange` and `compare_exchange_weak`. Both compile down to a `lock cmpxchg` instruction.

Load-Linked and Store-Conditional Instructions

The closest thing to a compare-and-exchange loop on a RISC architecture is a *load-linked/store-conditional* (LL/SC) loop. It involves two special instructions that come in a pair: a load-linked instruction, which mostly behaves like a regular load instruction, and a store-conditional instruction, which mostly behaves like a regular store instruction. They are used in a pair, with both instructions targeting the same memory address. The key difference to the regular load and store instructions is that the store is conditional: it refuses to store to memory if any other thread has overwritten that memory since the load-linked instruction.

These two instructions allow us to load a value from memory, modify it, and store the new value back only if nobody has overwritten the value since we loaded it. If that fails, we can simply retry. Once it succeeds, we can safely pretend the whole operation was atomic, since it didn't get disrupted.

The key to making these instructions feasible and efficient to implement is twofold: (1) only one memory address (per core) can be tracked at a time, and (2) the store-conditional is allowed to have false negatives, meaning that it may fail to store even though nothing has changed that particular piece of memory.

This makes it possible to be less precise when tracking changes to memory, at the cost of perhaps a few extra cycles through an LL/SC loop. Access to memory could be tracked not per byte, but per chunk of 64 bytes, or per kilobyte, or even the entire memory as a whole. Less accurate memory tracking results in more unnecessary cycles through LL/SC loops, significantly reducing performance, but also reducing implementation complexity.

Taking things to the extreme, a basic, hypothetical single-core system could use a strategy where it does not track writes to memory at all. Instead, it could track interrupts or context switches, the events that can cause the processor to switch to another thread. If, in a system without any parallelism, no such event happened, it could safely assume no other thread could have touched the memory. If any such event happened, it could just assume the worst, refuse the store, and hope for better luck in the next iteration of the loop.

ARM load-exclusive and store-exclusive

On ARM64, or at least in the first version of ARMv8, no atomic fetch-and-modify or compare-and-exchange operation can be represented by a single instruction. True to its RISC nature, the load and store steps are separate from the calculation and comparison.

ARM64's load-linked and store-conditional instructions are called ldxr (load exclusive register) and stxr (store exclusive register). In addition, the clrex (clear exclusive) instruction can be used as an alternative to stxr to stop tracking writes to memory without storing anything.

To see them in action, let's see what happens when we do an atomic addition on ARM64:

Rust source	Compiled ARM64

<pre>pub fn a(x: &AtomicI32) {
    x.fetch_add(10, Relaxed);
}</pre>
	<pre>a:
	.L1:
	    ldxr w8, [x0]
	    add w9, w8, #10
	    stxr w10, w9, [x0]
	    cbnz w10, .L1
	    ret</pre>

We get something that looks quite similar to the non-atomic version we got before (in "Read-Modify-Write Operations" on page 133): a load instruction, an add instruction, and a store instruction. The load and store instructions have been replaced by their "exclusive" LL/SC version, and a new cbnz (compare and branch on nonzero) instruction appeared. The stxr instruction stores a zero in w10 if it succeeded, or a one if it didn't. The cbnz instruction uses this to restart the whole operation if it failed.

Note that unlike with lock add on x86-64, we don't need to do anything special to retrieve the old value. In the example above, the old value will still be available in register w8 after the operation succeeds, so there's no need for a specialized instruction like xadd.

This LL/SC pattern is quite flexible: it doesn't just work for a limited set of operations like add and or, but for virtually any operation. We can just as easily implement an atomic fetch_divide or fetch_shift_left by putting the corresponding instruction(s) between the ldxr and stxr instructions. However, if there are too many instructions between them, there's an increasingly high chance of disruption resulting in extra cycles. Generally, the compiler will attempt to keep the number of instructions in an LL/SC pattern as small as possible, to avoid LL/SC loops that would rarely—or even never—succeed and thus could spin forever.

ARMv8.1 Atomic Instructions

A later version of ARM64, part of ARMv8.1, also includes new CISC style instructions for common atomic operations. For example, the new ldadd (load and add) instruction is equivalent to an atomic fetch_add operation, without the need for an LL/SC loop. It even includes instructions for operations like fetch_max, which don't exist on x86-64.

It also includes a cas (compare and swap) instruction corresponding to compare_exchange. When this instruction is used, there's no difference between com pare_exchange and compare_exchange_weak, just like on x86-64.

While the LL/SC pattern is quite flexible and nicely fits the general RISC pattern, these new instructions can be more performant, as they can be easier to optimize for with specialized hardware.

Compare-and-exchange on ARM

The compare_exchange operation maps quite nicely onto this LL/SC pattern by using a conditional branch instruction to skip the store instruction if the comparison failed. Let's look at the generated assembly:

Rust source	Compiled ARM64

<pre>pub fn a(x: &AtomicI32) {
    x.compare_exchange_weak(5, 6, Relaxed, Relaxed);
}</pre>
	<pre>a:
	    ldxr w8, [x0]
	    cmp w8, #5
	    b.ne .L1
	    mov w8, #6
	    stxr w9, w8, [x0]
	    ret
	.L1:
	    clrex
	    ret</pre>

Note that a compare_exchange_weak operation is normally used in a loop that repeats if the comparison fails. For this example, however, we only call it once and ignore its return value, which shows us the relevant assembly without distractions.

The `ldxr` instruction loads the value, which is then immediately compared with the `cmp` (compare) instruction to the expected value of 5. The `b.ne` (branch if not equal) instruction will cause a jump to the `.L1` label if the value was not as expected, at which point the `clrex` instruction is used to abort the LL/SC pattern. If the value was five, the flow continues through the `mov` and `stxr` instructions to store the new value of six in memory, but only if nothing has overwritten the five in the meantime.

Remember that `stxr` is allowed to have false negatives; it might fail here even if the five wasn't overwritten. That's okay, because we're using `compare_exchange_weak`, which is allowed to have false negatives too. In fact, this is the reason why a weak version of `compare_exchange` exists.

If we replace `compare_exchange_weak` with `compare_exchange`, we get nearly identical assembly, except for an extra branch to restart the operation if it failed:

Rust source	Compiled ARM64
```pub fn a(x: &AtomicI32) { x.compare_exchange(5, 6, Relaxed, Relaxed); }```	```a: mov w8, #6 .L1: ldxr w9, [x0] cmp w9, #5 b.ne .L2 stxr w9, w8, [x0] cbnz w9, .L1 ret .L2: clrex ret```

As expected, there's now an extra `cbnz` (compare and branch on nonzero) instruction to restart the LL/SC loop on failure. Additionally, the `mov` instruction has been moved out of the loop, to keep the loop as short as possible.

Optimization of Compare-and-Exchange Loops

As we saw in "x86 compare-and-exchange instruction" on page 135, a `fetch_or` operation and the equivalent `compare_exchange` loop compile down to the exact same instructions on x86-64. One might expect the same to happen on ARM, at least with `compare_exchange_weak`, as the load and weak compare-and-exchange operations could directly be mapped to the LL/SC instructions.

Unfortunately, this is currently (as of Rust 1.66.0) not what happens.

While this might change in the future as the compiler is always improving, it's quite hard for a compiler to safely turn a manually written compare-and-exchange loop into the corresponding LL/SC loop. One of the reasons is that there's a limit on the number and type of instructions that can be put between the `stxr` and `ldxr` instructions, which is not something that the compiler is designed to keep in mind while applying other optimizations. At the time where patterns like a compare-and-exchange loop are still recognizable, the exact instructions that an expression will compile down to are not known yet, making this a very tricky optimization to implement for the general case.

So, at least until we get even smarter compilers, it's advisable to use the dedicated fetch-and-modify methods rather than a compare-and-exchange loop, if possible.

Caching

Reading and writing memory is slow, and can easily cost as much time as executing tens or hundreds of instructions. This is why all performant processors implement *caching*, to avoid interacting with the relatively slow memory as much as possible. The exact implementation details of memory caches in modern processors are complex, partially proprietary, and, most importantly, mostly irrelevant to us when writing software. After all, the name *cache* comes from the French word *caché*, meaning *hidden*. Nevertheless, understanding the basic principles behind how most processors implement caching can be extremely useful when optimizing software for performance. (Not that we need an excuse to learn more about an interesting topic, of course.)

Except for very small microcontrollers, virtually all modern processors use caching. Such a processor never interacts directly with main memory, but instead routes every single read and write request through its cache. If an instruction needs to read something from memory, the processor will ask its cache for that data. If it is already cached, the cache will quickly respond with the cached data, avoiding interacting with main memory. Otherwise, it'll have to take the slow path, where the cache might have to ask the main memory for a copy of the relevant data. Once the main memory responds, not only will the cache finally respond to the original read request, but it will also remember the data, such that it can respond more quickly the next time this data is requested. If the cache becomes full, it makes space by dropping some old data it deems least likely to be useful.

When an instruction wants to write something to memory, the cache could decide to hold on to the modified data without writing it to main memory. Any subsequent read requests for the same memory address will then get a copy of the modified data, ignoring the outdated data in main memory. It would only actually write the data back to main memory when the modified data needs to be dropped from the cache to make space.

In most processor architectures, the cache reads and writes memory in blocks of 64 bytes, even if only a single byte was requested. These blocks are often called *cache lines*. By caching the entire 64-byte block that surrounds the requested byte, any subsequent instructions that need to access any of the other bytes in that block will not have to wait for main memory.

Cache Coherence

In modern processors, there is usually more than one layer of caching. The first cache, or *level one (L1) cache* is the smallest and fastest. Instead of talking to the main memory, it talks to the level two (L2) cache, which is much larger, but slower. The L2 cache might be the one to talk to main memory, or there might be yet another, larger and slower, L3 cache—perhaps even an L4 cache.

Adding extra layers doesn't change much about how they work; each layer can operate independently. Where things get interesting, however, is when there are multiple processor cores that each have their own cache. In a multi-core system, each processor core usually has its own L1 cache, while the L2 or L3 caches are often shared with some or all of the other cores.

A naive caching implementation would break down under these conditions, as the cache can no longer assume it controls all interactions with the next layer. If one cache would accept a write and mark some cache line as modified without informing the other caches, the state of the caches could become inconsistent. Not only would the modified data not be available to the other cores until the cache writes the data down to the next level(s), it could end up conflicting with different modifications cached in other caches.

To solve this problem, a *cache coherence protocol* is used. Such a protocol defines how exactly the caches operate and communicate with each other to keep everything in a consistent state. The exact protocol used varies per architecture, processor model, and even per cache level.

We'll discuss two basic cache coherence protocols. Modern processors use many variations of these.

The write-through protocol

In caches that implement the *write-through cache coherence protocol*, writes are not cached but immediately sent through to the next layer. The other caches are connected to the next layer through the same shared communication channel, which means that they can observe the other caches' communications to the next layer. When a cache observes a write for an address it currently has cached, it immediately either drops or updates its own cache line to keep everything consistent.

Using this protocol, caches never contain any cache lines in a modified state. While this simplifies things significantly, it nullifies any benefits of caching for writes. When optimizing just for reading, this can be a great choice.

The MESI protocol

The *MESI cache coherence protocol* is named after the four possible states it defines for cache line: modified, exclusive, shared and invalid. Modified (M) is used for cache lines that contain data that has been modified but not yet written to memory (or the next level cache). Exclusive (E) is used for cache lines that contain unmodified data that's not cached in any other cache (at the same level). Shared (S) is used for unmodified cache lines that might also appear in one or more of the other (same level) caches. Invalid (I) is used for unused (empty or dropped) cache lines, which do not contain any useful data.

Caches that use this protocol communicate with all the other caches at the same level. They send each other updates and requests to make it possible for them to stay consistent with each other.

When a cache gets a request for an address it has not yet cached, also called a *cache miss*, it does not immediately request it from the next layer. Instead, it first asks the other caches (at the same level) if any of them have this cache line available. If none of them have it, the cache will continue to request the address from the (slower) next layer, and mark the resulting new cache line as exclusive (E). When this cache line is then modified by a write operation, the cache can change the state to modified (M) without informing the others, since it knows none of the others have the same cache line cached.

When requesting a cache line that's already available in any of the other caches, the result is a shared (S) cache line, obtained directly from the other cache(s). If the cache line was in the modified (M) state, it'll first be written (or *flushed*) to the next layer, before changing it to shared (S) and sharing it. If it was in the exclusive (E) state, it'll be changed to shared (S) immediately.

If the cache wants exclusive rather than shared access (for example, because it is going to modify the data right after), the other cache(s) will not keep the cache line in shared (S) state, but instead drop it entirely by changing it to invalid (I). In this case, the result is an exclusive (E) cache line.

If a cache needs exclusive access to a cache line it already has available in the shared (S) state, it simply tells the others to drop the cache line before upgrading it to exclusive (E).

There are several variations of this protocol. For example, the *MOESI* protcol adds an extra state to allow sharing of modified data without immediately writing it to the next layer, and the *MESIF* protcol uses an extra state to decide which cache responds to a request for a shared cache line that's available in multiple caches. Modern processors often use more elaborate and proprietary cache coherence protocols.

Impact on Performance

While caching is mostly hidden from us, caching behavior can have significant effects on the performance of our atomic operations. Let's try to measure some of those effects.

Measuring the speed of a single atomic operation is very tricky, since they are extremely fast. To be able to get some useful numbers, we'll have to repeat an operation, say, a billion times, and measure how long that takes in total. For example, we could try to measure the time it takes for a billion load operations like this:

```
static A: AtomicU64 = AtomicU64::new(0);

fn main() {
    let start = Instant::now();
    for _ in 0..1_000_000_000 {
        A.load(Relaxed);
    }
    println!("{:?}", start.elapsed());
}
```

Unfortunately, this does not work as expected.

When running this with optimizations turned on (e.g., with `cargo run --release` or `rustc -O`), we'll see an unreasonably low measured time. What happened is that the compiler was smart enough to understand that we're not using the loaded values, so it decided to completely optimize the "unnecessary" loop away.

To avoid this, we can use the special `std::hint::black_box` function. This function takes an argument of any type, which it just returns without doing anything. What makes this function special is that the compiler will try its best not to assume anything about what the function does; it treats it like a "black box" that could do anything.

We can use this to avoid certain optimizations that would render a benchmark useless. In this case, we can pass the result of the load operation to `black_box()` to stop any optimizations that assume we don't actually need the loaded values. That's not enough, though, since the compiler could still assume that A is always zero, making the load operations unnecessary. To avoid that, we can pass a reference to A to `black_box()` at the start, such that the compiler may no longer assume there's only one thread that accesses A. After all, it must assume that `black_box(&A)` might have spawned an extra thread that interacts with A.

Let's try that out:

```
use std::hint::black_box;

static A: AtomicU64 = AtomicU64::new(0);

fn main() {
    black_box(&A); // New!
    let start = Instant::now();
    for _ in 0..1_000_000_000 {
        black_box(A.load(Relaxed)); // New!
    }
    println!("{:?}", start.elapsed());
}
```

The output fluctuates a bit when running this multiple times, but on a not-so-recent x86-64 computer, it seems to give a result of about 300 milliseconds.

To see any caching effects, we'll spawn a background thread that interacts with the atomic variable. That way, we can see if it affects the load operations of the main thread or not.

First, let's try that with just load operations on the background thread, as follows:

```
static A: AtomicU64 = AtomicU64::new(0);

fn main() {
    black_box(&A);

    thread::spawn(|| { // New!
        loop {
            black_box(A.load(Relaxed));
        }
    });

    let start = Instant::now();
    for _ in 0..1_000_000_000 {
        black_box(A.load(Relaxed));
    }
    println!("{:?}", start.elapsed());
}
```

Note that we're not measuring the performance of the operations on the background thread. We're still only measuring how long it takes for the main thread to perform a billion load operations.

Running this program results in similar measurements as before: it fluctuates a bit around 300 milliseconds when tested on the same x86-64 computer. The background thread has no significant effect on the main thread. They presumably each run on a separate processor core, but the caches of *both* cores contain a copy of A, allowing for very fast access.

Now let's change the background thread to perform store operations instead:

```
static A: AtomicU64 = AtomicU64::new(0);

fn main() {
    black_box(&A);
    thread::spawn(|| {
        loop {
            A.store(0, Relaxed); // New!
        }
    });
    let start = Instant::now();
    for _ in 0..1_000_000_000 {
        black_box(A.load(Relaxed));
    }
    println!("{:?}", start.elapsed());
}
```

This time, we do see a significant difference. Running this program on the same x86-64 machine now results in an output that fluctuates around three whole seconds, almost ten times as much as before. More recent computers will show a less significant but still very measurable difference. For example, it went from 350 milliseconds to 500 milliseconds on a recent Apple M1 processor, and from 250 milliseconds to 650 milliseconds on a very recent x86-64 AMD processor.

This behavior matches our understanding of cache coherence protocols: a store operation requires exclusive access to a cache line, which slows down subsequent load operations on other cores that no longer share the cache line.

Failing Compare-and-Exchange Operations

Interestingly, on most processor architectures, the same effect we saw with store operations also happens when the background thread performs only compare-and-exchange operations, even if they all fail.

To try that out, we can replace the store operation (of the background thread) with a call to compare_exchange that will never succeed:

```
    ...
    loop {
        // Never succeeds, because A is never 10.
        black_box(A.compare_exchange(10, 20, Relaxed, Relaxed).is_ok());
    }
    ...
```

Because A is always zero, this compare_exchange operation will never succeed. It'll load the current value of A, but never update it to a new value.

One might reasonably expect this to behave the same as a load operation, since it does not modify the atomic variable. However, on most processor architectures, the instruction(s) of `compare_exchange` will claim exclusive access of the relevant cache line regardless of whether the comparison succeeds or not.

This means that it can be beneficial to not use `compare_exchange` (or `swap`) in a spin loop like we did for our `SpinLock` in Chapter 4, but instead use a `load` operation first to check if the lock has been unlocked. That way, we avoid unnecessarily claiming exclusive access to the relevant cache line.

Since caching happens per cache line, not per individual byte or variable, we should be able to see the same effect using adjacent variables rather than the same one. To try this out, let's use three atomic variables instead of one, have the main thread use only the middle variable, and make the background thread use only the other two, as follows:

```
static A: [AtomicU64; 3] = [
    AtomicU64::new(0),
    AtomicU64::new(0),
    AtomicU64::new(0),
];

fn main() {
    black_box(&A);
    thread::spawn(|| {
        loop {
            A[0].store(0, Relaxed);
            A[2].store(0, Relaxed);
        }
    });
    let start = Instant::now();
    for _ in 0..1_000_000_000 {
        black_box(A[1].load(Relaxed));
    }
    println!("{:?}", start.elapsed());
}
```

Running this produces similar results as before: it takes several seconds on that same x86-64 computer. Even though A[0], A[1], and A[2] are each used by only one thread, we still see the same effects as if we're using the same variable on both threads. The reason is that A[1] shares a cache line with either or both of the others. The processor core running the background thread repeatedly claims exclusive access to the cache line(s) containing A[0] and A[2], which also contains A[1], slowing down "unrelated" operations on A[1]. This effect is called *false sharing*.

We can avoid this by spacing the atomic variables further apart, so they each get their own cache line. As mentioned before, 64 bytes is a reasonable guess for the size of a cache line, so let's try wrapping our atomics in a 64-byte aligned struct, as follows:

```
#[repr(align(64))] // This struct must be 64-byte aligned.
struct Aligned(AtomicU64);

static A: [Aligned; 3] = [
    Aligned(AtomicU64::new(0)),
    Aligned(AtomicU64::new(0)),
    Aligned(AtomicU64::new(0)),
];

fn main() {
    black_box(&A);
    thread::spawn(|| {
        loop {
            A[0].0.store(1, Relaxed);
            A[2].0.store(1, Relaxed);
        }
    });
    let start = Instant::now();
    for _ in 0..1_000_000_000 {
        black_box(A[1].0.load(Relaxed));
    }
    println!("{:?}", start.elapsed());
}
```

The #[repr(align)] attribute enables us to tell the compiler the (minimal) alignment of our type, in bytes. Since an AtomicU64 is only 8 bytes, this will add 56 bytes of padding to our Aligned struct.

Running this program no longer gives slow results. Instead, we get the same results as when we had no background thread at all: about 300 milliseconds when run on the same x86-64 computer as before.

Depending on the type of processor you're trying this on, you might need to use 128-byte alignment to see the same effect.

The experiment above shows that it can be advisable not to put unrelated atomic variables close to each other. For example, a dense array of small mutexes might not always perform as well as an alternative structure that keeps the mutexes are spaced further apart.

On the other hand, when multiple (atomic) variables are related and often accessed in quick succession, it can be good to put them close together. For example, our SpinLock<T> from Chapter 4 stores the T right next to the AtomicBool, which means it's likely that the cache line containing the AtomicBool will also contain the T, such that a claim for (exclusive) access to one also includes the other. Whether this is beneficial depends entirely on the situation.

Reordering

Consistent caching, for example through the MESI protocol we explored earlier in this chapter, generally does not affect correctness of a program, even when multiple threads are involved. The only observable differences caused by consistent caching come down to differences in timing. However, modern processors implement many more optimizations that can have a big impact on correctness, at least when multiple threads are involved.

At the start of Chapter 3, we briefly discussed *instruction reordering*, how both the compiler and the processor can change the order of instructions. Focusing just on the processor, here are some examples of various ways in which instructions, or their effects, might happen *out of order*:

Store buffers
> Since writes can be slow, even with caching, processor cores often include a *store buffer*. Write operations to memory can be stored in this store buffer, which is very quick, to allow the processor to immediately continue with the instructions that follow. Then, in the background, the write operation is completed by writing to the (L1) cache, which can be significantly slower. This way, the processor does not have to wait while the cache coherence protocol jumps into action to get exclusive access to the relevant cache line.

> As long as special care is taken to handle subsequent read operations from the same memory address, this is entirely invisible for instructions running as part of the same thread, on the same processor core. However, for a brief moment, the write operation is not yet visible to the other cores, resulting in an inconsistent view of what the memory looks like from different threads running on different cores.

Invalidation queues
> Regardless of the exact coherency protocol, caches that operate in parallel need to process invalidation requests: instructions to drop a specific cache line because it's about to be modified and become invalid. As a performance optimization, it's common for such requests not to be processed immediately, but to be queued for (slightly) later processing instead. When such invalidation queues are in use, the caches are no longer always consistent, as cache lines might be briefly outdated before they are dropped. However, this has no impact on a single threaded program, other than speeding it up. The only impact is the visibility of write operations from other cores, which might now appear as (very slightly) delayed.

Pipelining
> Another very common processor feature that significantly improves performance is *pipelining*: executing consecutive instructions in parallel, if possible. Before an instruction finishes executing, the processor might already start executing

the next one. Modern processors can often start the execution of quite a few instructions in series while the first one is still in progress.

If each instruction operates on the result from the previous one, this doesn't help much; they each still need to wait on the result of the one before it. But when an instruction can be executed independently of the previous one, it might even finish first. For example, an instruction that just increments a register might finish very quickly, while a previously started instruction might still be waiting on reading something from memory, or some other slow operation.

While this doesn't affect a single threaded program (other than speed), interaction with other cores might happen out of order when an instruction that operates on memory finishes executing before a preceding one does.

There are many ways in which a modern processor might end up executing instructions in an entirely different order than expected. There are many proprietary techniques involved, some of which become public only when a subtle mistake is found that can be exploited by malicious software. When they work as expected, however, they all have one thing in common: they do not affect single threaded programs, other than timing, but can cause interaction with other cores to appear to happen in an inconsistent order.

Processor architectures that allow for memory operations to be reordered also provide a way to prevent this through special instructions. These instructions might, for example, force the processor to flush its store buffer, or to finish any pipelined instructions, before continuing. Sometimes, these instructions only prevent a certain type of reordering. For example, there might be an instruction to prevent store operations from being reordered with respect to each other, while still allowing load operations to be reordered. Which types of reordering might happen, and how they can be prevented, depends on the processor architecture.

Memory Ordering

When performing any atomic operation in a language like Rust or C, we specify a memory ordering to inform the compiler of our ordering requirements. The compiler will generate the right instructions for the processor to prevent it from reordering instructions in ways that would break the rules.

Which types of instruction reordering are allowed depends on the kind of memory operation. For non-atomic and relaxed atomic operations, any type of reordering is acceptable. At the other extreme, sequentially consistent atomic operations don't allow for any type of reordering at all.

An acquire operation may not get reordered with any memory operations that follow, while a release operation may not be reordered with any memory operations that precede it. Otherwise, some mutex-protected data might be accessed before acquiring—or after releasing—its mutex, resulting in a data race.

Other-Multi-Copy Atomicity

The ways in which the order of memory operations is affected on some processor architectures, such as those one might find in graphics cards, cannot always be explained by instruction reordering. The effect of two consecutive store operations on one core might become visible in the same order on a second core, but in opposite order on a third core. This could happen, for example, because of inconsistent caching or shared store buffers. This effect can't be explained by the instructions on the first core being reordered, as that doesn't explain the inconsistency between the second and third core's observations.

The theoretical memory model we discussed in Chapter 3 leaves space for such processor architectures by not requiring a globally consistent order for anything but sequentially consistent atomic operations.

The architectures we're focusing on in this chapter, x86-64 and ARM64, are *other-multi-copy atomic*, which means that write operations, once they are visible to any core, become visible to all cores at the same time. For other-multi-copy atomic architectures, memory ordering is only a matter of instruction reordering.

Some architectures, such as ARM64, are called *weakly ordered*, as they allow the processor to freely reorder any memory operation. On the other hand, *strongly ordered* architectures, such as x86-64, are very restrictive about which memory operations may be reordered.

x86-64: Strongly Ordered

On an x86-64 processor, a load operation will never appear to have happened after a memory operation that follows. Similarly, this architecture doesn't allow for a store operation to appear to have happened before a preceding memory operation. The only kind of reordering you might see on x86-64 is a store operation getting delayed until after a later load operation.

Because of the reordering restrictions of the x86-64 architecture, it is often described as a *strongly ordered* architecture, although some prefer to reserve this term for architectures that preserve the order of *all* memory operations.

These restrictions satisfy all the needs of acquire-loads (because a load is never reordered with a later operation), and of release-stores (because a store is never reordered with an earlier operation). This means that on x86-64, we get release and acquire semantics "for free": release and acquire operations are identical to relaxed operations.

We can verify this by seeing what happens to a few of the snippets from "Load and Store" on page 132 and "x86 lock prefix" on page 134 when we change Relaxed to Release, Acquire, or AcqRel:

Rust source	Compiled x86-64

<pre>pub fn a(x: &AtomicI32) {
    x.store(0, Release);
}</pre>
	<pre>a:
	    mov dword ptr [rdi], 0
	    ret</pre>

<pre>pub fn a(x: &AtomicI32) -> i32 {
    x.load(Acquire)
}</pre>
	<pre>a:
	    mov eax, dword ptr [rdi]
	    ret</pre>

<pre>pub fn a(x: &AtomicI32) {
    x.fetch_add(10, AcqRel);
}</pre>
	<pre>a:
	    lock add dword ptr [rdi], 10
	    ret</pre>

As expected, the assembly is identical, even though we specified a stronger memory ordering.

We can conclude that on x86-64, ignoring potential compiler optimizations, acquire and release operations are just as cheap as relaxed operations. Or, perhaps more accurately, that relaxed operations are just as expensive as acquire and release operations.

Let's check out what happens for SeqCst:

Rust source	Compiled x86-64

<pre>pub fn a(x: &AtomicI32) {
    x.store(0, SeqCst);
}</pre>
	<pre>a:
	    xor eax, eax
	    xchg dword ptr [rdi], eax
	    ret</pre>

<pre>pub fn a(x: &AtomicI32) -> i32 {
    x.load(SeqCst)
}</pre>
	<pre>a:
	    mov eax, dword ptr [rdi]
	    ret</pre>

<pre>pub fn a(x: &AtomicI32) {
    x.fetch_add(10, SeqCst);
}</pre>
	<pre>a:
	    lock add dword ptr [rdi], 10
	    ret</pre>

The `load` and `fetch_add` operations still result in the same assembly as before, but assembly for `store` changed completely. The `xor` instruction looks a bit out of place, but is just a common way to set the `eax` register to zero by xor'ing it with itself, which always results in zero. A `mov eax, 0` instruction would've worked as well, but takes a bit more space.

The interesting part is the `xchg` instruction, which is normally used for a swap operation: a store operation that also retrieves the old value.

A regular `mov` instruction like before wouldn't suffice for a `SeqCst` store, because it would allow reordering it with a later load operation, breaking the globally consistent order. By changing it to an operation that also performs a load, even though we don't care about the value it loads, we get the additional guarantee of our instruction not getting reordered with later memory operations, solving the issue.

 A `SeqCst` load operation can still be a regular `mov`, exactly because `SeqCst` stores are upgraded to `xchg`. `SeqCst` operations guarantee a globally consistent order only with other `SeqCst` operations. The `mov` from a `SeqCst` load might still be reordered with the `mov` of an earlier non-`SeqCst` store operation, but that's perfectly fine.

On x86-64, a store operation is the only atomic operation for which there's a difference between `SeqCst` and weaker memory ordering. In other words, x86-64 `SeqCst` operations other than stores are just as cheap as `Release`, `Acquire`, `AcqRel`, and even `Relaxed` operations. Or, if you prefer, x86-64 makes `Relaxed` operations other than stores as expensive as `SeqCst` operations.

ARM64: Weakly Ordered

On a *weakly ordered* architecture such as ARM64, all memory operations can potentially be reordered with each other. This means that unlike x86-64, acquire and release operations will not be identical to relaxed operations.

Let's take a look at what happens on ARM64 for `Release`, `Acquire`, and `AcqRel`:

Rust source	Compiled ARM64
```pub fn a(x: &AtomicI32) { x.store(0, Release); }```	```a: stlr wzr, [x0] ❶ ret```
```pub fn a(x: &AtomicI32) -> i32 { x.load(Acquire) }```	```a: ldar w0, [x0] ❷ ret```

Rust source	Compiled ARM64
```pub fn a(x: &AtomicI32) { x.fetch_add(10, AcqRel); }```	```a: .L1: ldaxr w8, [x0] ❸ add w9, w8, #10 stlxr w10, w9, [x0] ❹ cbnz w10, .L1 ret```

The changes, compared to the Relaxed versions we saw earlier, are very subtle:

❶ str (store register) is now stlr (store-release register).

❷ ldr (load register) is now ldar (load-acquire register).

❸ ldxr (load exclusive register) is now ldaxr (load-acquire exclusive register).

❹ stxr (store exclusive register) is now stlxr (store-release exclusive register).

As this shows, ARM64 has special versions of its load and store instructions for acquire and release ordering. Unlike an ldr or ldxr instruction, an ldar or ldxar instruction will never be reordered with any later memory operation. Similarly, unlike an str or stxr instruction, an stlr or stxlr instruction will never be reordered with any earlier memory operation.

 A fetch-and-modify operation using only Release or Acquire ordering instead of AcqRel uses only one of the stlxr and ldxar instructions, respectively, paired with a regular ldxr or stxr instruction.

In addition to the restrictions required for release and acquire semantics, none of the special acquire and release instructions is ever reordered with any other of these special instructions, making them also suitable for SeqCst.

As demonstrated below, upgrading to SeqCst results in the exact same assembly as before:

Rust source	Compiled ARM64
```pub fn a(x: &AtomicI32) { x.store(0, SeqCst); }```	```a: stlr wzr, [x0] ret```
```pub fn a(x: &AtomicI32) -> i32 { x.load(SeqCst) }```	```a: ldar w0, [x0] ret```

Rust source	Compiled ARM64

`pub fn a(x: &AtomicI32) {`
`    x.fetch_add(10, SeqCst);`
`}`
	`a:`
	`.L1:`
	`    ldaxr w8, [x0]`
	`    add w9, w8, #10`
	`    stlxr w10, w9, [x0]`
	`    cbnz w10, .L1`
	`    ret`

This means that on ARM64, sequentially consistent operations are exactly as cheap as acquire and release operations. Or, rather, that ARM64 `Acquire`, `Release`, and `AcqRel` operations are as expensive as `SeqCst`. Unlike x86-64, however, `Relaxed` operations are relatively cheap, as they don't result in stronger ordering guarantees than necessary.

ARMv8.1 Atomic Release and Acquire Instructions

As discussed in "ARMv8.1 Atomic Instructions" on page 139, the ARMv8.1 version of ARM64 includes CISC style instructions for atomic operations such as `ldadd` (load and add) as an alternative to an `ldxr`/`stxr` loop.

Just like the load and store operations have special versions with acquire and release semantics, these instructions also have variants for stronger memory ordering. Because these instructions involve both a load and a store, they each have three additional variants: one for release (`-l`), one for acquire (`-a`), and one for combined release and acquire (`-al`) semantics.

For example, for `ldadd`, there is also `ldaddl`, `ldadda`, and `ldaddal`. Similarly, the `cas` instruction comes with the `casl`, `casa`, and `casal` variants.

Just like for the load and store instructions, the combined release and acquire (`-al`) variants also suffice for `SeqCst` operations.

An Experiment

An unfortunate consequence of the popularity of strongly ordered architectures is that certain classes of memory ordering bugs can easily stay undiscovered. Using `Relaxed` where `Acquire` or `Release` is necessary is incorrect, but could accidentally end up working just fine in practice on x86-64, assuming the compiler doesn't reorder your atomic operations.

Remember that it's not only the processor that can cause things to happen out of order. The compiler is also allowed to reorder the instructions it produces, as long as it takes the memory ordering constraints into account.

In practice, compilers tend to be very conservative about optimizations involving atomic operations, but that might very well change in the future.

This means one can easily write incorrect concurrent code that (accidentally) works perfectly fine on x86-64, but might break down when compiled for and run on an ARM64 processor.

Let's try to do exactly that.

We'll create a spin lock–protected counter, but change all the memory orderings to Relaxed. Let's not bother with creating a custom type or unsafe code. Instead, let's just use an AtomicBool for the lock and an AtomicUsize for the counter.

To be sure the compiler won't be the one to reorder our operations, we'll use the std::sync::compiler_fence() function to inform the compiler of the operations that should have been Acquire or Release, without telling the processor.

We'll make four threads repeatedly lock, increment the counter, and unlock—a million times each. Putting that all together, we end up with the following code:

```
fn main() {
    let locked = AtomicBool::new(false);
    let counter = AtomicUsize::new(0);

    thread::scope(|s| {
        // Spawn four threads, that each iterate a million times.
        for _ in 0..4 {
            s.spawn(|| for _ in 0..1_000_000 {
                // Acquire the lock, using the wrong memory ordering.
                while locked.swap(true, Relaxed) {}
                compiler_fence(Acquire);

                // Non-atomically increment the counter, while holding the lock.
                let old = counter.load(Relaxed);
                let new = old + 1;
                counter.store(new, Relaxed);

                // Release the lock, using the wrong memory ordering.
                compiler_fence(Release);
                locked.store(false, Relaxed);
            });
        }
    });
```

```
    println!("{}", counter.into_inner());
}
```

If the lock works properly, we'd expect the final value of the counter to be exactly four million. Note how incrementing the counter happens in a non-atomic way, with a separate `load` and `store` rather than a single `fetch_add`, to make sure that any problems with the spin lock could result in missed increments and thus a lower total value of the counter.

Running this program a few times on a computer with an x86-64 processor gives:

```
4000000
4000000
4000000
```

As expected, we get release and acquire semantics for "free," and our mistake does not cause any issues.

Trying this on an Android phone from 2021 and a Raspberry Pi 3 model B, which both use an ARM64 processor, results in the same output:

```
4000000
4000000
4000000
```

This suggests that not all ARM64 processors make use of all forms of their instruction reordering, although we can't assume much based on this experiment.

When trying this out on an 2021 Apple iMac, which contains an ARM64-based Apple M1 processor, we get something different:

```
3988255
3982153
3984205
```

Our previously hidden mistake suddenly turned into an actual issue—an issue that is only visible on a weakly ordered system. The counter is only off by about 0.4%, showing how subtle such an issue can be. In a real-life scenario, an issue like this might stay undiscovered for a very long time.

 Don't forget to enable optimization (with `cargo run --release` or `rustc -O`) when trying to replicate the results above. Without optimization, the same code often results in many more instructions, which can hide the subtle effects of instruction reordering.

Memory Fences

There is one type of memory ordering related instruction we haven't seen yet: memory fences. A *memory fence* or *memory barrier* instruction is used to represent a std::sync::atomic::fence, which we discussed in "Fences" on page 67.

As we've seen before, memory ordering on x86-64 and ARM64 is all about instruction reordering. A fence instruction prevents certain types of instructions from being reordered past it.

An acquire fence must prevent preceding load operations from getting reordered with any memory operations that follow. Similarly, a release fence must prevent subsequent store operations from getting reordered with any preceding memory operations. A sequentially consistent fence must prevent all memory operations that precede it from being reordered with memory operations after the fence.

On x86-64, the basic memory ordering semantics already satisfy the needs of acquire and release fences. This architecture doesn't allow the types of reordering that these fences prevent, regardless.

Let's dive right in and see what instructions the four different fences compile to on both x86-64 and ARM64:

Rust source	Compiled x86-64	Compiled ARM64

`pub fn a() {`
`    fence(Acquire);`
`}`
	`a:`
	`        ret`
		`a:`
		`        dmb ishld`
		`        ret`

`pub fn a() {`
`    fence(Release);`
`}`
	`a:`
	`        ret`
		`a:`
		`        dmb ish`
		`        ret`

`pub fn a() {`
`    fence(AcqRel);`
`}`
	`a:`
	`        ret`
		`a:`
		`        dmb ish`
		`        ret`

`pub fn a() {`
`    fence(SeqCst);`
`}`
	`a:`
	`        mfence`
	`        ret`
		`a:`
		`        dmb ish`
		`        ret`

Unsurprisingly, release and acquire fences on x86-64 do not result in any instruction. We get release and acquire semantics "for free" on this architecture. Only a SeqCst fence results in an mfence (memory fence) instruction. This instruction makes sure that all memory operations before it have been completed before continuing.

On ARM64, the equivalent instruction is dmb ish (data memory barrier, inner shared domain). Unlike on x86-64, it is used for Release and AcqRel as well, since this architecture doesn't implicitly provide acquire and release semantics. For Acquire, a slightly less impactful variant is used: `dmb ishld`. This variant only waits for load operations to complete, but freely allows preceding store operations to be reordered past it.

Similar to what we saw before with the atomic operations, we see that x86-64 gives us release and acquire fences "for free," while on ARM64, sequentially consistent fences come at the same cost as release fences.

Summary

- On x86-64 and ARM64, relaxed load and store operations are identical to their non-atomic equivalents.

- The common atomic fetch-and-modify and compare-and-exchange operations on x86-64 (and ARM64 since ARMv8.1) have their own instructions.

- On x86-64, an atomic operation for which there is no equivalent instruction compiles down to a compare-and-exchange loop.

- On ARM64, any atomic operation can be represented by a load-linked/store-conditional loop: a loop that automatically restarts if the attempted memory operation was disrupted.

- Caches operate on cache lines, which are often 64 bytes in size.

- Caches are kept consistent with a cache coherence protocol, such as write-through or MESI.

- Padding, for example through #[repr(align(64))], can be useful for improving performance by preventing *false sharing*.

- A load operation can be significantly cheaper than a failed compare-and-exchange operation, in part because the latter often demands exclusive access to a cache line.

- Instruction reordering is invisible within a single threaded program.

- On most architectures, including x86-64 and ARM64, memory ordering is about preventing certain types of instruction reordering.

- On x86-64, every memory operation has acquire and release semantics, making it exactly as cheap or expensive as a relaxed operation. Everything other than stores and fences also has sequentially consistent semantics at no extra cost.

- On ARM64, acquire and release semantics are not as cheap as relaxed operations, but do include sequentially consistent semantics at no extra cost.

A summary of the assembly instructions we've seen in this chapter can be found in Figure 7-1.

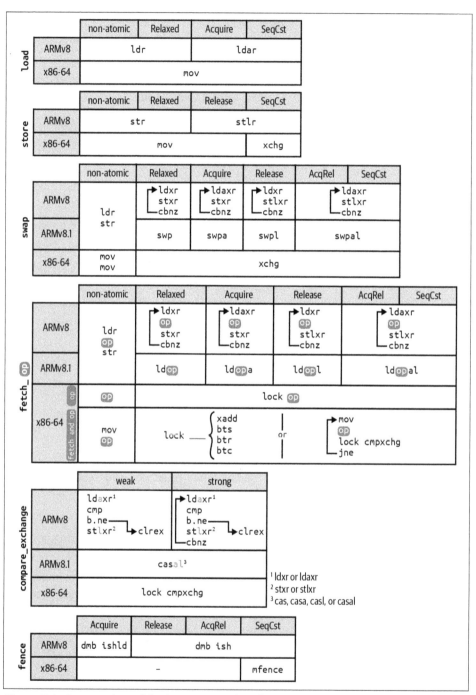

Figure 7-1. An overview of the instructions that the various atomic operations compile down to on ARM64 and x86-64 for each memory ordering

CHAPTER 8

Operating System Primitives

So far, we've mostly focused on non-blocking operations. If we want to implement something like a mutex or condition variable, something that can wait for another thread to unlock or notify it, we need a way to efficiently block the current thread.

As we saw in Chapter 4, we can do this ourselves without the help of the operating system by *spinning*, repeatedly trying something over and over again, which can easily waste a lot of processor time. If we want to block efficiently, however, we need the help of the operating system's kernel.

The kernel, or more specifically the *scheduler* part of it, is responsible for deciding which process or thread gets to run when, for how long, and on which processor core. While a thread is waiting for something to happen, the kernel can stop giving it any processor time, prioritizing other threads that can make better use of this scarce resource.

We'll need a way to inform the kernel that we're waiting for something and ask it to put our thread to sleep until something relevant happens.

Interfacing with the Kernel

The way things are communicated with the kernel depends heavily on the operating system, and often even its version. Usually, the details of how this works are hidden behind one or more libraries that handle this for us. For example, using the Rust standard library, we can just call File::open() to open a file, without having to know any details about the operating system's kernel interface. Similarly, using the C standard library, libc, one can call the standard fopen() function to open a file. Calling such a function will eventually result in a call into the operating system's kernel, also known as a *syscall*, which is usually done through a specialized processor instruction. (On some architectures, that instruction is literally called syscall.)

Programs are generally expected, sometimes even required, to not make any syscalls directly, but to make use of higher level libraries that shipped with the operating system. On Unix systems, such as those based on Linux, libc takes this special role of providing the standard interface to the kernel.

The "Portable Operating System Interface" standard, more commonly known as the POSIX standard, includes additional requirements for libc on Unix systems. For example, next to the fopen() function from the C standard, POSIX additionally requires the existence of the lower-level open() and openat() functions for opening files, which often correspond directly with a syscall. Because of the special status of libc on Unix systems, programs written in languages other than C usually still use libc for all their interactions with the kernel.

Rust software, including the standard library, often makes use of libc through the identically named libc crate.

For Linux specifically, the syscall interface is guaranteed to be stable, allowing us to make syscalls directly, without using libc. While that's not the most common or most advised route, it is slowly becoming more popular.

However, on macOS, also a Unix operating system that follows the POSIX standard, the syscall interface of the kernel is not stable, and we're not supposed to use it directly. The only stable interfaces that programs are allowed to use are provided through the libraries that ship with the system, such as libc, libc++, and various other libraries for C, C++, Objective-C, and Swift, Apple's programming languages of choice.

Windows does not follow the POSIX standard. It does not ship with an extended libc that serves as the main interface to the kernel, but instead ships with a separate set of libraries, such as kernel32.dll, that provide Windows-specific functions, such as CreateFileW for opening files. Just like on macOS, we're not supposed to make use of undocumented lower-level functions or make syscalls directly.

Through their libraries, operating systems provide us with synchronization primitives that need to interact with the kernel, such as mutexes and condition variables. Which part of their implementation is part of such a library or part of the kernel varies heavily per operating system. For example, sometimes the mutex lock and unlock operations correspond directly with a kernel syscall, whereas on other systems, the library handles most of the operations and will only perform a syscall when a thread needs to be blocked or woken up. (The latter tends to be more efficient, as making a syscall can be slow.)

POSIX

As part of the POSIX Threads extensions, better known as pthreads, POSIX specifies data types and functions for concurrency. While technically specified as part of a separate system library, libpthread, this functionality is nowadays often included in libc directly.

Next to functionality like spawning and joining threads (pthread_create and pthread_join), pthread provides the most common synchronization primitives: mutexes (pthread_mutex_t), reader-writer locks (pthread_rwlock_t), and condition variables (pthread_cond_t).

pthread_mutex_t
> Pthread's mutex must be initialized by calling pthread_mutex_init() and destroyed with pthread_mutex_destroy(). The initialization function takes an argument of type pthread_mutexattr_t that can be used to configure some of the properties of the mutex.
>
> One of those properties is its behavior on *recursive locking*, which happens when the same thread that already holds a lock, attempts to lock it again. This results in undefined behavior when using the default setting (PTHREAD_MUTEX_DEFAULT), but it can also be configured to result in an error (PTHREAD_MUTEX_ERRORCH ECK), in a deadlock (PTHREAD_MUTEX_NORMAL), or in a successful second lock (PTHREAD_MUTEX_RECURSIVE).
>
> These mutexes are locked through pthread_mutex_lock() or pthread_mutex_trylock(), and unlocked through pthread_mutex_unlock(). Additionally, unlike Rust's standard mutex, they also support locking with a time limit, through pthread_mutex_timedlock().
>
> A pthread_mutex_t can be statically initialized without a call to pthread_mutex_init() by assigning it the value PTHREAD_MUTEX_INITIALIZER. However, this is only possible for a mutex with default settings.

pthread_rwlock_t
> Pthread's reader-writer lock is initialized and destroyed through pthread_rwlock_init() and pthread_rwlock_destroy(). Similar to a mutex, a default pthread_rwlock_t can also be initialized statically with PTHREAD_RWLOCK_INITIALIZER.
>
> A pthread reader-writer lock has significantly fewer properties that can be configured through its initialization function, compared to a pthread mutex. Most notably, attempting to recursively write-lock it will always result in a deadlock.

Attempts to recursively acquire additional read locks, however, are guaranteed to succeed, even if there are writers waiting. This effectively rules out any efficient implementation that prioritizes writers over readers, which is why most pthread implementations prioritize readers.

Its interface is nearly identical to that of pthread_mutex_t, including support for time limits, except each locking function comes in two variants: one for readers (pthread_rwlock_rdlock), and one for writers (pthread_rwlock_wrlock). Perhaps surprisingly, there is only one unlock function (pthread_rwlock_unlock) that's used for unlocking a lock of either kind.

pthread_cond_t

A pthread condition variable is used together with a pthread mutex. It is initialized and destroyed through pthread_cond_init and pthread_cond_destroy, and has a few attributes that can be configured. Most notably, we can configure whether time limits will use a monotonic clock (like Rust's Instant) or real-time clock (like Rust's SystemTime, somtimes called "wall-clock time"). A condition variable with default settings, such as one statically initialized by PTHREAD_COND_INITIALIZER, uses the real-time clock.

Waiting for such a condition variable, optionally with a time limit, is done through pthread_cond_timedwait(). Waking up a waiting thread is done by calling pthread_cond_signal(), or, to wake all waiting threads at once, pthread_cond_broadcast().

The remaining synchronization primitives provided by pthread are barriers (pthread_barrier_t), spin locks (pthread_spinlock_t), and one-time initialization (pthread_once_t), which we will not discuss.

Wrapping in Rust

It might seem like we could easily expose these pthread synchronization primitives to Rust by conveniently wrapping their C type (through the libc crate) in a Rust struct, like this:

```
pub struct Mutex {
    m: libc::pthread_mutex_t,
}
```

However, there are a few issues with that, as this pthread type was designed for C, not for Rust.

First of all, Rust has rules about mutability and borrowing, which normally don't allow for mutations to something when shared. Since functions like pthread_mutex_lock will most likely mutate the mutex, we'll need interior mutability to make sure that's acceptable. So, we'll have to wrap it in an UnsafeCell:

```
pub struct Mutex {
    m: UnsafeCell<libc::pthread_mutex_t>,
}
```

A much bigger problem is related to *moving*.

In Rust, we move objects around all the time. For example, by returning an object from a function, passing it as an argument, or simply assigning it to a new place. Everything that we own (and that isn't borrowed by anything else), we can freely move into a new place.

In C, however, that's not universally true. It's quite common for a type in C to depend on its memory address staying constant. For example, it might contain a pointer that points into itself, or store a pointer to itself in some global data structure. In that case, moving it to a new place could result in undefined behavior.

The pthread types we discussed do not guarantee they are *movable*, which becomes quite a problem in Rust. Even a simple idiomatic `Mutex::new()` function is a problem: it would return a mutex object, which would move it into a new place in memory.

Since a user could always move around any mutex object they own, we either need to make them promise they won't do that, by making the interface `unsafe`; or we need to take away their ownership and hide everything behind a wrapper (something that `std::pin::Pin` can be used for). Neither of these are good solutions, as they impact the interface of our mutex type, making it very error-prone and/or inconvenient to use.

A solution to this problem is to wrap the mutex in a `Box`. By putting the pthread mutex in its own allocation, it stays in the same location in memory, even if its owner is moved around.

```
pub struct Mutex {
    m: Box<UnsafeCell<libc::pthread_mutex_t>>,
}
```

 This is how `std::sync::Mutex` was implemented on all Unix platforms before Rust 1.62.

The downside of this approach is the overhead: every mutex now gets its own allocation, adding significant overhead to creating, destroying, and using the mutex. Another downside is that it prevents the `new` function from being `const`, which gets in the way of having a `static` mutex.

Even if pthread_mutex_t was movable, a const fn new could only initialize it with default settings, which results in undefined behavior when locking recursively. There is no way to design a safe interface that prevents locking recursively, so this means we'd need to make the lock function unsafe to make the user promise they won't do that.

A problem that remains with our Box approach occurs when dropping a locked mutex. It might seem that, with the right design, it would not be possible to drop a Mutex while locked, since it's impossible to drop it while it's still borrowed by a MutexGuard. The MutexGuard would have to be dropped first, unlocking the Mutex. However, in Rust, it's safe to forget (or leak) an object, without dropping it. This means one could write something like this:

```
fn main() {
    let m = Mutex::new(..);

    let guard = m.lock(); // Lock it ..
    std::mem::forget(guard); // .. but don't unlock it.
}
```

In the example above, m will be dropped at the end of the scope while it is still locked. This is fine, according to the Rust compiler, because the guard has been leaked and can't be used anymore.

However, pthread specifies that calling pthread_mutex_destroy() on a locked mutex is not guaranteed to work and might result in undefined behavior. One work-around is to first attempt to lock (and unlock) the pthread mutex when dropping our Mutex, and panic (or leak the Box) when it is already locked, but that adds even more overhead.

These issues don't just apply to pthread_mutex_t, but to the other types we discussed as well. Overall, the design of the pthread synchronization primitives is fine for C, but just not a great fit for Rust.

Linux

On Linux systems, the pthread synchronization primitives are all implemented using the *futex* syscall. Its name comes from "fast user-space mutex," as the original motivation for adding this syscall was to allow libraries (like pthread implementations) to include a fast and efficient mutex implementation. It's much more flexible than that though and can be used to build many different synchronization tools.

The futex syscall was added to the Linux kernel in 2003 and has seen several improvements and extensions since then. Some other operating systems have since also added similar functionality, most notably Windows 8 in 2012 with the addition of WaitOnAddress (which we'll discuss a bit later, in "Windows" on page 175). In 2020, the C++ language even added support for basic futex-like operations to its standard library, with the addition of the `atomic_wait` and `atomic_notify` functions.

Futex

On Linux, `SYS_futex` is a syscall that implements various operations that all operate on a 32-bit atomic integer. The main two operations are `FUTEX_WAIT` and `FUTEX_WAKE`. The wait operation puts a thread to sleep, and a wake operation on the same atomic variable wakes the thread up again.

These operations don't store anything in the atomic integer. Instead, the kernel remembers which threads are waiting on which memory address to allow a wake operation to wake up the right threads.

In "Waiting: Parking and Condition Variables" on page 24, we saw how other mechanisms for blocking and waking up threads need a way to make sure that wake operations don't get lost in a race. For thread parking, that issue is solved by making the `unpark()` operation also apply to future `park()` operations as well. And for condition variables, that's taken care of by the mutex that is used together with the condition variable.

For the futex wait and wake operations, another mechanism is used. The wait operation takes an argument which specifies the value we expect the atomic variable to have and will refuse to block if it doesn't match. The wait operation behaves atomically with respect to the wake operation, meaning that no wake signal can get lost between the check of the expected value and the moment it actually goes to sleep.

If we make sure that the value of the atomic variable is changed right before a wake operation, we can be sure that a thread that's about to start waiting will not go to sleep, such that potentially missing the futex wake operation no longer matters.

Let's go over a minimal example to see this in practice.

First, we need to be able to invoke these syscalls. We can use the `syscall` function from the `libc` crate to do so, and wrap each of them in a convenient Rust function, as follows:

```
#[cfg(not(target_os = "linux"))]
compile_error!("Linux only. Sorry!");

pub fn wait(a: &AtomicU32, expected: u32) {
    // Refer to the futex (2) man page for the syscall signature.
    unsafe {
        libc::syscall(
            libc::SYS_futex, // The futex syscall.
            a as *const AtomicU32, // The atomic to operate on.
            libc::FUTEX_WAIT, // The futex operation.
            expected, // The expected value.
```

```
                std::ptr::null::<libc::timespec>(), // No timeout.
            );
        }
    }

    pub fn wake_one(a: &AtomicU32) {
        // Refer to the futex (2) man page for the syscall signature.
        unsafe {
            libc::syscall(
                libc::SYS_futex, // The futex syscall.
                a as *const AtomicU32, // The atomic to operate on.
                libc::FUTEX_WAKE, // The futex operation.
                1, // The number of threads to wake up.
            );
        }
    }
```

Now, as a usage example, let's use these to make a thread wait for another. We'll use an atomic variable that we initialize at zero, which the main thread will futex-wait on. A second thread will change the variable to one, and then run a futex wake operation on it to wake up the main thread.

Just like thread parking and waiting on a condition variable, a futex wait operation can *spuriously* wake up, even when nothing happened. Therefore, it is most commonly used in a loop, repeating it if the condition we're waiting for isn't met yet.

Let's take a look at the example below:

```
fn main() {
    let a = AtomicU32::new(0);

    thread::scope(|s| {
        s.spawn(|| {
            thread::sleep(Duration::from_secs(3));
            a.store(1, Relaxed); ❶
            wake_one(&a); ❷
        });

        println!("Waiting...");
        while a.load(Relaxed) == 0 { ❸
            wait(&a, 0); ❹
        }
        println!("Done!");
    });
}
```

❶ The spawned thread will set the atomic variable to one after a few seconds.

❷ It then executes a futex wake operation to wake up the main thread, in case it was sleeping, so it can see that the variable has changed.

❸   The main thread waits as long as the variable is zero, before continuing to print its final message.

❹   The futex wait operation is used to put the thread to sleep. Very importantly, this operation will check whether a is still zero before going to sleep, which is the reason that the signal from the spawned thread cannot get lost between ❸ and ❹. Either ❶ (and therefore ❷) did not happen yet and it goes to sleep, or ❶ (and maybe ❷) already happened, and it immediately continues.

An important observation to make here is that the `wait` call is avoided entirely if a was already set to one before the `while` loop. In a similar fashion, if the main thread had also stored in the atomic variable whether it started waiting for the signal (by setting it to a value other than zero or one), the signaling thread could skip the futex wake operation if the main thread hadn't started waiting yet. This is what makes futex-based synchronization primitives so fast: since we manage the state ourselves, we don't need to rely on the kernel, except when we actually need to block.

Since Rust 1.48, the standard library's thread parking functions on Linux are implemented like this. They use one atomic variable per thread, with three possible states: zero for the idle and initial state, one for "unparked but not yet parked," and minus one for "parked but not yet unparked."

In Chapter 9, we'll implement mutexes, condition variables, and reader-writer locks using these operations.

Futex Operations

Next to the wait and wake operations, the futex syscall supports several other operations. In this section, we'll briefly discuss every operation supported by this syscall.

The first argument to the futex is always a pointer to the 32-bit atomic variable to operate on. The second argument is a constant representing the operation, such as FUTEX_WAIT, to which up to two flags can be added: FUTEX_PRIVATE_FLAG and/or FUTEX_CLOCK_REALTIME, which we will discuss below. The remaining arguments depend on the operation and are described for each of the operations below.

FUTEX_WAIT
    This operation takes two additional arguments: the value the atomic variable is expected to have and a pointer to a `timespec` representing the maximum time to wait.

    If the value of the atomic variable matches the expected value, the wait operation blocks until woken up by one of the wake operations, or until the duration specified by the timespec has passed. If the pointer to the timespec is null, there is no time limit. Additionally, the wait operation might spuriously wake up and return without a corresponding wake operation, before the time limit is reached.

The check and blocking operation happens as a single atomic operation with respect to other futex operations, meaning that no wake signals can get lost between them.

The duration specified by the timespec represents a duration on the monotonic clock (like Rust's Instant) by default. By adding the FUTEX_CLOCK_REALTIME flag, the real-time clock (like Rust's SystemTime) is used instead.

The return value indicates whether the expected value matched and whether the timeout was reached or not.

FUTEX_WAKE

This operation takes one additional argument: the number of threads to wake up, as an i32.

This wakes up as many threads as specified that are blocked in a wait operation on the same atomic variable. (Or fewer if there are not that many waiting threads.) Most commonly, this argument is either one to wake up just one thread, or i32::MAX to wake up all threads.

The number of awoken threads is returned.

FUTEX_WAIT_BITSET

This operation takes four additional arguments: the value the atomic variable is expected to have, a pointer to a timespec representing the maximum time to wait, a pointer that's ignored, and a 32-bit "bitset" (a u32).

This operation behaves the same as FUTEX_WAIT, with two differences.

The first difference is that it takes a bitset argument that can be used to wait for only specific wake operations, rather than all wake operations on the same atomic variable. A FUTEX_WAKE operation is never ignored, but a signal from a FUTEX_WAKE_BITSET operation is ignored if the wait bitset and the wake bitset do not have any 1-bit in common.

For example, a FUTEX_WAKE_BITSET operation with a bitset of 0b0101 will wake up a FUTEX_WAIT_BITSET operation with a bitset of 0b1100, but not one with a bitset of 0b0010.

This might be useful when implementing something like a reader-writer lock, to wake up a writer without waking up any readers. However, note that using two separate atomic variables can be more efficient than using a single one for two different kinds of waiters, since the kernel will keep a single list of waiters per atomic variable.

The other difference with FUTEX_WAIT is that the timespec is used as an absolute timestamp, rather than a duration. Because of this, FUTEX_WAIT_BITSET is often used with a bitset of u32::MAX (all bits set), effectively turning it into a regular FUTEX_WAIT operation, but with an absolute timestamp for the time limit.

FUTEX_WAKE_BITSET
This operation takes four additional arguments: the number of threads to wake up, two pointers that are ignored, and a 32-bit "bitset" (a u32).

This operation is identical to FUTEX_WAKE, except it does not wake up FUTEX_WAIT_BITSET operations with a bitset that does not overlap. (See FUTEX_WAIT_BITSET above.)

With a bitset of u32::MAX (all bits set), this is identical to FUTEX_WAKE.

FUTEX_REQUEUE
This operation takes three additional arguments: the number of threads to wake up (an i32), the number of threads to requeue (an i32), and the address of a secondary atomic variable.

This operation wakes up a given number of waiting threads, and then *requeues* a given number of remaining waiting threads to instead wait on another atomic variable.

Waiting threads that are requeued continue to wait, but are no longer affected by wake operations on the primary atomic variable. Instead, they are now woken up by wake operations on the secondary atomic variable.

This can be useful for implementing something like the "notify all" operation of a condition variable. Instead of waking up all threads, which will subsequently try to lock a mutex, most likely making all but one thread wait for that mutex right afterwards, we could only wake up a single thread and requeue all the others to directly wait for the mutex without waking them up first.

Just like with the FUTEX_WAKE operation, the value of i32::MAX can be used to requeue all waiting threads. (Specifying a value of i32::MAX for the number of threads to wake up is not very useful, since that will make this operation equivalent to FUTEX_WAKE.)

The number of awoken threads is returned.

FUTEX_CMP_REQUEUE

This operation takes four additional arguments: the number of threads to wake up (an i32), the number of threads to requeue (an i32), the address of a secondary atomic variable, and the value the primary atomic variable is expected to have.

This operation is nearly identical to FUTEX_REQUEUE, except it refuses to operate if the value of the primary atomic variable does not match the expected value. The check of the value and the requeueing operation happens atomically with respect to other futex operations.

Unlike FUTEX_REQUEUE, this returns the sum of the number of awoken and requeued threads.

FUTEX_WAKE_OP

This operation takes four additional arguments: the number of threads to wake up on the primary atomic variable (an i32), the number of threads to potentially wake up on the second atomic variable (an i32), the address of a secondary atomic variable, and a 32-bit value encoding both an operation and a comparison to be made.

This is a very specialized operation that modifies the secondary atomic variable, wakes a number of threads waiting on the primary atomic variable, checks if the previous value of the atomic variable matches a given condition, and if so, also wakes a number of threads on a secondary atomic variable.

In other words, it is identical to the following code, except the entire operation behaves atomically with respect to other futex operations:

```
let old = atomic2.fetch_update(Relaxed, Relaxed, some_operation);
wake(atomic1, N);
if some_condition(old) {
    wake(atomic2, M);
}
```

The modifying operation to perform and the condition to check are both specified by the last argument to the syscall, encoded in its 32 bits. The operation can be one of the following: assignment, addition, binary or, binary and-not, and binary xor, with either a 12-bit argument or a 32-bit argument that's a power of two. The comparison can be chosen from ==, !=, <, <=, >, and >=, with a 12-bit argument.

See the futex(2) Linux man page for details on the encoding of this argument, or use the linux-futex crate on crates.io, which includes a convenient way to construct this argument.

This operation returns the total number of awoken threads.

At first glance this may seem like a flexible operation with many use cases. However, it was designed for just one specific use case in GNU libc where two threads had to be woken up from two separate atomic variables. That specific case has been replaced by a different implementation that no longer makes use of FUTEX_WAKE_OP.

The FUTEX_PRIVATE_FLAG can be added to any of these operations to enable a possible optimization if all relevant futex operations on the same atomic variable(s) come from threads of the same process, which is usually the case. To make use of it, every relevant futex operation must include this same flag. By allowing the kernel to assume there will be no interactions with other processes, it can skip some otherwise potentially expensive steps in performing futex operations, improving performance.

In addition to Linux, NetBSD also supports all the futex operations described above. OpenBSD also has a futex syscall, but only supports the FUTEX_WAIT, FUTEX_WAKE, and FUTEX_REQUEUE operations. FreeBSD does not have a native futex syscall, but does include a syscall called _umtx_op, which includes functionality nearly identical to FUTEX_WAIT and FUTEX_WAKE: UMTX_OP_WAIT (for 64-bit atomics), UMTX_OP_WAIT_UINT (for 32-bit atomics), and UMTX_OP_WAKE. Windows also includes functions that behave very similarly to the futex wait and wake operations, which we will discuss later in this chapter.

New Futex Operations

As of Linux 5.16, released in 2022, there is an additional futex syscall: futex_waitv. This new syscall allows waiting for more than one futex at once, by providing it a list of atomic variables (and their expected values) to wait on. A thread blocked on futex_waitv can be woken up by a wake operation on any of the specified variables.

This new syscall also leaves space for future extensions. For example, it's possible to specify the size of the atomic variable to wait on. While the initial implementation only supports 32-bit atomics, just like the original futex syscall, this might be extended in the future to include 8-bit, 16-bit, and 64-bit atomics.

Priority Inheritance Futex Operations

Priority inversion is a problem that occurs when a high priority thread is blocked on a lock held by a low priority thread. The high priority thread effectively has its priority "inverted," since it now has to wait for the low priority thread to release the lock before it can make progress.

A solution to this problem is *priority inheritance*, in which the blocking thread inherits the priority of the highest priority thread that is waiting for it, temporarily increasing the priority of the low priority thread while it holds the lock.

In addition to the seven futex operations we discussed before, there are six priority inheriting futex operations specifically designed for implementing *priority inheriting locks*.

The general futex operations we discussed before do not have any requirements for the exact contents of the atomic variable. We got to choose ourselves what the 32 bits represent. However, for a priority inheriting mutex, the kernel needs to be able to understand whether the mutex is locked, and if so, which thread has locked it.

To avoid having to make a syscall on every state change, the priority inheritance futex operations specify the exact contents of the 32-bit atomic variable, so the kernel can understand it: the highest bit represents whether there are any threads waiting to lock the mutex, and the lowest 30 bits contain the thread ID (the Linux `tid`, not the Rust `ThreadId`) of the thread that holds the lock, or zero when unlocked.

As an extra feature, the kernel will set the second highest bit if the thread that holds the lock terminates without unlocking it, but only if there are any waiters. This allows for the mutex to be *robust*: a term used to describe a mutex that can gracefully handle a situation where its "owning" thread unexpectedly terminates.

The priority inheriting futex operations have a one to one correspondence to the standard mutex operations: `FUTEX_LOCK_PI` for locking, `FUTEX_UNLOCK_PI` for unlocking, and `FUTEX_TRYLOCK_PI` for locking without blocking. Additionally, the `FUTEX_CMP_REQUEUE_PI` and `FUTEX_WAIT_REQUEUE_PI` operations can be used to implement a condition variable that pairs with a priority inheriting mutex.

We'll not discuss these operations in detail. See the `futex(2)` Linux man page or the `linux-futex` crate on crates.io for their details.

macOS

The kernel that's part of macOS supports various useful low-level concurrency related syscalls. However, just like most operating systems, the kernel interface is not considered stable, and we're not supposed to use it directly.

The only way software should interact with the macOS kernel is through the libraries that ship with the system. These libraries include its standard library implementations for C (libc), C++ (libc++), Objective-C, and Swift.

As a POSIX-compliant Unix system, the macOS C library includes a full pthread implementation. The standard locks in other languages tend to use pthread's primitives under the hood.

Pthread's locks tend to be relatively slow on macOS compared to the equivalent on other operating systems. One of the reasons is that the locks on macOS behave as *fair locks* by default. This means that when several threads attempt to lock the same mutex, they are served in order of arrival, like a perfect queue. While fairness can be a desirable property, it can significantly reduce performance, especially under high contention.

os_unfair_lock

Next to the pthread primitives, macOS 10.12 introduced a new lightweight platform-specific mutex, which is not fair: os_unfair_lock. It is just 32 bits in size, initialized statically with the OS_UNFAIR_LOCK_INIT constant, and does not require destruction. It can be locked through os_unfair_lock_lock() (blocking) or os_unfair_lock_try lock() (non-blocking), and is unlocked through os_unfair_lock_unlock().

Unfortunately, it does not come with a condition variable, nor does it have a reader-writer variant.

Windows

The Windows operating system ships with a set of libraries that together form the *Windows API*, often called the "Win32 API" (even on 64-bit systems). This forms a layer on top of the "Native API": the largely undocumented interface with the kernel, which we're not supposed to use directly.

The Windows API is made available to Rust programs through Microsoft's official windows and windows-sys crates, which are available on crates.io.

Heavyweight Kernel Objects

Many of the older synchronization primitives available on Windows are managed fully by the kernel, making them quite heavyweight, and giving them similar properties as other kernel-managed objects, such as files. They can be used by multiple processes, they can be named and located by their name, and they support fine-grained permissions, similar to files. For example, it's possible to allow a process to wait on some object, without allowing it to send signals through it to wake others.

These heavyweight kernel-managed synchronization objects include Mutex (which can be locked and unlocked), Event (which can be signalled and waited for), and WaitableTimer (which can be automatically signalled after a chosen time, or periodically). Creating such an object results in a HANDLE, just like opening a file, that can be easily passed around and used with the regular HANDLE functions; most notably the family of wait functions. These functions allow us to wait for one or more objects of various types, including the heavyweight synchronization primitives, processes, threads, and various forms of I/O.

Lighter-Weight Objects

A lighter-weight synchronization primitive included in the Windows API is the "critical section."

The term *critical section* refers to a part of a program, a "section" of code, that may not be entered concurrently by more than one thread. The mechanism for protecting a critical section is often called a mutex. In this case, however, Microsoft used the name "critical section" for the mechanism, quite possibly because the name "mutex" was already taken by the heavyweight Mutex object discussed above.

A Windows CRITICAL_SECTION is effectively a *recursive mutex*, except it uses the terms "enter" and "leave" rather than "lock" and "unlock." As a recursive mutex, it is designed to only protect against other threads. It allows the same thread to lock (or "enter") it more than once, requiring it to also unlock (leave) it the same number of times.

This is something to keep in mind when wrapping this type in Rust. Successfully locking (entering) a CRITICAL_SECTION shouldn't result in an exclusive reference (&mut T) to data protected by it. Otherwise, a thread could use this to create two exclusive references to the same data, which immediately results in undefined behavior.

A CRITICAL_SECTION is initialized using the InitializeCriticalSection() function, destroyed with DeleteCriticalSection(), and may not be moved. It is locked through EnterCriticalSection() or TryEnterCriticalSection(), and unlocked with LeaveCriticalSection().

Until Rust 1.51, std::sync::Mutex on Windows XP was based on a (Box-allocated) CRITICAL_SECTION object. (Rust 1.51 dropped support for Windows XP.)

Slim reader-writer locks

As of Windows Vista (and Windows Server 2008), the Windows API includes a much nicer locking primitive that's very lightweight: the *slim reader-writer lock*, or *SRW lock* for short.

The SRWLOCK type is just one pointer in size, can be statically initialized with SRWLOCK_INIT, and does not require destruction. While not in use (borrowed), we're even allowed to move it, making it an excellent candidate for being wrapped in a Rust type.

It provides exclusive (writer) locking and unlocking through AcquireSRWLockEx clusive(), TryAcquireSRWLockExclusive(), and ReleaseSRWLockExclusive(), and provides shared (reader) locking and unlocking through AcquireSRWLockShared(), TryAcquireSRWLockShared(), and ReleaseSRWLockShared(). It is often used as a regular mutex, simply by ignoring the shared (reader) locking functions.

An SRW lock prioritizes neither writers nor readers. While not guaranteed, it attempts to serve all lock requests in order, as far as possible without reducing performance. One must not attempt to acquire a second shared (reader) lock on a thread that already holds one. Doing so could lead to a permanent deadlock if the operation gets queued behind an exclusive (writer) lock operation of another thread, which would be blocked because of the first shared (reader) lock that the first thread already holds.

The SRW lock was introduced to the Windows API together with the condition variable. Similar to an SRW lock, a CONDITION_VARIABLE is just one pointer in size, can be initialized statically with CONDITION_VARIABLE_INIT, and does not require destruction. We're also allowed to move it, as long as it isn't in use (borrowed).

This condition variable can not only be used together with an SRW lock, through SleepConditionVariableSRW, but also with a critical section, through SleepCondi tionVariableCS.

Waking up waiting threads is done either through WakeConditionVariable to wake a single thread, or WakeAllConditionVariable to wake all waiting threads.

Originally, Windows SRW locks and condition variables used in the standard library were wrapped in a Box to avoid moving the objects. Microsoft didn't document the movability guarantees until we requested that in 2020. Since then, as of Rust 1.49, std::sync::Mutex, std::sync::RwLock, and std::sync::Condvar on Windows Vista and later directly wrap an SRWLOCK or CONDI TION_VARIABLE, without any allocations.

Address-Based Waiting

Windows 8 (and Windows Server 2012) introduced a new, more flexible, type of synchronization functionality that is very similar to the Linux FUTEX_WAIT and FUTEX_WAKE operations we discussed earlier in this chapter.

The WaitOnAddress function can operate on an 8-bit, 16-bit, 32-bit, or 64-bit atomic variable. It takes four arguments: the address of the atomic variable, the address of a variable that holds the expected value, the size of the atomic variable (in bytes), and the maximum number of milliseconds to wait before giving up (or u32::MAX for an infinite timeout).

Just like the FUTEX_WAIT operation, it compares the value of the atomic variable with the expected value, and goes to sleep if they match, waiting for a corresponding wake operation. The check and sleep operation happens atomically with respect to wake operations, meaning no wake signal can get lost in between.

Waking a thread that's waiting on WaitOnAddress is done through either WakeByAddressSingle to wake a single thread, or WakeByAddressAll to wake all waiting threads. These two functions take just a single argument: the address of the atomic variable, which was also passed to WaitOnAddress.

Some, but not all, of the synchronization primitives of the Windows API are implemented using these functions. More importantly, they are a great building block for building our own primitives, which we will do in Chapter 9.

Summary

- A *syscall* is a call into the operating system's kernel and is relatively slow compared to a regular function call.

- Usually, programs don't make syscalls directly, but instead go through the operating system's libraries (e.g., `libc`) to interface with the kernel. On many operating systems, this is the only supported way of interfacing with the kernel.

- The `libc` crate gives Rust code access to `libc`.

- On POSIX systems, `libc` includes more than what's required by the C standard to comply with the POSIX standard.

- The POSIX standard includes *pthreads*, a library with concurrency primitives such as `pthread_mutex_t`.

- Pthread types are designed for C, not for Rust. For example, they are not movable, which can be a problem.

- Linux has a *futex* syscall supporting several waiting and waking operations on an `AtomicU32`. The wait operation verifies the expected value of the atomic, which is used to avoid missing notifications.

- In addition to pthread, macOS also provides `os_unfair_lock` as a lightweight locking primitive.

- Windows heavyweight concurrency primitives always require interacting with the kernel, but can be passed between processes and used with the standard Windows waiting functions.

- Windows lightweight concurrency primitives include a "slim" reader-writer lock (*SRW lock*) and a condition variable. These are easily wrapped in Rust, as they are movable.

- Windows also provides basic futex-like functionality, through `WaitOnAddress` and `WakeByAddress`.

CHAPTER 9

Building Our Own Locks

In this chapter, we'll build our own mutex, condition variable, and reader-writer lock. For each of them, we'll start with a very basic version, and then extend it to make it more efficient.

Since we're not going to use the lock types from the standard libary (which would be cheating), we're going to have to use the tools from Chapter 8 to be able to make threads wait without busy-looping. However, as we saw in that chapter, the available tools the operating system provides vary a lot per platform, making it hard to build something that works cross-platform.

Fortunately, most modern operating systems support futex-like functionality, or at least the wake and wait operations. As we saw in Chapter 8, Linux has supported them since 2003 with the `futex` syscall, Windows since 2012 with the `WaitOnAddress` family of functions, FreeBSD since 2016 as part of the `_umtx_op` syscall, and so on.

The most notable exception is macOS. While its kernel does support these operations, it is not exposed through any stable, publicly usable, C function that we can use. However, macOS does ship with a recent version of libc++, an implementation of the C++ standard library. This library includes support for C++20, which is the version of C++ that comes with built-in support for very basic atomic wait and wake operations (like `std::atomic<T>::wait()`). While it's somewhat tricky to make use of that from Rust for a variety of reasons, it is certainly possible, giving us access to basic futex-like wait and wake functionality on macOS as well.

We'll not dive into the dirty details, but instead make use of the atomic-wait crate from crates.io to provide us with the building blocks for our locking primitives. This crate provides just three functions: wait(), wake_one(), and wake_all(). It implements these for all the major platforms, using the various platform-specific implementations we've discussed above. This means we no longer have to think about any platform-specific details, as long as we stick to these three functions.

These functions behave like the identically named ones we implemented in "Futex" on page 167 for Linux, but let's quickly recall how they work:

wait(&AtomicU32, u32)

This function is used to wait until the atomic variable no longer contains the given value. It blocks if the value stored in the atomic variable is equal to the given value. When another thread modifies the value of the atomic variable, that thread needs to call one of the wake functions below, on the same atomic variable, to wake up the waiting thread from its sleep.

This function might return spuriously, without a corresponding wake operation. So make sure to check the value of the atomic variable after it returns, and repeat the wait() call if necessary.

wake_one(&AtomicU32)

This wakes up a single thread that's currently blocked on wait() on the same atomic variable. Use this right after modifying the atomic variable, to inform one waiting thread of the change.

wake_all(&AtomicU32)

This wakes up all threads that are currently blocked on wait() on the same atomic variable. Use this right after modifying the atomic variable, to inform the waiting threads of the change.

Only 32-bit atomics are supported, because that's the only size that's supported on all major platforms.

In "Futex" on page 167, we discussed a very minimal example that shows how these functions are used in practice. If you've forgotten, make sure you check out that example before continuing.

To use the atomic-wait crate, add atomic-wait = "1" to the [dependencies] section in your Cargo.toml; or run cargo add atomic-wait@1, which will do that for you. The three functions are defined in the root of the crate and can be imported with use atomic_wait::{wait, wake_one, wake_all};.

There might be later versions of this crate available by the time you're reading this, but only major version 1 is made for this chapter. Later versions might not have a compatible interface.

Now that we have our basic building blocks ready, let's get started.

Mutex

We'll take our SpinLock<T> type from Chapter 4 as our reference while building our Mutex<T>. The parts not involved in blocking, such as the design of the guard type, will remain unchanged.

Let's start with the type definition. We'll have to make one change compared to the spin lock: instead of an AtomicBool set to false or true, we'll use an AtomicU32 set to zero or one, so we can use it with the atomic wait and wake functions.

```
pub struct Mutex<T> {
    /// 0: unlocked
    /// 1: locked
    state: AtomicU32,
    value: UnsafeCell<T>,
}
```

Just like for the spin lock, we need to promise that a Mutex<T> can be shared between threads, even though it contains a scary UnsafeCell:

```
unsafe impl<T> Sync for Mutex<T> where T: Send {}
```

We'll also add a MutexGuard type that implements the Deref traits to provide a fully safe locking interface, like we did in "A Safe Interface Using a Lock Guard" on page 80:

```
pub struct MutexGuard<'a, T> {
    mutex: &'a Mutex<T>,
}

impl<T> Deref for MutexGuard<'_, T> {
    type Target = T;
    fn deref(&self) -> &T {
        unsafe { &*self.mutex.value.get() }
    }
}

impl<T> DerefMut for MutexGuard<'_, T> {
    fn deref_mut(&mut self) -> &mut T {
        unsafe { &mut *self.mutex.value.get() }
    }
}
```

For the design and operation of a lock guard type, see "A Safe Interface Using a Lock Guard" on page 80.

Let's also get the `Mutex::new` function out of the way before we move on to the interesting part.

```
impl<T> Mutex<T> {
    pub const fn new(value: T) -> Self {
        Self {
            state: AtomicU32::new(0), // unlocked state
            value: UnsafeCell::new(value),
        }
    }

    …
}
```

Now that we have all that out of the way, there are two remaining pieces left: locking (`Mutex::lock()`) and unlocking (`Drop for MutexGuard<T>`).

The lock function we implemented for our spin lock uses an atomic swap operation to attempt to obtain the lock, returning if it succesfully changed the state from "unlocked" to "locked." If unsuccessful, it immediately tries again.

To lock our mutex we'll do almost the same, except we use `wait()` to wait before trying again:

```
pub fn lock(&self) -> MutexGuard<T> {
    // Set the state to 1: locked.
    while self.state.swap(1, Acquire) == 1 {
        // If it was already locked..
        // .. wait, unless the state is no longer 1.
        wait(&self.state, 1);
    }
    MutexGuard { mutex: self }
}
```

For the memory ordering, the same reasoning applies as with our spin lock. Refer back to Chapter 4 for the details.

Note how the wait() function will only block if the state is still set to 1 (locked) at the time we call it, such that we don't have to worry about the possibility of missing a wake-up call between the swap and the wait calls.

The Drop implementation of the guard type is responsible for unlocking the mutex. Unlocking our spin lock was easy: just set the state back to false (unlocked). For our mutex, however, that won't suffice. If there's a thread waiting to lock the mutex, it won't know that the mutex has been unlocked unless we notify it using a wake operation. If we don't wake it up, it will most likely stay asleep forever. (Maybe it is lucky and is spuriously woken up at the right time, but let's not count on that.)

So, we'll not only set the state back to 0 (unlocked), but also call wake_one() right afterwards:

```
impl<T> Drop for MutexGuard<'_, T> {
    fn drop(&mut self) {
        // Set the state back to 0: unlocked.
        self.mutex.state.store(0, Release);
        // Wake up one of the waiting threads, if any.
        wake_one(&self.mutex.state);
    }
}
```

Waking one thread is enough, because even if there are multiple threads waiting, only one of them will be able to claim the lock. The next thread to lock it will wake up another thread when it's done with the lock, and so on. Waking up more than one thread at once will just set those threads up for disappointment, wasting valuable processor time when all but one of them realize their chance at locking has been snatched away by another lucky thread, before they go back to sleep again.

Note that there is no guarantee that the one thread that we wake up will be able to grab the lock. Another thread might still grab the lock right before it gets the chance.

An important observation to make here is how this mutex implementation would still be technically correct (that is, memory safe) without the wait and wake functions. Because the wait() operation can spuriously wake up, we can't make any assumptions about when it returns. We still have to manage the state of our locking primitives ourselves. If we were to remove the wait and wake function calls, our mutex would be basically identical to our spin lock.

In general, the atomic wait and wake functions never play a factor in correctness, from a memory safety perspective. They are only a (very serious) optimization to avoid busy-looping. This doesn't mean that an unusably inefficient lock would be considered "correct" by any practical standards, but this insight can be helpful when trying to reason about unsafe Rust code.

Lock API

If you're planning to take on implementing Rust locks as a new hobby, you might quickly get bored with the boilerplate code involved in providing a safe interface. That is, the `UnsafeCell`, the `Sync` implementation, the guard type, the `Deref` implementations, and so on.

The `lock_api` crate on crates.io can be used to automatically take care of all these things. You'll only have to make a type that represents the lock state, and provide (unsafe) lock and unlock functions through the (unsafe) `lock_api::RawMutex` trait. In return, the `lock_api::Mutex` type will provide you with a fully safe and ergonomic mutex type, including a mutex guard, based on your lock implementation.

Avoiding Syscalls

By far the slowest part of our mutex are the wait and wake, since those (can) result in a *syscall*, a call into the operating system's kernel. Talking with the kernel like that is quite an involved process that tends to be quite slow, especially compared to atomic operations. So, for a performant mutex implementation, we should try to avoid wait and wake calls as much as possible.

Luckily, we're already halfway there. Because the `while` loop in our locking function checks the state before the `wait()` call, the wait operation is skipped entirely in the situation where we don't need to wait, when the mutex wasn't locked. We do, however, unconditionally call the `wake_one()` function when unlocking.

We can skip the `wake_one()` if we know there are no other threads waiting. To know whether there are waiting threads, we need to keep track of this information ourselves.

We can do this by splitting the "locked" state into two separate states: "locked without waiters" and "locked with waiter(s)." We'll use the values 1 and 2 for that, and update our documentation comment of the `state` field in the struct definition:

```
pub struct Mutex<T> {
    /// 0: unlocked
    /// 1: locked, no other threads waiting
    /// 2: locked, other threads waiting
    state: AtomicU32,
    value: UnsafeCell<T>,
}
```

Now, for an unlocked mutex, our lock function still needs to set the state to 1 to lock it. However, if it was already locked, our lock function now needs to set the state to 2 before going to sleep, so that the unlock function can tell there's a waiting thread.

To do this, we'll first use a compare-and-exchange function to attempt to change the state from 0 to 1. If that succeeds, we've locked the mutex, and we know there are no other waiters, since the mutex wasn't locked before. If it fails, that must be because the mutex is currently locked (in state 1 or 2). In that case, we'll use an atomic swap operation to set it to 2. If that swap operation returns an old value of 1 or 2, that means the mutex was indeed still locked, and only then do we use wait() to block until it changes. If the swap operation returns 0, that means we've succesfully locked the mutex by changing its state from 0 to 2.

```
pub fn lock(&self) -> MutexGuard<T> {
    if self.state.compare_exchange(0, 1, Acquire, Relaxed).is_err() {
        while self.state.swap(2, Acquire) != 0 {
            wait(&self.state, 2);
        }
    }
    MutexGuard { mutex: self }
}
```

Now, our unlock function can make use of the new information by skipping the wake_one() call when it's unnecessary. Instead of just storing a 0 to unlock the mutex, we'll now use a swap operation so we can check out its previous value. Only if that value was 2, will we continue to wake up a thread:

```
impl<T> Drop for MutexGuard<'_, T> {
    fn drop(&mut self) {
        if self.mutex.state.swap(0, Release) == 2 {
            wake_one(&self.mutex.state);
        }
    }
}
```

Note that after setting the state back to zero, it no longer indicates whether there are any waiting threads. The thread that's woken up is responsible for setting the state back to 2, to make sure any other waiting threads are not forgotten. This is why the compare-and-exchange operation is not part of the while loop in our lock function.

This does mean that for every time a thread had to wait() while locking, it will also call wake_one() when unlocking, even when that's not necessary. However, what's most important is that in the *uncontended case*, the ideal situation where threads are not attempting to acquire the lock simultaneously, both the wait() and wake_one() calls are entirely avoided.

Figure 9-1 visualizes the operations and happens-before relationships in a situation where two threads concurrently attempt to lock our Mutex. The first thread locks the mutex by changing the state from 0 to 1. At that point, the second thread will not be able to acquire the lock and therefore goes to sleep after changing the state from 1 to 2. When the first thread unlocks the Mutex, it swaps the state back to 0. Because it was 2, indicating a waiting thread, it calls wake_one() to wake up the second thread. Note how we do not depend on any happens-before relationship between the wake and wait operations. While it's likely that the wake operation is the one responsible for waking up the waiting thread, the happens-before relationship is established through the acquire swap operation observing the value stored by the release swap operation.

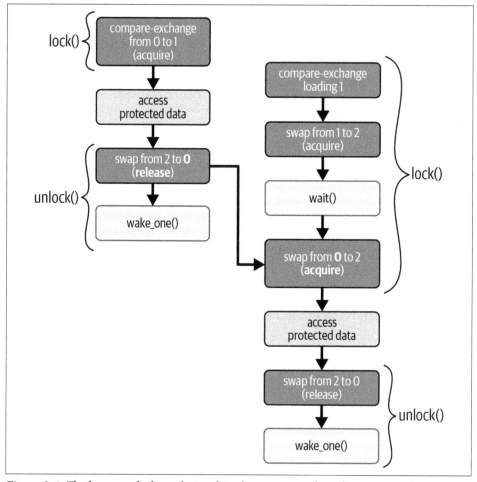

Figure 9-1. The happens-before relationships between two threads concurrently attempting to lock our Mutex

Optimizing Further

At this point, it might seem like there's not much else we could optimize further. In the uncontended case, we perform zero syscalls, and all that's left are just two very simple atomic operations.

The only way to avoid the wait and wake operations is to go back to our spin lock implementation. While spinning is usually very inefficient, it at least does avoid the potential overhead of a syscall. The only situation where spinning can be more efficient is when waiting for only a very short time.

For locking a mutex, that happens only in situations where the thread that currently holds the lock is running in parallel on a different processor core and will keep the lock only very briefly. This is, however, a very common case.

We can try to combine the best of both approaches by spinning for a very short amount of time before resorting to calling wait(). That way, if the lock is released very quickly, we don't need to call wait() at all, but we still avoid consuming an unreasonable amount of processor time that other threads could make better use of.

Implementing this only requires changes to our lock function.

To keep things as performant as possible in the uncontended case, we'll keep the original compare-and-exchange operation at the start of the lock function. We'll leave spinning waiting to a separate function.

```
impl<T> Mutex<T> {
    …

    pub fn lock(&self) -> MutexGuard<T> {
        if self.state.compare_exchange(0, 1, Acquire, Relaxed).is_err() {
            // The lock was already locked. :(
            lock_contended(&self.state);
        }
        MutexGuard { mutex: self }
    }
}

fn lock_contended(state: &AtomicU32) {
    …
}
```

In lock_contended, we could simply repeat the same compare-and-exchange operation a few hundred times before continuing to the wait loop. However, a compare-and-exchange operation generally attempts to get exclusive access to the relevant cache line (see "The MESI protocol" on page 143), which can be more expensive than a simple load operation when executed repeatedly.

With that in mind, we come to the following lock_contended implementation:

```
fn lock_contended(state: &AtomicU32) {
    let mut spin_count = 0;

    while state.load(Relaxed) == 1 && spin_count < 100 {
        spin_count += 1;
        std::hint::spin_loop();
```

```
        }

        if state.compare_exchange(0, 1, Acquire, Relaxed).is_ok() {
            return;
        }

        while state.swap(2, Acquire) != 0 {
            wait(state, 2);
        }
    }
```

First, we spin up to 100 times, making use of a *spin loop hint* like we did in Chapter 4. We only spin as long as the mutex is locked and has no waiters. If another thread is already waiting, it means it gave up spinning because it took too long, which can be an indication that spinning will likely not be very useful for this thread either.

 The spin duration of a hundred cycles is chosen mostly arbitrarily. The time an iteration takes and the duration of a syscall (which we're trying to avoid) depend heavily on the platform. Extensive benchmarking can help with choosing the right number, but unfortunately there's not a single correct answer.

The Linux implementation of std::sync::Mutex in the Rust standard library, at least the one in Rust 1.66.0, uses a spin count of 100.

After the lock state has changed, we try once more to lock it by setting it to 1, before we give up and start waiting. As we discussed before, after we call wait() we can no longer lock the mutex by setting its state to 1, since that might result in other waiters being forgotten.

Cold and Inline Attributes

You could add the #[cold] attribute to the lock_contended function definition to help the compiler understand that this function is not called in the common (uncontended) case, which can help with optimizations for the lock method.

Additionally, you could add the #[inline] attribute to the Mutex and MutexGuard methods to inform the compiler that it might be a good idea to *inline* them: to put the resulting instructions directly at the place where the method is called. Whether that increases performance is hard to say in general, but for very small functions like these, it usually does.

Benchmarking

Testing the performance of a mutex implementation is hard. It's easy to write a benchmark test and get some numbers, but it's very hard to get any meaningful numbers.

Optimizing a mutex implementation to perform very well in a specific benchmark test is relatively easy, but not very useful. After all, the point is to make something that performs well in real-world programs, not just in test programs.

We'll attempt to write two simple benchmark tests showing that our optimizations at least had some positive effect on some use cases, but keep in mind that any conclusions won't necessarily hold up in different scenarios.

For our first test, we'll create a `Mutex` and lock and unlock it a few million times, all on the same thread, measuring the total time it takes. This is a test for the trivial uncontended scenario, where there are never any threads that need to be woken up. Hopefully, this will show us a significant difference between our 2-state and 3-state versions.

```
fn main() {
    let m = Mutex::new(0);
    std::hint::black_box(&m);
    let start = Instant::now();
    for _ in 0..5_000_000 {
        *m.lock() += 1;
    }
    let duration = start.elapsed();
    println!("locked {} times in {:?}", *m.lock(), duration);
}
```

 We use `std::hint::black_box` (like we did in "Impact on Performance" on page 144) to force the compiler to assume there might be more code that accesses the mutex, preventing it from optimizing away the loop or locking operations.

Results will vary heavily depending on hardware and operating system. Trying this on one particular Linux computer with a recent AMD processor results in a total time of about 400 milliseconds for our unoptimized 2-state mutex, and about 40 milliseconds for our more optimized 3-state mutex. A factor ten improvement! On another Linux computer with an older Intel processor, the difference is even bigger: about 1800 milliseconds versus 60 milliseconds. This confirms that the addition of the third state can indeed be a very significant optimization.

Running this on a computer that runs macOS, however, produces completely different results: about 50 milliseconds for both versions, showing that it's all highly platform-dependent.

As it turns out, the implementation of libc++'s `std::atomic<T>::wake()`, which we use on macOS, already performs its own bookkeeping, independent from the kernel, to avoid unnecessary syscalls. The same holds for `WakeByAddressSingle()` on Windows.

Avoiding a call to those functions can still result in slightly better performance, since their implementation is far from trivial, especially because they can't store any information in the atomic variable itself. However, if we'd only be targeting only these operating systems, we should question whether adding a third state to our mutex was really worth the effort.

To see if our spinning optimization made any positive difference, we need a different benchmark test: one with lots of contention, with multiple threads repeatedly trying to lock an already locked mutex.

Let's try a scenario where four threads all concurrently attempt to lock and unlock the mutex a few million times:

```
fn main() {
    let m = Mutex::new(0);
    std::hint::black_box(&m);
    let start = Instant::now();
    thread::scope(|s| {
        for _ in 0..4 {
            s.spawn(|| {
                for _ in 0..5_000_000 {
                    *m.lock() += 1;
                }
            });
        }
    });
    let duration = start.elapsed();
    println!("locked {} times in {:?}", *m.lock(), duration);
}
```

Note that this is an extreme and unrealistic scenario. The mutex is only kept for an extremely short time (only to increment an integer), and the threads will immediately attempt to lock the mutex again after unlocking. A different scenario will most likely result in very different results.

Let's run this benchmark on the same two Linux computers as before. On the one with the older Intel processor, this results in about 900 milliseconds for the version of our mutex that doesn't spin, and about 750 milliseconds when using the spinning version. An improvement! On the computer with the newer AMD processor, however, we get opposite results: about 650 milliseconds without spinning and about 800 milliseconds with.

In conclusion, the answer as to whether spinning actually increases performance is, unfortunately, "it depends," even when looking at just one scenario.

Condition Variable

Let's move on to something more fun: implementing a condition variable.

As we saw in "Condition Variables" on page 26, a condition variable is used together with a mutex to wait until the mutex-protected data matches some condition. It has a wait method that unlocks a mutex, waits for a signal, and locks the same mutex again. Signals are sent by other threads, usually right after modifying the mutex-protected data, to either one waiting thread (often called "notify one" or "signal") or all waiting threads (often called "notify all" or "broadcast").

While a condition variable attempts to keep a waiting thread asleep until it is signalled, it is possible for a waiting thread to be woken up spuriously, without a corresponding signal. The condition variable's wait operation will still relock the mutex before returning, though.

Notice how this interface is nearly identical to our futex-like wait(), wake_one(), and wake_all() functions. The main difference is the mechanism used to prevent lost signals. A condition variable will start "listening" to signals before unlocking the mutex to not miss any signals right after, while our futex-style wait() function relies on a check of the state of the atomic variable to make sure waiting is still a good idea.

This leads to the following minimal implementation idea for a condition variable: if we make sure that every notification changes an atomic variable (like a counter), then all our Condvar::wait() method needs to do is check the value of that variable before unlocking the mutex, and pass it to the futex-style wait() function after unlocking it. That way, it will not go to sleep if any notification signal arrived since unlocking the mutex.

Let's try that out!

We start with a Condvar struct that just contains a single AtomicU32, which we initialize at zero:

```
pub struct Condvar {
    counter: AtomicU32,
}

impl Condvar {
    pub const fn new() -> Self {
        Self { counter: AtomicU32::new(0) }
    }

    ...
}
```

The notify methods are simple. They just need to change the counter and use the corresponding wake operation to notify any waiting thread(s):

```
pub fn notify_one(&self) {
    self.counter.fetch_add(1, Relaxed);
    wake_one(&self.counter);
}

pub fn notify_all(&self) {
    self.counter.fetch_add(1, Relaxed);
    wake_all(&self.counter);
}
```

(We'll discuss the memory ordering in a moment.)

The wait method will take a MutexGuard, since that represents proof of a locked mutex. It will also return a MutexGuard, since it'll make sure the mutex is locked again before returning.

As we sketched out above, the method will first check the current value of the counter before unlocking the mutex. After unlocking the mutex, it should only wait if the counter hasn't changed, to make sure we didn't miss any signals. Here's what that looks like as code:

```
pub fn wait<'a, T>(&self, guard: MutexGuard<'a, T>) -> MutexGuard<'a, T> {
    let counter_value = self.counter.load(Relaxed);

    // Unlock the mutex by dropping the guard,
    // but remember the mutex so we can lock it again later.
    let mutex = guard.mutex;
    drop(guard);

    // Wait, but only if the counter hasn't changed since unlocking.
    wait(&self.counter, counter_value);

    mutex.lock()
}
```

 This makes use of the private mutex field of the MutexGuard. Privacy in Rust is based on modules, so if you're defining this in a different module than the MutexGuard, you'll need to mark the mutex field of the MutexGuard as, for example, pub(crate) to make it available to other modules in the crate.

Before we celebrate our success in finishing our condition variable, let's think for a second about memory ordering.

While the mutex is locked, no other thread can change the mutex-protected data. Therefore, we don't need to worry about notifications from before we unlock the mutex, since, as long as we hold the mutex locked, nothing can happen to the data that would make us change our mind about wanting to go to sleep and wait.

The only situation we're interested in is when, after we release the mutex, another thread comes along and locks the mutex, changes the protected data, and signals us (hopefully after unlocking the mutex).

In this situation, there's a happens-before relationship between unlocking the mutex in `Condvar::wait()` and locking the mutex in the notifying thread. This happens-before relationship is what guarantees that our relaxed load, which happens before unlocking, will observe the value *before* the notification's relaxed increment operation, which happens after locking.

We don't know whether the `wait()` operation will see the value before or after incrementing, since there's nothing that guarantees any ordering at that point. However, that doesn't matter, since `wait()` behaves atomically with respect to corresponding wake operations. Either it sees the new value, in which case it does not go to sleep at all, or it sees the old value, in which case it goes to sleep and will be woken up by the corresponding `wake_one()` or `wake_all()` call from the notification.

Figure 9-2 shows the operations and happens-before relationships for a situation in which one thread uses `Condvar::wait()` to wait for some mutex-protected data to change and gets woken up by a second thread that modifies the data and calls `Condvar::wake_one()`. Note how the first load operation is guaranteed to observe the value before it gets incremented, thanks to the unlock and lock operations.

We should also consider what happens if the counter overflows.

The actual value of the counter doesn't matter as long as it is different after each notification. Unfortunately, after a bit more than four billion notifications, the counter will overflow and restart at zero, going back to values that have been used before. Technically, it is possible for our `Condvar::wait()` implementation to go to sleep when it shouldn't: if it misses exactly 4,294,967,296 notifications (or any multiple of that), it will overflow the counter all the way around to the value it had before.

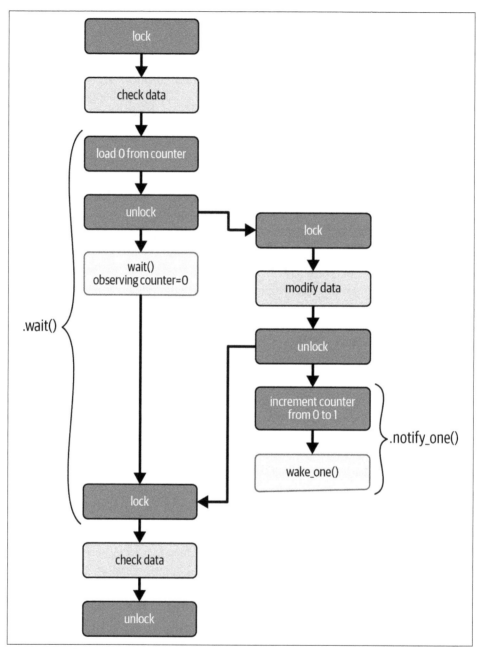

Figure 9-2. The operations and happens-before relationships of one thead using `Con` `dvar::wait()` that's woken up by another thread using `Condvar::notify_one()`

It's entirely reasonable to consider the chance of that happening to be negligible. In contrtast to what we did in our mutex locking method, we don't recheck the state and repeat the `wait()` call after waking up here, so we only need to worry about an overflow round-trip happening in the moment between the relaxed load of the counter and the `wait()` call. If a thread can be interrupted for so long that it allows for (exactly) that many notifications to happen, something has probably already gone terribly wrong, and the program has already turned unresponsive. At that point, one might reasonably argue, a microscopic additional risk of a thread staying asleep no longer matters.

 On platforms that support futex-style waiting with a time limit, the risk of overflowing can be mitigated by using a timeout for the wait operation of a few seconds. Sending four billion notifications will take significantly longer, at which point the risk of a few additional seconds will have very little impact. This completely removes any risk of the program locking up due to a waiting thread wrongly staying asleep forever.

Let's see if it works!

```rust
#[test]
fn test_condvar() {
    let mutex = Mutex::new(0);
    let condvar = Condvar::new();

    let mut wakeups = 0;

    thread::scope(|s| {
        s.spawn(|| {
            thread::sleep(Duration::from_secs(1));
            *mutex.lock() = 123;
            condvar.notify_one();
        });

        let mut m = mutex.lock();
        while *m < 100 {
            m = condvar.wait(m);
            wakeups += 1;
        }

        assert_eq!(*m, 123);
    });

    // Check that the main thread actually did wait (not busy-loop),
    // while still allowing for a few spurious wake ups.
    assert!(wakeups < 10);
}
```

We count the number of times the condition variable returns from its wait method, to make sure it actually goes to sleep. If that number would be very high, it would indicate that we are accidentally spin-looping instead. It's important to test this, since a condition variable that never sleeps still results in "correct" behavior, but would effectively turn the waiting loop into a spin loop.

If we run this test, we see that it compiles and passes just fine, confirming that our condition variable did actually put the main thread to sleep. Of course, this doesn't prove that its implementation is correct. A long stress test that involves many threads, ideally run on a computer with a weakly ordered processor architecture, can be used to gain more confidence if necessary.

Avoiding Syscalls

As we realized in "Avoiding Syscalls" on page 186, optimizing a locking primitive is mainly about avoiding unnecessary wait and wake operations.

In the case of our condition variable, there is not much use in trying to avoid the wait() call in our Condvar::wait() implementation. By the time a thread decides to wait on a condition variable, it has already checked that the thing it's waiting for hasn't happened yet, and it needs to go to sleep. If the wait wasn't necessary, it wouldn't have called Condvar::wait() at all.

We can, however, avoid the wake_one() and wake_all() calls if there are no waiting threads, similar to what we did for our Mutex.

A simple way to do this is to keep track of the number of waiting threads. Our wait method will need to increment it before waiting, and decrement it when it's done. Then our notify methods can skip sending their signal if that number is zero.

So, we add a new field to our Condvar struct to track the number of active waiters:

```
pub struct Condvar {
    counter: AtomicU32,
    num_waiters: AtomicUsize, // New!
}

impl Condvar {
    pub const fn new() -> Self {
        Self {
            counter: AtomicU32::new(0),
            num_waiters: AtomicUsize::new(0), // New!
        }
    }

    …
}
```

By using an AtomicUsize for num_waiters, we don't have to worry about it overflowing. A usize is big enough to count every byte in memory, so if we assume that every active thread takes up at least a single byte of memory, it's definitely big enough to count any number of concurrently existing threads.

Next, we update our notification functions to not do anything if there are no waiters:

```
pub fn notify_one(&self) {
    if self.num_waiters.load(Relaxed) > 0 { // New!
        self.counter.fetch_add(1, Relaxed);
        wake_one(&self.counter);
    }
}

pub fn notify_all(&self) {
    if self.num_waiters.load(Relaxed) > 0 { // New!
        self.counter.fetch_add(1, Relaxed);
        wake_all(&self.counter);
    }
}
```

(We'll discuss the memory ordering in a moment.)

And finally, most importantly, we increment it at the start of our wait method and decrement as soon as it wakes up:

```
pub fn wait<'a, T>(&self, guard: MutexGuard<'a, T>) -> MutexGuard<'a, T> {
    self.num_waiters.fetch_add(1, Relaxed); // New!

    let counter_value = self.counter.load(Relaxed);

    let mutex = guard.mutex;
    drop(guard);

    wait(&self.counter, counter_value);

    self.num_waiters.fetch_sub(1, Relaxed); // New!

    mutex.lock()
}
```

We should again ask ourselves carefully if relaxed memory ordering is enough for all these atomic operations.

A new potential risk we've introduced, is one of the notify methods observing a zero in num_waiters, skipping its wake operation, while there was actually a thread to wake up. This can happen when a notify method observes the value either before the increment operation or after the decrement operation.

Just as with the relaxed load from the counter, the fact that the waiter still holds the mutex locked while incrementing num_waiters makes sure that any load of num_waiters that happens after unlocking the mutex will not see a value from before it was incremented.

We also don't need to worry about the notifying thread observing the decremented value "too soon," because once the decrementing operation is executed, perhaps after a spurious wake-up, the waiting thread no longer needs to be woken up anyway.

In other words, the happens-before relationship that the mutex establishes still provides all the guarantees we need.

Avoiding Spurious Wake-ups

Another way in which we could optimize our condition variable is by avoiding spuriously waking up. Every time a thread is woken up, it'll try to lock the mutex, potentially competing with other threads, which can have a big impact on performance.

It's quite uncommon for the underlying wait() operation to spuriously wake up, but our condition variable implementation easily allows for notify_one() to cause more than one thread to stop waiting. If a thread is in the process of going to sleep, has just loaded the counter value, but hasn't gone to sleep yet, a call to notify_one() will prevent that thread from going to sleep due to the updated counter, but it'll also cause a second thread to wake up because of the wake_one() operation that follows. Both of those threads will then compete to lock the mutex, wasting valuable processor time.

This might sound like a rarely occurring situation, but this can actually happen quite easily, due to how the mutex ends up synchronizing the threads. A thread that will call notify_one() on the condition variable will most likely lock and unlock the mutex right before, to change something about the data that the waiting thread is waiting for. This means that as soon as the Condvar::wait() method unlocks the mutex, that might immediately unblock a notifying thread that was waiting for the mutex. At that point the two threads are racing: the waiting thread to go to sleep, and the notifying thread to lock and unlock the mutex and notify the condition variable. If the notifying thread wins that race, the waiting thread will not go to sleep because of the incremented counter, but the notifying thread will still call wake_one(). This is exactly the problematic situation described above, where it might unnecessarily wake up an extra waiting thread.

A relatively straightforward solution would be to keep track of the number of threads that are allowed to wake up (that is, return from Condvar::wait()). The notify_one method would increase it by one, and the wait method would attempt to decrease it by one if it's not zero. If the counter is at zero, it could go (back) to sleep, instead of attempting to relock the mutex and returning. (Notifying all threads could be done by adding another counter specifically for notify_all that is never decremented.)

This approach works, but comes with a new and more subtle issue: a notification might wake up a thread that hasn't even called `Condvar::wait()` yet, including itself. A call to `Condvar::notify_one()` would increment the number of threads that should be woken up and use `wake_one()` to wake up one waiting thread. Then, if another (or even the same) thread calls `Condvar::wait()` afterwards, before the thread that was already waiting has a chance to wake up, the newly waiting thread could see that there's one notification pending and claim it by decrementing the counter to zero, returning immediately. The first thread that was waiting would then go back to sleep, since another thread already took the notification.

Depending on the use case, this might be perfectly fine, or it might be a big problem, causing some threads to never make progress.

GNU libc's `pthread_cond_t` implementation used to suffer from this issue. After much discussion on whether or not this was allowed by the POSIX specification, the issue was eventually resolved with the release of GNU libc 2.25 in 2017, which included a completely new condition variable implementation.

In many situations where a condition variable is used, it's perfectly fine for a waiter to snatch away an earlier notification. However, when implementing a condition variable for general use rather than a specific kind of use case, this behavior might be unacceptable.

Again, we must come to the conclusion that the answer to whether we should use an optimized aproach is, unsurprisingly, "it depends."

There are ways to avoid this problem while still avoiding spurious wake-ups, but those are significantly more complicated than other approaches.

The solution used by GNU libc's new condition variable involves categorizing waiters into two groups, only allowing the first group to consume notifications and swapping the groups around when the first one has no waiters left.

A downside of this approach is not only the complexity of the algorithm, but also that it significantly increases the size of the condition variable type, since it now needs to keep track of much more information.

Thundering Herd Problem

Another performance problem that one might encounter when using a condition variable occurs when using `notify_all()` to wake up many threads waiting for the same thing.

The problem is that, after waking up, all those threads will immediately try to lock the same mutex. Most likely, only one thread will succeed, and all the others will have to go back to sleep. This resource-wasting problem of many threads all rushing to claim the same resource is referred to as the *thundering herd problem*.

It's not unreasonable to argue that `Condvar::notify_all()` is fundamentally an anti-pattern not worth optimizing for. A condition variable's purpose is to unlock a mutex and relock it when notified, so perhaps notifying more than one thread at once will never lead to anything good.

Even so, if we want to optimize for this situation, we can do so on operating systems that support a futex-like *requeuing* operation, like `FUTEX_REQUEUE` on Linux. (See "Futex Operations" on page 169.)

Instead of waking up many threads of which all but one will immediately go back to sleep once they realize the lock has already been taken, we can *requeue* all but one thread such that their futex wait operations no longer wait for the condition variable's counter, but start waiting for the mutex state instead.

Requeueing a waiting thread doesn't wake it up. In fact, the thread won't even know that it has been requeued. Unfortunately, this can lead to some very subtle pitfalls.

For example, remember how a three-state mutex always must be locked to the right state ("locked with waiters") after waking up, to make sure other waiters aren't forgotten about? This means we should no longer use the regular mutex lock method in our `Condvar::wait()` implementation, which might set the mutex to the wrong state.

A requeueing condition variable implementation would need to store a pointer to the mutex used by the waiting threads. Otherwise, the notify methods wouldn't know which atomic variable (the mutex state) to requeue the waiting threads to. This is why a condition variable generally does not allow two threads to wait for different mutexes. Even though many condition variable implementations do not make use of requeueing, it can be useful to keep open the possibility for a future version to do so.

Reader-Writer Lock

It's time to implement a reader-writer lock!

Recall how, unlike a mutex, a reader-writer lock supports two types of locking: read-locking and write-locking, sometimes called shared locking and exclusive locking. Write-locking behaves identically to locking a mutex, only allowing one lock at a time, while read-locking allows for multiple readers to hold a lock at once. In other words, it closely matches how exclusive references (&mut T) and shared references (&T) work in Rust, allowing only one exclusive reference, or any number of shared references, to be active at the same time.

For our mutex, we needed to track only whether it was locked or not. For our reader-writer lock, however, we also need to know how many (reader) locks are currently held, to make sure write-locking only happens after all readers have released their locks.

Let's start with a RwLock struct that uses a single AtomicU32 as its state. We'll use it to represent the number of currently acquired read locks, such that a value of zero means it's unlocked. To represent the write-locked state, let's use a special value of u32::MAX.

```
pub struct RwLock<T> {
    /// The number of readers, or u32::MAX if write-locked.
    state: AtomicU32,
    value: UnsafeCell<T>,
}
```

For our Mutex<T>, we had to restrict its Sync implementation to types T that implement Send, to make sure it can't be used to send, for example, an Rc to another thread. For our new RwLock<T>, we additionally need to require that T also implements Sync, because multiple readers will be able to access the data at once:

```
unsafe impl<T> Sync for RwLock<T> where T: Send + Sync {}
```

Because our RwLock can be locked in two different ways, we'll have two separate lock functions, each with its own type of guard:

```
impl<T> RwLock<T> {
    pub const fn new(value: T) -> Self {
        Self {
            state: AtomicU32::new(0), // Unlocked.
            value: UnsafeCell::new(value),
        }
    }

    pub fn read(&self) -> ReadGuard<T> {
        ...
    }
```

```
        pub fn write(&self) -> WriteGuard<T> {
            …
        }
    }

    pub struct ReadGuard<'a, T> {
        rwlock: &'a RwLock<T>,
    }

    pub struct WriteGuard<'a, T> {
        rwlock: &'a RwLock<T>,
    }
```

The write guard should behave like an exclusive reference (&mut T), which we do by implementing both Deref and DerefMut for it:

```
    impl<T> Deref for WriteGuard<'_, T> {
        type Target = T;
        fn deref(&self) -> &T {
            unsafe { &*self.rwlock.value.get() }
        }
    }

    impl<T> DerefMut for WriteGuard<'_, T> {
        fn deref_mut(&mut self) -> &mut T {
            unsafe { &mut *self.rwlock.value.get() }
        }
    }
```

However, the read guard should only implement Deref, not DerefMut, because it doesn't have exclusive access to the data, making it behave like a shared reference (&T):

```
    impl<T> Deref for ReadGuard<'_, T> {
        type Target = T;
        fn deref(&self) -> &T {
            unsafe { &*self.rwlock.value.get() }
        }
    }
```

Now that we got all that boilerplate code out of the way, let's get to the interesting parts: locking and unlocking.

To read-lock our RwLock, we must increment the state by one, but only if it wasn't already write-locked. We'll use a compare-and-exchange loop ("Compare-and-Exchange Operations" on page 42) to do so. In case the state is u32::MAX, meaning the RwLock is write-locked, we'll use a wait() operation to sleep and retry later.

```
pub fn read(&self) -> ReadGuard<T> {
    let mut s = self.state.load(Relaxed);
    loop {
        if s < u32::MAX {
            assert!(s != u32::MAX - 1, "too many readers");
            match self.state.compare_exchange_weak(
                s, s + 1, Acquire, Relaxed
            ) {
                Ok(_) => return ReadGuard { rwlock: self },
                Err(e) => s = e,
            }
        }
        if s == u32::MAX {
            wait(&self.state, u32::MAX);
            s = self.state.load(Relaxed);
        }
    }
}
```

Write-locking is easier; we just need to change the state from zero to u32::MAX, or wait() if it was already locked:

```
pub fn write(&self) -> WriteGuard<T> {
    while let Err(s) = self.state.compare_exchange(
        0, u32::MAX, Acquire, Relaxed
    ) {
        // Wait while already locked.
        wait(&self.state, s);
    }
    WriteGuard { rwlock: self }
}
```

Note how the exact state value of a locked RwLock varies, but the wait() operation expects us to give it an exact value to compare the state with. This is why we use the return value from the compare-and-exchange operation for the wait() operation.

Unlocking a reader involves decrementing the state by one. The reader that ends up unlocking the RwLock, the one that changes the state from one to zero, is responsible for waking up a waiting writer, if any.

Waking up just one thread is enough, because we know there cannot be any waiting readers at this point. There would simply be no reason for a reader to be waiting on a read-locked RwLock.

```
impl<T> Drop for ReadGuard<'_, T> {
    fn drop(&mut self) {
        if self.rwlock.state.fetch_sub(1, Release) == 1 {
            // Wake up a waiting writer, if any.
            wake_one(&self.rwlock.state);
        }
    }
}
```

A writer must reset the state to zero to unlock, after which it should wake either one waiting writer or all waiting readers.

We don't know whether readers or writers are waiting, nor do we have a way to wake up only a writer or only the readers. So, we'll just wake all threads:

```
impl<T> Drop for WriteGuard<'_, T> {
    fn drop(&mut self) {
        self.rwlock.state.store(0, Release);
        // Wake up all waiting readers and writers.
        wake_all(&self.rwlock.state);
    }
}
```

And that's it! We've built a very simple but perfectly usable reader-writer lock.

Time to fix some issues.

Avoiding Busy-Looping Writers

One issue with our implementation is that write-locking might result in an accidental busy-loop.

If we have an RwLock with a lot of readers repeatedly locking and unlocking it, the lock state might be continuously in flux, rapidly going up and down. For our write method, this results in a high chance of the lock state changing between the compare-and-exchange operation and the subsequent wait() operation, especially if the wait() operation is directly implemented as a (relatively slow) syscall. This means that the wait() operation will often return immediately, even though the lock was never unlocked; it just had a different number of readers than expected.

A solution can be to use a different AtomicU32 for the writers to wait on, and only change the value of that atomic when we actually want to wake up a writer.

Let's try that, by adding a new writer_wake_counter field to our RwLock:

```
pub struct RwLock<T> {
    /// The number of readers, or u32::MAX if write-locked.
    state: AtomicU32,
    /// Incremented to wake up writers.
    writer_wake_counter: AtomicU32, // New!
    value: UnsafeCell<T>,
}

impl<T> RwLock<T> {
    pub const fn new(value: T) -> Self {
        Self {
            state: AtomicU32::new(0),
            writer_wake_counter: AtomicU32::new(0), // New!
            value: UnsafeCell::new(value),
        }
    }

    …
}
```

The `read` method remains unchanged, but the `write` method now needs to wait for the new atomic variable instead. To make sure we don't miss any notifications between seeing that the RwLock is read-locked and actually going to sleep, we'll use a pattern similar to the one we used for implementing our condition variable: check the `writer_wake_counter` before checking if we still want to sleep:

```
pub fn write(&self) -> WriteGuard<T> {
    while self.state.compare_exchange(
        0, u32::MAX, Acquire, Relaxed
    ).is_err() {
        let w = self.writer_wake_counter.load(Acquire);
        if self.state.load(Relaxed) != 0 {
            // Wait if the RwLock is still locked, but only if
            // there have been no wake signals since we checked.
            wait(&self.writer_wake_counter, w);
        }
    }
    WriteGuard { rwlock: self }
}
```

The acquire-load operation of `writer_wake_counter` will form a happens-before relationship with a release-increment operation that's executed right after unlocking the state, before waking up a waiting writer:

```
impl<T> Drop for ReadGuard<'_, T> {
    fn drop(&mut self) {
        if self.rwlock.state.fetch_sub(1, Release) == 1 {
            self.rwlock.writer_wake_counter.fetch_add(1, Release); // New!
            wake_one(&self.rwlock.writer_wake_counter); // Changed!
        }
    }
}
```

The happens-before relationship makes sure that the `write` method cannot observe the incremented `writer_wake_counter` value while still seeing the not-yet-decremented `state` value afterwards. Otherwise, the write-locking thread might conclude the RwLock is still locked while having missed the wake-up call.

As before, write-unlocking should wake either one waiting writer or all waiting readers. Since we still don't know whether there are writers or readers waiting, we have to wake both one waiting writer (through `wake_one`) and all waiting readers (using `wake_all`):

```
impl<T> Drop for WriteGuard<'_, T> {
    fn drop(&mut self) {
        self.rwlock.state.store(0, Release);
        self.rwlock.writer_wake_counter.fetch_add(1, Release); // New!
        wake_one(&self.rwlock.writer_wake_counter); // New!
        wake_all(&self.rwlock.state);
    }
}
```

On some operating systems, the operation behind the wake operations returns the number of threads it woke up. It might indicate a lower number than the actual number of awoken threads (due to spuriously awoken threads), but its return value can still be useful as an optimization.

In the drop implementation above, for example, we could skip the `wake_all()` call if the `wake_one()` operation would indicate it actually woke up a thread.

Avoiding Writer Starvation

A common use case for an RwLock is a situation with many frequent readers, but very few, often only one, infrequent writer. For example, one thread might be responsible for reading out some sensor input or periodically downloading some new data that many other threads need to use.

In such a situation, we can quickly run into an issue called *writer starvation*: a situation where the writer(s) never get a chance to lock the RwLock because there are always readers around to keep the RwLock read-locked.

One solution to this problem is to prevent any new readers from acquiring a lock when there is a writer waiting, even when the RwLock is still read-locked. That way, all new readers will have to wait until the writer has had its turn, making sure that readers will get access to the latest data that the writer wanted to share.

Let's implement this.

To do this, we need to keep track of whether there are any waiting writers. To make space for this information in the state variable, we can multiply the reader count by 2, and add 1 for situations where there is a writer waiting. This means that a state of 6 or 7 both represent a situation with three active read locks: 6 without a waiting writer, and 7 with a waiting writer.

If we keep u32::MAX, which is an odd number, as the write-locked state, then readers will have to wait if the state is odd, but are free to acquire a read lock by incrementing it by two if the state is even.

```
pub struct RwLock<T> {
    /// The number of read locks times two, plus one if there's a writer waiting.
    /// u32::MAX if write locked.
    ///
    /// This means that readers may acquire the lock when
    /// the state is even, but need to block when odd.
    state: AtomicU32,
    /// Incremented to wake up writers.
    writer_wake_counter: AtomicU32,
    value: UnsafeCell<T>,
}
```

We'll have to change the two if statements in our read method to no longer compare the state against u32::MAX, but instead check whether the state is even or odd. We also need to change the upper bound in the assert statement and make sure we lock by incrementing by two instead of one.

```
pub fn read(&self) -> ReadGuard<T> {
    let mut s = self.state.load(Relaxed);
    loop {
        if s % 2 == 0 { // Even.
            assert!(s != u32::MAX - 2, "too many readers");
            match self.state.compare_exchange_weak(
                s, s + 2, Acquire, Relaxed
            ) {
                Ok(_) => return ReadGuard { rwlock: self },
                Err(e) => s = e,
            }
        }
        if s % 2 == 1 { // Odd.
            wait(&self.state, s);
            s = self.state.load(Relaxed);
        }
    }
}
```

Our write method has to undergo bigger changes. We'll use a compare-and-exchange loop, just like our read method above. If the state is 0 or 1, which means the RwLock is unlocked, we'll attempt to change the state to u32::MAX to write-lock it. Otherwise, we'll have to wait. Before doing so, however, we need to make sure the state is odd, to stop new readers from acquiring the lock. After making sure the state is odd, we wait for the `writer_wake_counter` variable, while making sure that the lock hasn't been unlocked in the meantime.

In code, that looks like this:

```
pub fn write(&self) -> WriteGuard<T> {
    let mut s = self.state.load(Relaxed);
    loop {
        // Try to lock if unlocked.
        if s <= 1 {
            match self.state.compare_exchange(
                s, u32::MAX, Acquire, Relaxed
            ) {
                Ok(_) => return WriteGuard { rwlock: self },
                Err(e) => { s = e; continue; }
            }
        }
        // Block new readers, by making sure the state is odd.
        if s % 2 == 0 {
            match self.state.compare_exchange(
                s, s + 1, Relaxed, Relaxed
            ) {
                Ok(_) => {}
                Err(e) => { s = e; continue; }
            }
        }
        // Wait, if it's still locked
        let w = self.writer_wake_counter.load(Acquire);
        s = self.state.load(Relaxed);
        if s >= 2 {
            wait(&self.writer_wake_counter, w);
            s = self.state.load(Relaxed);
        }
    }
}
```

Since we now track whether there are any waiting writers, read-unlocking can now skip the wake_one() call when unnecessary:

```
impl<T> Drop for ReadGuard<'_, T> {
    fn drop(&mut self) {
        // Decrement the state by 2 to remove one read-lock.
        if self.rwlock.state.fetch_sub(2, Release) == 3 {
            // If we decremented from 3 to 1, that means
            // the RwLock is now unlocked _and_ there is
            // a waiting writer, which we wake up.
            self.rwlock.writer_wake_counter.fetch_add(1, Release);
            wake_one(&self.rwlock.writer_wake_counter);
        }
    }
}
```

While write-locked (a state of u32::MAX), we do not track any information on whether any thread is waiting. So, we have no new information to use for write-unlocking, which will remain identical:

```
impl<T> Drop for WriteGuard<'_, T> {
    fn drop(&mut self) {
        self.rwlock.state.store(0, Release);
        self.rwlock.writer_wake_counter.fetch_add(1, Release);
        wake_one(&self.rwlock.writer_wake_counter);
        wake_all(&self.rwlock.state);
    }
}
```

For a reader-writer lock that's optimized for the "frequent reading and infrequent writing" use case, this would be quite acceptable, since write-locking (and therefore write-unlocking) happens infrequently.

For a more general purpose reader-writer lock, however, it is definitely worth optimizing further, to bring the performance of write-locking and -unlocking near the performance of an efficient 3-state mutex. This is left as a fun exercise for the reader.

Summary

- The atomic-wait crate provides basic futex-like functionality that works on (recent versions of) all major operating systems.

- A minimal mutex implementation only needs two states, like our SpinLock from Chapter 4.

- A more efficient mutex tracks whether there are any waiting threads, so it can avoid an unnecessary wake operation.

- Spinning before going to sleep might in some cases be beneficial, but it depends heavily on the situation, operating system, and hardware.

- A minimal condition variable only needs a notification counter, which Condvar::wait will have to check both before and after unlocking the mutex.

- A condition variable could track the number of waiting threads to avoid unnecessary wake operations.

- Avoiding spuriously waking up from Condvar::wait can be tricky, requiring extra bookkeeping.

- A minimal reader-writer lock requires only an atomic counter as its state.

- An additional atomic variable can be used to wake writers independently from readers.

- To avoid writer starvation, extra state is required to prioritize a waiting writer over new readers.

CHAPTER 10

Ideas and Inspiration

There are an infinite number of concurrency related topics, algorithms, data structures, anecdotes, and other potential chapters that could be part of this book. However, we've arrived at the final chapter and it's almost time for us to part ways, hopefully leaving you with an excited feeling of new possibilities and ready to apply new knowledge and skills in practice.

This final chapter's purpose is to provide inspiration for your own creations and future work by showing you some ideas that you can study, explore, and build on your own.

Semaphore

A *semaphore* is effectively just a counter with two operations: *signal* (also called *up* or *V*) and *wait* (also called *down* or *P*). The signal operation increments the counter up to a certain maximum, while a wait operation decrements the counter. If the counter is zero, a wait operation will block and wait for a matching signal operation, preventing the counter from ever becoming negative. It is a flexible tool that can be used to implement other synchronization primitives.

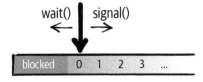

A semaphore can be implemented as a combination of a Mutex<u32> for the counter and a Condvar for wait operations to wait for. However, there are several ways to implement it more efficiently. Most notably, on platforms that support futex-like operations ("Futex" on page 167), it can be implemented more efficiently as a single AtomicU32 (or even AtomicU8).

A semaphore with a maximum value of one is sometimes called a *binary semaphore*, and can be used as a building block with which to build other primitives. For example, it can be used as a mutex by initializing the counter at one, using the wait operation for locking, and the signal operation for unlocking. By initializing it at zero, it can also be used for signaling, like a condition variable. For example, the standard park() and unpark() functions in std::thread can be implemented as wait and signal operations on a binary semaphore associated with the thread.

 Note how a mutex can be implemented using a semaphore, while a semaphore can be implemented using a mutex (and a condition variable). It's advisable to avoid using a mutex-based semaphore to implement a semaphore-based mutex, and the other way around.

Further reading:

- Wikipedia article on semaphores (*https://oreil.ly/_rSRZ*)
- Stanford University course notes on semaphores (*https://oreil.ly/ZVaei*)

RCU

If you want to allow multiple threads to (mostly) read and (sometimes) mutate some data, you can use an RwLock. When this data is just a single integer, you can use an atomic variable (such as AtomicU32) to avoid locking, which is more efficient. However, for larger chunks of data, like a struct with many fields, there's no available atomic type that allows for lock-free atomic operations on the entire object.

Just like every other problem in computer science, this problem can be solved by adding a layer of indirection. Instead of the struct itself, you can use an atomic variable to store a pointer to it. This still doesn't allow you to modify the struct as a whole atomically, but it does allow you to replace the entire struct atomically, which is nearly as good.

This pattern is often called *RCU*, which stands for "read, copy, update," the steps necessary to replace the data. After reading the pointer, the struct can be copied into a new allocation that can be modified without worrying about other threads. When ready, the atomic pointer can be updated using a compare-and-exchange operation ("Compare-and-Exchange Operations" on page 42), which will only succeed if no other thread has replaced the data in the meantime.

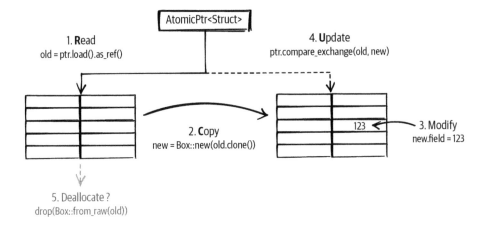

The most interesting part about the RCU pattern is the last step, which does not have a letter in the acronym: deallocating the old data. After a successful update, other threads might still be reading the old copy, if they read the pointer before the update. You'll have to wait for all those threads to be done before the old copy can be deallocated.

There are many possible solutions for this issue, including reference counting (like Arc), leaking memory (ignoring the problem), garbage collection, hazard pointers (a way for threads to tell the others what pointers they are currently using), and quiescent state tracking (waiting for each thread to reach a point at which it is definitely not using any pointers). The last one can be extremely efficient in certain conditions.

Many data structures in the Linux kernel are RCU based, and there are many interesting talks and articles about their implementation details that can provide a great deal of inspiration.

Further reading:

- Wikipedia article on the read-copy-update pattern (*https://oreil.ly/egIIi*)
- LWN article "What is RCU, Fundamentally?" (*https://oreil.ly/GQZ6r*)

Lock-Free Linked List

Expanding on the basic RCU pattern, you can add an atomic pointer to the struct to point to the next one, to turn it into a *linked list*. This allows for threads to atomically add or remove elements on this list, without having to copy the entire list for every update.

To insert a new element at the start of the list, you only have to allocate that element and point its pointer at the first element in the list, and then atomically update the initial pointer to point to your newly allocated element.

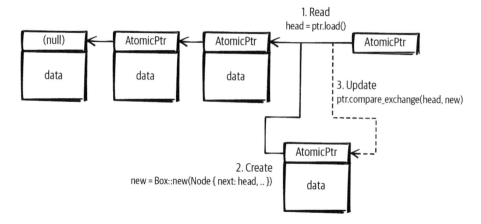

Similarly, removing an element can be done by atomically updating the pointer before it to point to the element after it. However, when multiple writers are involved, care must be taken to handle concurrent insertion or removal operations on neighboring elements. Otherwise, you might accidentally also remove a concurrently newly inserted element, or undo the removal of a concurrently removed element.

To keep things simple, you can use a regular mutex to avoid concurrent mutations. That way, reading is still a lock-free operation, but you don't have to worry about handling concurrent mutation.

After detaching an element from the linked list, you'll run into the same issue as before: waiting until you can deallocate it (or otherwise claim ownership). The same solutions we discussed for the basic RCU pattern can work in this case as well.

In general, you can build a wide variety of elaborate lock-free data structures based on compare-and-exchange operations on atomic pointers, but you'll always need a good strategy for deallocating or otherwise reclaiming ownership of the allocations.

Further reading:

- Wikipedia article on non-blocking linked lists (*https://oreil.ly/kVQ1O*)
- LWN article "Using RCU for Linked Lists—A Case Study" (*https://oreil.ly/H0lt4*)

Queue-Based Locks

For most standard locking primitives, the operating system's kernel keeps track of the threads that are blocked on it, and is responsible for picking one to wake up when asked to do so. An interesting alternative is to implement a mutex (or other locking primitive), by manually keeping track of the queue of waiting threads.

Such a mutex could be implemented as a single `AtomicPtr` that can point to a (list of) waiting threads.

Each element in this list needs to contain something that can be used to wake up the corresponding thread, such as a `std::thread::Thread` object. Some unused bits of the atomic pointer can be used to store the state of the mutex itself, and whatever is necessary for managing the state of the queue.

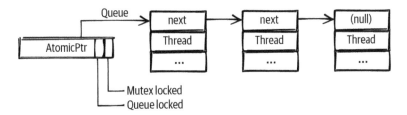

There are many variations possible. The queue could be protected by its own lock bit or it could be implemented as a (partially) lock-free structure. The elements don't have to be allocated on the heap, but could be local variables of the threads that are waiting. The queue could be a doubly-linked list with not only pointers to the next element, but also to the previous element. The first element could also include a pointer to the last element to allow efficiently appending an element at the end.

This pattern allows for implementing efficient locking primitives using only something that can be used to block and wake up a single thread, such as thread parking.

Windows SRW locks ("Slim reader-writer locks" on page 176) are implemented using this pattern.

Further reading:

- Notes on the implementation of Windows SRW locks (*https://oreil.ly/El8GA*)
- A Rust implementation of queue-based locks (*https://oreil.ly/aFyg1*)

Parking Lot–Based Locks

To make a highly efficient mutex that's as small as possible, you can build upon the queue-based locks idea by moving the queue into a global data structure, leaving only one or two bits inside the mutex itself. This way, the mutex only needs to be a single byte. You could even put it in some unused bits of a pointer, allowing for very fine-grained locking at almost no extra cost.

The global data structure can be a `HashMap` that maps memory addresses to a queue of threads waiting on the mutex at that address. This global data structure is often called a *parking lot*, since it's a collection of parked threads.

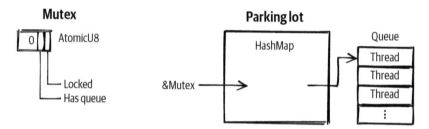

The pattern can be generalized by not only tracking queues for mutexes, but also for condition variables and other primitives. By tracking a queue for any atomic variable, this effectively provides a way to implement futex-like functionality on platforms that don't natively support that.

This pattern is most well known from its 2015 implementation in WebKit, where it was used for locking JavaScript objects. Its implementation inspired other implementations, such as the popular `parking_lot` Rust crate.

Further reading:

- WebKit blog post, "Locking in WebKit" (*https://oreil.ly/6dPim*)
- Documentation of the `parking_lot` crate (*https://oreil.ly/UPcXu*)

Sequence Lock

A sequence lock is another solution to the problem of atomically updating (larger) data without using traditional (blocking) locks. It uses an atomic counter that is odd while the data is being updated, and even when the data is ready to be read.

The writing thread will have to increment the counter from even to odd before mutating the data, after which it has to increment the counter again to leave it at a (different) even value.

Any reading thread can, at any point and without blocking, read the data by reading the counter both before and after. If the two values from the counter are equal and even, there was no concurrent mutation, meaning you read a valid copy of the data. Otherwise, you might have read data that was concurrently being modified, in which case you should just try again.

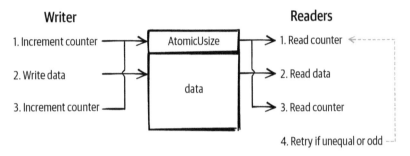

This is a great pattern for making data available to other threads, without the possibility of the reading threads blocking the writing thread. It is often used in operating systems kernels and many embedded systems. Since the readers need only read access to the memory and no pointers are involved, this can be a great data structure to safely use in shared memory, between processes, without needing to trust the readers. For example, the Linux kernel uses this pattern to very efficiently provide timestamps to processes by providing them with read-only access to (shared) memory.

An interesting question is how this fits into the memory model. Concurrent non-atomic reads and writes to the same data result in undefined behavior, even if the read data is ignored. This means that, technically speaking, both reading and writing the data should be done using only atomic operations, even though the entire read or write does not have to be a single atomic operation.

Further reading:

- Wikipedia article on Linux's Seqlock (*https://oreil.ly/T28bW*)
- Rust RFC 3301, `AtomicPerByte` (*https://oreil.ly/Qavc7*)
- Documentation of the `seqlock` crate (*https://oreil.ly/yHd_7*)

Teaching Materials

It can be great fun to spend many hours—or years—inventing new concurrent data structures and designing ergonomic Rust implementations of them. If you're looking for something else to do with your knowledge on Rust, atomics, locks, concurrent data structures, and concurrency in general, it can also be very fulfilling to create new teaching materials to share your knowledge with others.

There is a great lack of accessible resources aimed at those new to these topics. Rust has played a significant role in making systems programming more accessible to everyone, but many programmers still shy away from low-level concurrency. Atomics are often thought of as a somewhat mystical topic that's best left to a very small group of experts, which is a shame.

I hope this very book makes a significant difference, but there is so much space for more books, blog posts, articles, video courses, conference talks, and other materials about Rust concurrency.

~

I'm excited to see what you create.

Good luck. ♥

Index

on x86-64, 153
shadowing, 10
shared ownership, 7-10
    leaking, 8
    reference counting, 8
    statics, 7
shared references, 13
    mutating atomics through, 31
slim reader-writer locks (Windows), 176, 217
spawning threads, 2
    failing to, 5
    happens-before relationship, 53
    scoped, 5
spin locks
    building our own, 75-83
    cache lines, effect of, 148
    compare-and-exchange, (not) using, 147
    experiment, using wrong memory ordering,
        155-157
    guard, 80
    memory ordering, 77
spin loop hint, 76, 190
spinning, 75, 123, 161
    avoiding accidental (reader-writer lock), 206
splitting (borrowing), 99
spurious wake-ups, 25, 168, 200
SRW locks (Windows), 176, 217
stack size, 5
starvation, 23, 208
static lifetime, 4
statics, 7
stlr (store-release register) instruction (ARM),
    154
stlxr (store-release exclusive register) instruc-
    tion (ARM), 154
stop flag, 32
store buffers, 149
store operations (atomic) (see load and store
    operations)
store-conditional (see load-linked/store-
    conditional)
str (store register) instruction (ARM), 131
stress, reducing, 91
strongly ordered architecture, 151
stxr (store exclusive register) instruction
    (ARM), 138
sub (subtract) instruction (x86), 135
swap operation (atomic), 37
    locking using, 76

Sync trait, 16, 86
    implementing for Arc, 106
    implementing for channel, 88
    implementing for mutex, 183
    implementing for reader-writer lock, 203
    implementing for spin lock, 78
    requirement by RwLock, 23
syscalls, 161
    avoiding, 186, 198
SYS_futex (Linux), 167
    (see also futex)
    arguments, 169

T
--target (rustc), 130
teaching, 219
thin air, out of, 56
thread builder, 5
thread name, 5
Thread object, 101
    id, 2
    unpark, 24, 101
thread parking, 24-26, 92, 101, 167
    spurious wake-ups, 25
    timeout, 28
        example, 34
thread safety, 9, 16-18
    (see also Send and Sync traits)
    keeping objects on one thread, 102
ThreadId, 2
threads, 1
    joining, 3
    panicking, 3, 5
    returning a value, 4
    scoped, 5-7
    spawning, 2
thundering herd problem, 202
time travel, 12
timeout
    condition variables, 28
    futex, 169, 197
    thread parking, 28
        example, 34
total modification order, 54, 59, 90, 91

U
uncontended (mutexes), 187, 189
    benchmarking, 191
undefined behavior, 12

About the Author

Mara Bos maintains the Rust standard library and builds real-time control systems in Rust. As team lead of the Rust library team, she knows all the ins and outs of the language and the standard library. In addition, she has been working with concurrent real-time systems for years at the company she founded. Maintaining the most-used library in the Rust ecosystem and working daily on safety critical systems has given her the hands-on experience to both understand the theory and bring it to practice.

Colophon

The animal on the cover of *Rust Atomics and Locks* is a Kodiak bear (*Ursus arctos middendorffi*). This species of brown bear is endemic to the Kodiak Archipelago of Alaska. They have been isolated from other bears for roughly 12,000 years.

Kodiak bears are one of the largest bears in the world. A male can stand 10 feet tall on his hind legs and 5 feet tall on all four. Males can weigh up to 1,500 pounds while females are 20% to 30% smaller. They are larger than black bears, showcasing a more prominent shoulder hump, less prominent ears, and longer, straighter claws. While they are a type of brown bear, they cannot be easily identified by the color of their fur, which can range from dark brown to light blonde.

The Kodiak Archipelago hosts a pristine landscape for the bears. Its temperate forests are full of lush greenery that flourishes due to ample amounts of rain. Winters on the archipelago are long and cold, followed by mild summers. The bears take advantage of the climate by optimizing their diet for whatever is in season. During spring and early summer they feed on rapidly growing grasses. Berries are consumed during late summer and early fall. Salmon runs last from May through September, and the bears feast on Pacific salmon that spawn in nearby lakes and streams. They are easily adaptable and can be drawn to improperly stored garbage and food at human campsites and homes.

Kodiak bears were once actively hunted to protect livestock, but hunting is now regulated to keep the population thriving. As a result, Kodiak bears have a conservation status of Least Concern. Many of the animals on O'Reilly covers are endangered; all of them are important to the world.

The cover illustration is by Karen Montgomery, based on a black-and-white engraving from *Zoology*. The cover fonts are Gilroy Semibold and Guardian Sans. The text font is Adobe Minion Pro; the heading font is Adobe Myriad Condensed; and the code font is Dalton Maag's Ubuntu Mono.

Milton Keynes UK
Ingram Content Group UK Ltd.
UKHW031011240924
448749UK00004B/9

9 781098 119447